The Genesis of Macroeconom

The Genesis
of Macroeconomics

New Ideas from Sir William Petty
to Henry Thornton

Antoin E. Murphy

OXFORD
UNIVERSITY PRESS

OXFORD
UNIVERSITY PRESS

Great Clarendon Street, Oxford OX2 6DP

Oxford University Press is a department of the University of Oxford.
It furthers the University's objective of excellence in research, scholarship,
and education by publishing worldwide in

Oxford New York

Auckland Cape Town Dar es Salaam Hong Kong Karachi
Kuala Lumpur Madrid Melbourne Mexico City Nairobi
New Delhi Shanghai Taipei Toronto

With offices in

Argentina Austria Brazil Chile Czech Republic France Greece
Guatemala Hungary Italy Japan Poland Portugal Singapore
South Korea Switzerland Thailand Turkey Ukraine Vietnam

Oxford is a registered trade mark of Oxford University Press
in the UK and in certain other countries

Published in the United States
by Oxford University Press Inc., New York

British Library Cataloguing in Publication Data
Data available

Library of Congress Cataloging in Publication Data
Data available

Typeset by SPI Publisher Services, Pondicherry, India
Printed in Great Britain
on acid-free paper by
CPI Antony Rowe

ISBN 978–0–19–954323–6 (Pbk.)
978–0–19–954322–9 (Hbk.)

1 3 5 7 9 10 8 6 4 2

Preface

This book builds on some of my previous work published by Oxford University Press: *Richard Cantillon: Entrepreneur and Economist* (1986) and *John Law: Economic Theorist and Policymaker* (1997). It aims to bring the reader into the excitement of the discovery of macroeconomic ideas by pioneers of the discipline writing between the late seventeenth and early nineteenth centuries. It is hoped that, by acquainting readers with the ideas and reasoning of these writers, they will discover that many of our ideas on macroeconomics have a long lineage and are not recent discoveries.

I wish to express my gratitude to the Arts, Humanities, and Social Sciences Benefactions Fund of Trinity College Dublin for providing financial assistance to research for this book in both the United Kingdom and France. I would like to thank the *European Journal of the History of Economic Thought* for permission to reproduce some parts of my paper on Henry Thornton in the penultimate chapter. I would also like to thank Ms Sarah Caro and the editorial team at Oxford University Press for the care and attention that they have devoted to book. Mr Michael Curran was of invaluable assistance through his reading of the text and his help with the presentation of diagrams. I am also indebted to the two anonymous referees for their suggestions on how to improve the text. The usual disclaimer applies.

A.E.M.

Contents

List of Plates

List of Figures

1

Introduction: The Genesis of Macroeconomics

Macroeconomics analyses fluctuations in aggregated economic activity. It deals with the big board issues in the economy such as the size and growth of national income (gross domestic product–gross national product), inflation, employment–unemployment, and balance of payments problems.

Daily media coverage makes it difficult to escape from macroeconomics as the media report on macroeconomic indicators: the growth rate, the inflation rate, the interest rate, the exchange rate, etc. Macroeconomics influences all our lives. If the growth rate is strong, it is generally a very positive indicator for the economy. A strong growth rate feeds into employment and generally reduces unemployment. If the inflation rate rises, it reduces the purchasing power of our money. If the exchange rate depreciates, we have less to spend on holidays and foreign goods. If the interest rate rises, the cost of loans and mortgages increases and the price of shares—an important element for future pensions—may fall.

Macroeconomic measurement of national income is vital for governments framing fiscal policy through the budget. It is also vital to central banks for the formulation of monetary policy. The links between financial markets and the real economy mean that, when financial markets become turbulent or face the prospect of crashing, it is necessary to resort to a wider range of macroeconomic policies to ensure that the incipient contagion emanating from the financial sector does not lead to serious disruptions of employment and economic growth. In a word, macroeconomics concerns us all. If the macroeconomy performs badly, politicians find themselves unemployed; if it performs satisfactorily, governments generally remain in office. 'It's the economy, stupid' summarized the political viewpoint of at least one successful presidential candidate in the United States.

Despite its universal importance, macroeconomics appears to have been a relatively recent discovery. National income accounts measuring the performance of the economy at a macro level are generally credited to the pioneering work of Simon Kuznets in the 1930s. At around the same time the term 'macroeconomics' was first coined by Ragnar Frisch (see Schumpeter 1954: 278). John Maynard Keynes provided a great impetus for the systematic study of macroeconomics with his book *The General Theory of Employment, Interest and Money* (1936). However, despite the strong claims for the view that macroeconomics was founded in the 1930s, it is the contention of this book that macroeconomics had effectively been founded many centuries before.

Macroeconomics received its initial impetus from Sir William Petty, who attempted to measure, for the first time, the wealth and income of the nation. Petty made key distinctions between income and wealth, presented the national income equals national expenditure identity, and introduced the velocity of circulation into monetary analysis. He showed that it was possible to aggregate and quantify economic phenomena under headings such as wealth, income, and expenditure. Aggregation and quantification of economic data, the essential ingredients of macroeconomics, were a key part of Petty's legacy.

Macroeconomics then developed with considerable rapidity through the Scotsman John Law's efforts to implement his macroeconomic theory as macroeconomic policy through the famous Mississippi System in France. Law introduced into his analysis a wide range of important concepts such as supply and demand, the demand for money, a rudimentary circular flow of income analysis, and the law of one price. Above all, he wanted to demonstrate that there was no need to base the monetary system on an intrinsically valuable paper money. However, the failure of Law's ambitious macroeconomic experiment, flagged by the collapse of the Mississippi System, caused a reaction against his plans to replace metallic money with paper money.

Richard Cantillon, an Irishman who made a considerable fortune through the Mississippi System, then tried to rationalize why the System had failed. He presented a coherent model of how the economy operated. Starting from a rudimentary barter, command, and closed economy, he demonstrated the way the system could be progressively developed into an entrepreneur-based market and open economy. Central to this analysis was his circular flow of income process and central to this circular flow of income was the role of the entrepreneur.

The Frenchman François Quesnay, building on Cantillon's work, presented the first diagrammatic outline of the circular flow of income process through the 'Tableau économique' (the 'Economic Picture'). Using this 'Tableau économique', Quesnay and his Physiocratic followers were able to show how economic surpluses could be produced, and how these, in turn, generated economic growth. Quesnay, while concentrating excessively on land as the unique source of the economic surplus, recognized, too, that entrepreneurs and 'advances' were also important to the growth-generating process.

A French contemporary of Quesnay, Anne Robert Jacques Turgot, in his *Réflexions sur la formation et la distribution des richesses* (1769–70; trans. as

Reflections on the Production and Distribution of Wealth, 1793), substituted the term 'capital' for 'advances', and outlined the importance of capital for economic growth. Turgot also presented a model of interest rate determination through the supply and demand for loanable funds and demonstrated how low interest rates were important in promoting economic growth. The publication of Cantillon's *Essai sur la nature du commerce en général* (1755), the appearance of Quesnay's 'Tableau économique', and the emergence of Turgot's *Réflexions* were all part of the economists' contributions to the French Enlightenment. Paralleling these developments, Scotland produced two key contributors to the Enlightenment, David Hume and Adam Smith. Hume, a strong advocate of international free trade, swept away a wide range of so-called mercantilist beliefs when showing the self-adjusting properties of the monetary system in an open economy. Adam Smith, combining his views on the importance of the division and specialization of labour, which he had earlier presented in his lectures in Glasgow, with the subsequent theoretical developments by Quesnay and Turgot on the importance of capital, presented an overall synthesis in the *Wealth of Nations* (1776) which enabled readers to see the importance of both labour and capital in the determination of economic growth.

Just as Petty, at the end of the seventeenth century, opened up a wide range of new vistas to be developed in the eighteenth century, so also did Henry Thornton at the start of the nineteenth century. Thornton's *Paper Credit of Great Britain* (1802) developed considerably monetary theory, a key part of macroeconomics. Indeed, Thornton, according to David Laidler, 'brought monetary theory to a level of sophistication that it was not to surpass until the end of the 19th century' (Eatwell et al. 1978: 634). Thornton was the first writer to show the key role that a central bank could play in acting as a lender of last resort to ensure that financial difficulties did not develop into a financial contagion that threatened the real economy.

Historians of economic thought will immediately ask why this early prehistory of macroeconomics has stopped with Henry Thornton, contending that the gap between Thornton and Keynes needs to be bridged with a range of nineteenth-century writers. Here I believe that macroeconomics went through a great sleep during the nineteenth century and the innovativeness and vitality shown with respect to macroeconomic issues in the works from Petty to Thornton would not reappear until the twentieth century. Aside from Malthus on 'gluts' and the continued Bullionist Controversy, economists concerned themselves with issues other than macroeconomics during this period.

The macroeconomic writings cited in this book cover a period of 140 years from Petty's *Treatise of Taxes and Contributions* (1662) to Henry Thornton's *Paper Credit* (1802). These economic writings occur against the backdrop of enormous changes at the political, religious, commercial, financial, and scientific levels. At the political level society was evolving towards the emergence of the early stages of parliamentary democracy. Britain had gone through a period of regicide (Charles I), progressing towards increased parliamentary participation followed by dictatorship (Oliver Cromwell), replacement of the king (William of Orange for James II), and an increasing strengthening of democratic principles based on the Lockean rights to personal freedom and property. By the end of the seventeenth century, at least in Britain, the doctrine of the divine right of monarchs had lost its pseudo-legitimacy and been replaced by one stressing the people's will as expressed by Parliament.

In France, by the middle of the eighteenth century, Montesquieu was demonstrating in *De l'esprit des lois* (1748) how society could function through a separation and balancing of powers between the executive, the legislature, and the judiciary. Combining elements of Montesquieu's approach with John Locke's principles on freedom and property, the American revolutionaries produced the constitution of the newly established United States of America. This constitution enshrined a wide range of democratic principles based on the concept of freedom—though freedom for its black community would have to wait for a later civil war in the nineteenth century.

Montesquieu's writings heralded the start of what became known as the French Enlightenment. Diderot and d'Alembert, the editors of the great *Encyclopédie*, provided a forum for the progression of democratic sentiments. The *Encyclopédie*, along with other Enlightenment writings, produced a corrosion of the authority and power of the institutions of the *ancien régime*. The king and the Church were challenged with the tension of this opposition, eventually leading to the start of the French Revolution in 1789. Although espousing the principles of liberty, equality, and fraternity, this revolution also produced a regicide (Louis XVI and his family), a stumbling towards democratic institutions, and a movement towards dictatorship as embodied in Napoleon's desire to become the emperor of the French.

Wars and revolutions need to be financed. Their financing would inspire and catalyse many of the writings covered in this book. Just as Keynes would later write, in the twentieth century, *How to Pay for the War* (1940), Sir William Petty was so concerned with the cost of the war against Holland that he determined to measure the national income of England and Wales. Once again, the issue of how to pay for the war came to the fore in the macroeconomic policy of John Law. Law would eventually become prime minister of France because he offered a new method to reduce the enormous public sector debt that had been accumulated by Louis XIV during the long and very costly War of the Spanish Succession against the British and their allies. It was during that war that Richard Cantillon developed some of his accounting expertise. Furthermore, in my opinion he wrote the *Essai sur la nature du commerce en général* to refute Law's attempts to reduce the French debt through the development of the Mississippi System.

Law's theories and policies also had a distinct influence on Hume, Turgot, and Smith. All three, it will be later contended, produced distinctly conservative approaches to monetary analysis that were in part fashioned by their negative reactions to Law and his System.

Later, at the start of the nineteenth century, Henry Thornton's *Paper Credit* was written against the background of the suspension of gold convertibility by the Bank of England, a suspension caused by the war against Napoleon and the very real fear of an invasion of the country.

The wars across the seventeenth, eighteenth, and nineteenth centuries fostered a new type of banking culture. Political revolution was accompanied by financial revolution. The transfer of power to a Dutch king, William of Orange, also involved the transfer of new banking principles to Britain. These new banking principles facilitated the establishment of the Bank of England, which was founded to finance the Dutch king's war against the French. The Bank of England ushered in a new age of financial revolution for Britain as new methods of banking and debt management enabled the British to compete with a smaller population and resource base against the French. Through the eighteenth century the British banking system, and in particular the Scottish banking system, innovated to provide new methods of credit to the government and entrepreneurs. Meanwhile, France, dogged by the anti-banking sentiments generated by the collapse of the Royal Bank and the Company of the West, regressed in the area of financial innovation and returned to a system based on metallic money. This regression influenced French writers such as Quesnay and Turgot, who did not perceive the massive new financing opportunities that had been created by the British banks. Though Quesnay and, in particular, Turgot were blinkered in their approach to banking and financial innovation, it is surprising to note that the Scottish economists Hume and Smith, as will be shown, were also distinctly conservative in their approach to the financial innovation that was developing in the Scottish cities of Edinburgh and Glasgow that they inhabited. The French revolutionaries resorted to issuing paper money (*les assignats*) to finance the French Revolution. This money, initially using as collateral the confiscated property of the Church and the aristocracy, was successful in financing the first three years of the revolution. However, over-issue created hyperinflation and, once again, an attendant animosity towards banks and financial innovation.

It was left to Henry Thornton to describe and analyse the benefits arising from the financial innovation of banks and other financial institutions, though even here he had difficulty in accepting the logic that this system would ultimately completely replace gold and silver as money.

An objective of this book is to involve readers in the excitement of the macroeconomic discoveries that were made and to show how some of these ideas were built on in some cases and forgotten in other instances. Economics had not yet been formalized as a separate subject area, and it must be kept in mind that the economics authors presented in this book were writing against a background of either total or partial ignorance of the subject. They did not have the benefit of any settled body of theory, nor did they have access to sizeable libraries of books and articles to help them develop their theories and policies. Instead they started out in the raw quarries of the mind, where they had to chisel out their own perceptions of the economic world. By examining their writings it is possible to observe the way a science such as economics emerges.

The impressive contributions to the formation of macroeconomics of these writers constitute the substantive part of this book. They will be outlined in chapters dealing with each of the specific authors that have been chosen. Historians of economic thought may disagree with the selection listed above; they will argue, perhaps, for the exclusion of some of the above and the inclusion of others. In my opinion there are strong cases to be made for the inclusion of writers such as Sir Dudley North, who, in the *Discourses upon Trade* (1692), made a very strong plea for free international trade; the French writer Pierre de Boisguilbert (1646–1714), an exponent of *laissez-faire* (he was the first economics writer to use the term), who conceptualized a rudimentary circular flow of income approach; and Sir James Steuart, the author of *An Inquiry into the Principles of Political Oeconomy* (1767), a work full of fascinating insights, particularly on money, which Adam Smith deliberately and disgracefully neglected to mention in the *Wealth of Nations*. Although these three writers have been omitted, they do constitute a panel of excellent substitutes in the history of the evolution of macroeconomics.

Economists produce models by inviting readers to assume. Their catch cry is 'let us assume'. In this book readers are asked to imagine prior to assuming. This invitation to imagine has been used so as to entice a duality of reflection for readers. At the first level of reflection it has been designed to encourage readers to become time travellers and position themselves during specific events relating to the life of each of the authors chosen. This reverse movement through time has the huge advantage of presenting the writers in the context of their historical period as well as showing how, in some instances, specific events may have shaped their ideas on macroeconomics. The second level of reflection is to encourage readers to imagine, alongside these writers, the way that they were conceptualizing economic ideas. By trying to put ourselves into the minds of these writers we can attempt to ask questions as to why they wrote on macroeconomics and envisage the types of problem that they faced when trying to conceptualize the key elements of the subject. We can also glimpse the brilliance with which they imagined the macroeconomy as well as the blockages and hang-ups that, in some cases, limited their imaginations and prevented them from developing more complete theories.

To facilitate readers in this dualistic process of imagination it is intended, at the start of each chapter, to situate them during some significant event in the lives of the economists who have been selected. This is a triggering technique to enable readers to participate in events that were important for the economists that are presented. In using this technique it is hoped to bring the reader into the living environment of these economists. Absolutists will dislike this approach. For them it should be a case of insisting on the theory and forgetting about the events in which the theory was formulated. But theories are inevitably a product of context, and I believe that it is important to try to involve the reader with aspects of the time and circumstances of the writers that are described in this book. Samuel Johnson wrote, 'Were it not for imagination, Sir, a man would be as happy in the arms of a chambermaid as of a Duchess.' Our imagination frequently takes us away from the pedestrian tracks that we stumble through in life. It enables the mind to soar intellectually. It enabled the writers that are presented in this book to soar above their contemporaries through the imaginative ways in which they viewed the macroeconomy. Economists need to imagine before they can start to assume.

Petty was able to imagine a way of conceptualizing the wealth and income of a country in a couple of pages. Law was able to imagine a world without intrinsically valuable money, one characterized by banks, paper money, and credit. Cantillon was able to imagine the skeletal structure of a primitive economy and then to develop it by stages into a model of the economy in which he lived. Hume was able to imagine a world of international free trade. Quesnay imagined a diagrammatic presentation of Cantillon's theory of the circular flow of income and expenditure, the 'Tableau économique'. Turgot imagined how he could analyse the role of savings and investment in the process of generating economic growth; his imagining enabled him to introduce the concept of capital into economic analysis. Smith imagined presenting a synthesis of all the ideas that he had read about and learnt from his travels; this would lead to the *Wealth of Nations*. Thornton disagreed with many elements of Smith's monetary theory. As a practising banker he was able to imagine outside the very limited parameters that Smith had established for the monetary system and to evaluate the new world of money and banking in the context of the suspension of convertibility of gold payments by the Bank of England.

These first macroeconomists were a motley lot. Their backgrounds were very diverse and, in most cases, gave little hint that they would become founders of the subject. Petty, in a very varied career, was, among other things, an anatomist and a physician, an inventor of catamarans and writing machines, a surveyor and mapper, a landowner and proto-industrialist. How did he have the time to write books? John Law transformed from a rake and philanderer to a professional oddsmaker-cum-gambler, from a man sentenced to the scaffold to the equivalent of the prime minister of France. Where would such a man find the inspiration to write so convincingly on the future of money? Richard Cantillon initially worked for one of the most corrupt war profiteers of the eighteenth century, became a merchant and a banker, and was classified as a 'millionaire' through his successful stock market and foreign exchange investments. The wealth he accumulated led to civil and criminal proceedings. He was apparently murdered in his bed. But, if this was the case, who was the mysterious chevalier de Louvigny who appeared in the Dutch South American colony of Surinam with Cantillon's papers some six months after his death? The twenty-first anniversary of his demise was marked by the appearance of his one and only book, which clinically analysed the way to model the macroeconomy.

David Hume was less mysterious and even left us a short autobiography of his life. Turned down for two professorial chairs in Scotland, he nevertheless wrote majestically on philosophy, politics, history, and economics. His sole book on economics, the *Political Discourses*, which, with the benefit of hindsight, could have been retitled the *Macroeconomic Discourses*, was far more successful at the time of its publication than his philosophical works. But he left it at that with just one work on economics. Why, aside from revising and editing further editions of the *Political Discourses*, did he stop writing on economic issues with this one work?

François Quesnay came to the subject as an old man. Up to the age of 60 he had pursued a successful career as a doctor, latterly in the court of Louis XV at Versailles. How could an old doctor—a man in his sixties would have been regarded as such in those days—suddenly have become the head of a new sect called the *économistes*? Around the same time, Anne Robert Jacques Turgot quit his ecclesiastical career, in which he had become a prior at the Sorbonne, to become a full-time public sector administrator. Economics was his new calling and, like John Law, he also became prime minister of France. Again like Law, his time in office proved to be extremely short.

Adam Smith, converted from an academic professor to a travelling tutor, would meet and be influenced by Quesnay and Turgot. His scholarly journey resembles most that of the modern academic, though he did have the enormous luxury of having the equivalent of a research grant for life owing to the generosity of his tutee the duke of Buccleuch. This lifetime pension would give him the time to read, reflect, and eventually write the *Wealth of Nations*.

Henry Thornton, a banker and Member of Parliament, would challenge many of Smith's economic tenets. There was little of the academic about this practising banker and philanthropist who was ultimately more concerned with saving his soul and the skin and souls of his fellow men (working closely with his great friend William Wilberforce, he was a brilliant anti-slavery agitator in Parliament) than with writing on economics. Thornton, in his diaries, reveals a man mentally flagellating himself for not praying more to God, while at the same time he was 'having a hard fag' writing his ideas for *Paper Credit*.

It will be seen in this book that we are dealing with a very heterogeneous range of individuals with barely an academic among them. Yet, it was this group that would build the foundations of the subject of macroeconomics. Why did they write on this subject? This book will show that they had a variety of motivations, for, like Molière's Monsieur Jourdain and his use of prose, they were not aware that they were writing and talking macroeconomics. They were not fully cognizant of the extent to which they were filling in a significant part of the giant and complex macroeconomic jigsaw by putting in place key conceptual developments.

Their motivations for writing about macroeconomics were multifaceted. In many cases the authors were not seeking to create macroeconomics, and their contributions to macroeconomics were by-products of the pursuit of other goals. Because of these other goals and the fact that most of these writers, with the exception of Adam Smith, were not academic economists, their writings did not link together to form a continuous academic debate. In many cases they were one-off contributions linked to specific issues that concerned each individual writer. Because of this, their writings lay scattered on a winding trail ready to be discovered by later generations of economists. These discoveries would take time in some cases.

Though adroitly used by Quesnay and Smith, Cantillon was not rediscovered until the late nineteenth century by Stanley Jevons, who highlighted the *Essai sur la nature du commerce en général* as the 'cradle of political economy'.

It took even longer for Petty's contributions to be fully recognized. He presented an outstanding outline of macroeconomics in a couple of paragraphs in the very brief, but analytically powerful, work *Verbum Sapienti*. This title may be translated as 'A Word to the Wise', or, more prosaically, a word in the ear of the ruling politicians. Posthumously published, it was not deemed worthy of a separate printing by Petty's publishers, equally oblivious of its future potential. They tacked it on as an addendum to the *Political Anatomy of Ireland* when it was published in 1691, and there it lay largely unrecognized until recent times. This was a big miss by the economics profession, for in a few pages in the very brief opening chapter of this book Petty, as will be shown, expertly distinguished between stocks and flows and between income and wealth. He produced the national income identity that income equals expenditure, and then presented ways of measuring both income and wealth. This led him to identify the key role that labour played in the generation of income. These were magisterial developments. Why were they not fully recognized earlier? Here Petty has to share some of the blame for not directing future generations onto the right track. For him, this work was not primarily motivated by a desire to sketch out the rudimentary outlines of the macroeconomy. It was, first and foremost, a lobbying exercise on his part to the politicians in London to mitigate the burden of taxation on landlords, of which he was one. Petty wanted to show that landlords were only one part of the taxable base of the economy and that the tax net could be widened. Driven into action by his own self-interest in trying to present a case against further taxation for landlords, he produced an embryonic model of the macroeconomy. He did not rush off to his friends of the Royal Society, of which he was a founding member, to announce the good news of his macroeconomic discoveries. Instead he directed all his attention to lobbying the political authorities in England on the need to widen the tax base, unsuccessfully as it turned out. After that Petty largely forgot about this work.

The extraordinarily colourful Scotsman John Law was motivated to design a system that would lead to the replacement of metallic money by paper money and the creation of a financial system capable of reducing the burden of the national debt and providing finance to develop extensive colonial trading opportunities. This was an enormous intellectual task, for Law, a man with a more than colourful past, was challenging the global monetary structure. In this challenge he asserted that mankind had adopted the wrong monetary standard, a metallic standard that hampered rather than developed the economy. He provided coherent arguments for the removal of metallic money and its replacement by paper money. Unlike most theorists, he was presented with the opportunity to remove metallic money from the economy, albeit for a brief period, in France.

Law was a very modern theorist, both in his ideas and in his prose. He was the first writer to use the term 'demand' in economic discourse; he was the first to use supply and demand analysis; and he was the first to introduce the concept of the demand for money into monetary analysis. He used the latter concept, as monetarists have done, to show how inflation could occur when the supply of money rose out of line with the demand for money. But he also recognized that, in situations where there was unemployment and underutilization of resources, money could be used as a catalyst to drive economic activity. The opening words of the title of *Money and Trade, Considered with a Proposal for Supplying the Nation with Money* (1705) said it all for him. If money was scarce in the economy, then trade could not be driven. To show the importance of money, Law designed a circular flow of income model for an island economy and showed how the introduction of money could increase the economic activity of the island. He provided a view of how society could function without metallic money and how macroeconomic policy instruments such as the money supply and the rate of interest could be used to grow the economy. He was further motivated to push his ideas from the theoretical arena into policy-making, attempting to have his ideas implemented in England in 1704, Scotland in 1705, and Savoy around 1710. Rejected by all of these countries, Law spent over ten years lobbying the French administration on the merits of his plans. In 1715, on the death of Louis XIV, he was given his window of opportunity by France's new Regent, Philippe, duc d'Orléans, who permitted him to establish a bank in 1716. By the end of 1719 Law had geared up from this bank to a giant conglomerate trading company, called the Mississippi Company, which controlled all of France's colonial trade, the tax farms, the mint, and the totality of the national debt. In the process, he succeeded, for a brief period, in replacing metallic money with paper money and producing Europe's first major stock market boom. One of his employees, Nicolas Du Tot, would later write that posterity would not believe that Law had created a functioning monetary system without specie in France. While prepared to design and introduce the template for these major transformations, Law was not averse to putting his own money into his schemes, investments that at one stage made him, in his own words, 'the richest man who has ever been'.

The enigmatic Irishman Richard Cantillon made a very great fortune out of Law's System and the South Sea Bubble between 1717 and 1720. The term 'millionaire' was even coined to describe the 'rich Mississippians', such as Cantillon, who amassed considerable wealth during this period. What motivated a busy Cantillon to write on macroeconomic issues? His *Essai sur la nature du commerce en général* was, in my opinion, written as an intellectual refutation of John Law's System. Cantillon, initially a friend and business partner of Law and then his enemy, was not prepared to accept that the model designed by Law, with its emphasis on monetary and financial innovation, was an appropriate one for the economy. To show the limitations of Law's approach he needed to design his own model of the way the economy worked.

Cantillon started by outlining his tabula rasa of a very primitive command, barter, and closed macroeconomy. Then, by degrees, he transformed it into a money-using, entrepreneurially driven market economy open to international trade and capital flows. To accomplish this he needed to design a circular flow of income model—a development that Law had already initiated in *Money and Trade*—showing the interrelationships between income, output, and expenditure. Then he attempted to detail the way money flowed through the circular model in order to calculate the amount of money that would be required to ensure an efficient income flow. Having shown these developments, he was then able to question whether additions to the money stock and financial innovations could increase income and output any further. Thus, without ever mentioning Law's name or the Mississippi System, he was able to produce his refutation of the System. Parts of Cantillon's analysis also served to strengthen his lawyer's brief, as may be seen in a legal factum, in the civil and criminal proceedings that Cantillon's former banking clients took against him.

Prior to the posthumous publication of Cantillon's book in 1755, the Scottish philosopher David Hume provided nine essays on economics in the *Political Discourses*. This book, intervening between Hume's great philosophical and political works and his later *History of England*, opened up new vistas for economic writers by exposing the fallacies of the so-called mercantilist approach that money was wealth and that the accumulation of money would increase the wealth of the nation. Adherence to these beliefs had produced restrictive trade policies in order to boost the stock of money in an economy through the encouragement of exports and prohibitions on imports. The accompanying mindset meant that economic activity was perceived as a zero sum game in which one nation could only benefit from trade at the expense of another. By showing such policies to be self-defeating, Hume opened up new scenarios for international trade, the positive elements of which would later be demonstrated by David Ricardo through his approach on the comparative trading advantage of nations. What motivated Hume to write so elegantly on economic issues? Could it have been the case that the great British philosopher needed the royalties that a successful book would generate? Turned down for two university chairs in Glasgow and Edinburgh, Hume's earlier philosophical and political works had sold badly and Hume's only paid employment in 1752, when the *Political Discourses* was published, was that of Librarian in the Faculty of Advocates in Edinburgh.

Fortunately for Hume, the tide started to change after the successful publication of the *Political Discourses,* which sold well and was quickly translated and published in two separate French editions. But why did Hume, after such a promising start in economics, not continue to write on the subject? Money was again probably the motivating factor because, switching to history, he was able to negotiate a contract in 1754 whereby he was to be paid £400 for the first volume of his *History of England* and a further £600 for the second volume if the first volume was a success (see Mossner 1980: 303). A second motivating factor may have been that economics had still not been formally discovered as a separate discipline and so was of less interest to the reading public than history. The formal launch of the new science of political economy was to take place in France at the very time Hume was writing his *History of England.*

Hume's dismantling of the mercantilist shibboleths was quickly followed by developments in France, where credit must go for the founding of economics in the 1750s to the activities of a former merchant, Vincent de Gournay, and François Quesnay. These two each motivated a group of young French administrators to write and translate works on economic issues. The first group, led by Gournay, was contemporaneously referred to as *les économistes*, thus bringing the name 'economist' for the first time into the economic discourse. These young administrators espoused a new doctrine, that of *laissez-faire, laissez-passer*, freedom to produce and freedom to trade. They passionately believed that they were founding a new science: that of political economy (*économie politique*). Indeed, one surly crypto-communist, the abbé Bonnot de Mably, remarked that he was fed up with these young administrators running around Paris shouting *laissez-faire, laissez-passer* as the solution to all economic problems. On the death of Gournay in 1759, effective leadership on economic issues passed to Quesnay, who, building on the earlier work of Cantillon, provided a diagrammatic representation of the circular flow of income in the 'Tableau économique'.

What motivated the ageing physician suddenly to develop a strong interest in economics? Undoubtedly the intellectual environment of the time embodied in the French Enlightenment played a key role here. Quesnay had been requested by Diderot and d'Alembert, the editors of the *Encyclopédie*, to contribute to this ambitious publication. His articles on farmers (*fermiers*) and cereals (*grains*) represented his entry into the realm of economics. After these articles, influenced by Cantillon's circular flow theory, he encapsulated the flows of income, output, and expenditure in the 'Tableau économique', which, as mentioned above, means the 'Economic Picture'. More accurately, it should be called the 'Macroeconomic Picture'. The 'Tableau' sparked Quesnay's interest in the subject to such an extent that he even attempted to proselytize Louis XV to the theories of the new school.

There was an important distinction between Cantillon's analysis of the circular flow of income and that of Quesnay as embodied in the 'Tableau économique'. Cantillon had analysed the circular flow of income in order to determine the equilibrium quantity of money required in the economy. Quesnay had a very different objective in that he wanted to show the huge productive potential of agriculture. His 'Tableau' showed how an agriculturally driven economic system could generate a surplus. The potential of this surplus, described as the net product (*produit net*), helped further to graduate economic theory from the mercantilist 'zero sum game' mentality. Quesnay raised the prospect of the surplus increasing thereby enabling economic growth to take place. Thus, a new spirit emerged with Quesnay and his followers providing an economic tool in the form of the 'Tableau économique' to show how the economy could achieve growth. These macroeconomic developments were accompanied by the liberal call of *laissez-faire*.

This new spirit of the age, which saw these exciting ideas published in books and journals such as the *Éphémérides* and debated in the Parisian literary salons, was to have a profound influence on the Scottish philosopher Adam Smith. Journeying through France in the early 1760s as the tutor to the young duke of Buccleuch, Smith, bored with the travelling, wrote to Hume that he had decided to write another book. Smith had already lectured in Glasgow on economic issues, most notably on the importance of the division and specialization of labour. The pin factory example that he used to show the huge increases in productivity generated by the division and specialization of labour came directly from an article on *l'épingle* (the pin) in the book that was central to the French Enlightenment, the *Encyclopédie*. So, even prior to moving to France, Smith was well acquainted with works published there. On moving from Toulouse to Paris, he was invited to some of the literary salons where economic ideas were openly discussed and debated. There he met, among others, Quesnay, Pierre-Samuel Du Pont (later to be called Du Pont de Nemours), and Turgot. He was also able to purchase for his library the books and journals published by the *économistes*. Thus, the work that ten years later would emerge as *An Inquiry into the Nature and Causes of the Wealth of Nations* was initially activated by Smith's boredom as he travelled through rural France and then stimulated by the exciting economics environment that he experienced at first hand in Paris. Such was the impression of this environment, and the friendships that emerged from meeting with Enlightenment thinkers, that he intended dedicating the *Wealth of Nations* to Quesnay, but unfortunately the latter died before its publication.

Prior to this, Anne Robert Jacques Turgot, whom Smith had met in France, wrote a series of articles with the title *Réflexions sur la formation et la distribution des richesses*, to appear in the new economics journal the *Éphémérides du citoyen* in 1769–70. Turgot was the *intendant* for the Limousin region at the time of writing this work. Although he mixed with the Physiocrats, he was not really a fully fledged member of the sect; he was his own man with a rigorous line of independent thought. He was the quintessential example of a hard-working and strongly motivated civil servant who believed that he could help redirect the French economy in a more positive way by the development of economics. Although extremely busy with his administrative duties in the Limousin, he found the time to put together some of his ideas on economic issues. The *Réflexions* were written for the instruction of two Chinese students who were returning home. Turgot used this type of literary genre probably to cover up the rushed nature of the work—he could argue that it was just a couple of articles that he had hastily put together for the benefit of these two students. His close links with Du Pont de Nemours and his selection of the latter's journal for the *Réflexions* probably indicate that he had a deeper mission to accomplish with this work. Despite its rushed nature, it is a masterpiece of economic reasoning and one that would have a lasting influence on economists over the following 150 years. In this work Turgot introduced the term 'capital' for the first time in economics. While Quesnay had discussed the concept of capital under the term *avance*, Turgot's use of the term 'capital' was more than a semantic addition to the economist's lexicon. His analysis showed how savings could be transformed into capital formation and how capital formation could generate economic growth. This savings–capital formation analysis would provide the basis for the classical theory of savings and investment for most of the nineteenth century.

What were Turgot's motivations in writing the *Réflexions*? Like Quesnay, he was part of the exciting intellectual environment in France in which the *philosophes* believed that they could, through their writings, change their society. Working as the *intendant* in the Limousin, Turgot saw all round him economic deprivation. He was strongly motivated to change the French economy and wrote many memorandums and books with a wide variety of economic proposals. There was no monetary recompense for writing in the *Éphémérides* as even its editor, Du Pont, was having difficulty making ends meet while publishing it. Instead, Turgot would have known that his work would be read by the *économistes* and *philosophes* and would influence their views on the workings of the economy. Change was in the air and he wanted to reform the French economy. Like John Law earlier in the century, Turgot was given the opportunity to implement his theories as policies when he was made prime minister of France for a short period between 24 August 1774 and 12 May 1776. However, he was deemed to be excessively reformist and when he was dismissed by Louis XVI, the reforms he had introduced were quickly reversed.

Despite all the brilliance of the *Réflexions*, the book showed that Turgot had a mental block in one important area: that of money. He was quite aware that he had to integrate his theory of capital with a theory of money. The transformation of savings into capital realistically necessitated the use of money. However, Turgot identified only one type of money to be used for this purpose: intrinsically valuable metallic money in the form of gold and silver. He was a metallist at heart and gave no role to paper money, credit, or banks. It is quite striking that the latter two are never mentioned once in the *Réflexions*. Why did he have this monetary block? It may be surmised that Law cast a long shadow over Turgot's reflections on the issue of money. Turgot's first writing on an economic issue, 'Lettre à l'abbé de Cicé', when he was a young seminarian at the Sorbonne, was devoted to a scathing critique of Law and his System. As already mentioned, a secondary development arising from the collapse of Law's System was that financial innovation had been stopped in its tracks and France had reverted to a quasi-banking system based around notaries (*les notaires*). The notaries acted as intermediaries between lenders and borrowers but were not credit-creating banks. This meant that Turgot was writing against a very limited monetary background, one dominated by metallic money and the limited financial intermediation of the notaries.

This fault line on the role of money, banking, and finance, characterized in the work of Turgot, was not unique to the economic writings of the eighteenth century. David Hume and Adam Smith would also suffer from this monetary block, though in both their cases it was a more serious problem in that Scotland had produced an emerging modern banking system featuring the development of overdrafts. Instead of welcoming the emergence of this modern banking tradition, both Hume and Smith expressed strong reservations about the benefits arising from a non-metallic monetary system. The analysis of the evolution of Smith's monetary theory from the *Lectures on Jurisprudence* to the *Wealth of Nations* (1776) indicates that there was a major change in his approach to monetary theory between the 1760s and the 1770s. It will be argued that the reason for this change, which transformed Smith from a relative liberal on monetary theory to a deep conservative, was the collapse of the Ayr Bank. This collapse had considerable financial repercussions across Great Britain. Although Smith was not a banker, he became heavily involved in this financial collapse through his close friendship with the duke of Buccleuch. The duke, then aged only 26, had become one of the bank's biggest partners, exposing him to sizeable capital losses. Henceforth he would become a critic of the 'Daedalian wings of paper credit' rather than a supporter of the new Scottish financial innovations. Smith's limitations in the area of money, credit, and banking would be quickly exposed by the banking practitioner Henry Thornton in his *Paper Credit of Great Britain*.

Before discussing this intellectual stand-off between Thornton and Smith, it is important to recognize the latter's contributions to macroeconomics, for he provided the overall setting for the classical analysis of the economy, one marked by competition in a free market environment with individuals pursuing their own self-interest. By synthesizing Cantillon's earlier work on the allocation of resources and combining it with Boisguilbert and the Physiocrats' analysis of the role of natural forces and *laissez-faire*, Smith argued that the market was inherently stable. Furthermore, the provision of information and incentives through the market mechanism implied that the market was self-adjusting and did not need the heavy hand of state intervention to guide it to its optimal position. Some of Smith's interpreters believe that the *Wealth of Nations* therefore provides the blueprint for only limited state intervention in the form of justice and the constable. However, Smith the philosopher had earlier shown, in the *Theory of Moral Sentiments* (1759), that institutions and civic virtues were important elements in providing the social cement necessary for the efficient working of the market economy. To define and confine Smith as just a free market ideologue is to do him a disservice.

At the turn of the nineteenth century Thornton's monetary world was in turbulence. There had been a political revolution in France that produced a regicide. New ideas were in the air on the Continent, and there was a fear that they might be imported into Great Britain. The recent rise to power of Napoleon in France had created the threat of an invasion of Britain. This threat had led to a run on the banking system and the suspension of the convertibility of the pound in 1797. This created a new monetary environment in that the Bank of England was no longer constrained to maintain the convertibility of the pound into gold. To conservative monetary writers, this removal of the link between the issue of banknotes and its gold backing provided an excessively lax scenario in which the Bank of England could be tempted to over-expand the note issue. To others, it was important that a nation at war had access to a banking system that was sufficiently flexible to finance the war effort and to combat the effects of poor harvests. Otherwise, it was argued, the nation could face defeat and/or famine. It was within these parameters that Thornton's brother Samuel had to operate as the Governor of the Bank of England (1799–1801). It was a veritable financial tightrope for the Governor, balancing between deflationary and inflationary policies, a case of damned if he did and damned if he didn't. Thornton attempted a reconciliation of this potential double damnation. There were arguments in favour of both approaches. An anti-deflationist policy could be justified in certain circumstances and an anti-inflationist policy could be recommended at other times. In this way he could provide an intellectual justification for his brother's handling of affairs. Just as Cantillon never mentioned Law in the *Essai*, so Thornton never mentioned his brother in *Paper Credit*. Both are nevertheless present in these respective works.

But an even greater presence in *Paper Credit* emerged in the form of Adam Smith. Thornton criticized monetary policies recommended by writers that drew their inspiration from the *Wealth of Nations*. Smith's work had been used by its proponents for the making of *ex cathedra* pronouncements with respect to monetary policy, which, by implication, were highly critical of the Bank of England's recent monetary stance. Thornton set out to show that there was a huge gulf between the monetary theory of Smith and the world of banking. As a practising banker, he could show the shallowness of Smith's ideas with respect to monetary theory and therefore the danger of basing monetary policy on them. He attacked Smith for his definition of the money supply, his neglect of the velocity of circulation, and his fallacious distinction between real and fictitious bills. In brief, Thornton believed that Smith did not understand that there was a huge and growing range of financial instruments (banknotes, bills of exchange, etc.), other than metallic money, that were being used as money. Furthermore, these different types of money had different velocities of circulation, which made it impossible to determine the equilibrium quantity of money for the economy.

In the first half of *Paper Credit* Thornton produced a number of strong arguments against deflationary monetary policies. These arguments could be construed as providing support for the actual policies implemented by his brother as Governor of the Bank of England, and which opponents of his brother felt were contrary to the implied recommendations on monetary policy to be found in the *Wealth of Nations*. The arguments provided by Thornton showed, for the first time, the circumstances in which the Bank of England, which was starting to emerge as a central bank, should act as a lender of last resort to the rest of the banking sector.

The paradox of Thornton's book is that, having argued strongly against deflationary policies in the first half, he then proceeded to attack inflationary type policies in the second half. Having shown the instability of the velocity of money, Thornton then used an outlandish estimate of velocity to show the inflationary effects that might emerge from an excessive increase in the money supply. Both David Laidler in private discussions and Neil Skaggs (2005) believe that this velocity estimate was a *reductio ad absurdum* adopted by Thornton to warn of the folly of increasing the money supply. For my own part, I do not believe that this type of genre was part of the literary bag of tricks of the serious-minded Thornton.

Intriguingly, Thornton analysed the monetary system at a time when there was no formal gold backing of the currency because of the suspension of convertibility. He could see the potential for the system to continue without the gold anchor, but he also recognized that such a system could not permanently prevail as long as the usury laws were in place. The usury laws had established a maximum rate of interest of 5 per cent, and Thornton understood that the Bank of England could not properly operate with such a limitation. The interest rate could be used to protect the exchange rate of sterling on the international markets provided there was no limitation to its movement. The usury laws prevented Thornton from conceptualizing further on the possibilities of such a monetary environment. This was a great pity, for he had the intellectual capability to become a third Mr Thornton of *Paper Credit*, namely a paper credit emancipationist theorizing monetary policy for a non-metallic monetary environment. Unfortunately, Thornton's imagination was constrained excessively by the usury laws and also by the position he held as a leading banker in the City of London. How could such a leading banker recommend the abolition of the gold standard? It would take until 1971 for economists and bankers to realize fully that John Law's simple change of a preposition—money is the value by which goods are exchanged and not the value for which goods are exchanged—was the right direction to take and that the world's monetary system could operate independently of an intrinsically valuable metal. It had taken a long time for one's man's imagination to win through.

The spirit of John Law lives through these chapters because, in many ways, he set the standard for others. He imagined and created an economy without gold and silver, an extraordinary achievement for the age he lived in. Ultimately he failed, but, more than any of the other writers in this book, he was able to imagine the type of monetary world that we live in today. By using him as a reference point, I may be accused of unfairness towards many of the other writers by implicitly benchmarking them against Law. This is not intended, because each of the writers selected made highly significant contributions to the development of macroeconomics. It may, of course, also be argued that writers such as Hume, Turgot, and Smith, in favouring metallism, adopted the appropriate approach for their times because Law's System had shown the dangers of introducing paper money into contemporary economies.

There is a strong message coming through this analysis of the emergence of macroeconomics, and it relates to the process of economic discovery. There has been a tendency on the part of some economists to take an absolutist approach to the history of economic thought. This approach identifies and highlights the 'correct' contributions of writers to the development of economic theory, a progression from error to truth. This book, while it presents the writers in a chronological format, will, it is hoped, force readers to rethink the absolutist approach. It will show enormous progress in the evolution of economic ideas through time, but it will also illustrate that this progress has not been linear. Sometimes ideas have lain forgotten, awaiting discovery many years later; other times ideas have been deemed to be the new orthodoxy, only to become obsolete when a new paradigm appeared. History should encourage reflection and teach caution. It should convince today's macroeconomic thinkers that modesty should be the hallmark of the profession, for in many cases they are only repackaging ideas that have long since been discovered, and in other cases they are presenting ideas that will end up in historical dustbins.

References

Eatwell, John, Murray Milgate, and Peter Newman (eds) (1978), *The New Palgrave: A Dictionary of Economics* (Basingstoke), iv.

Mossner, E. C. (1980), *The Life of David Hume* (Oxford).

Schumpeter, Joseph (1954), *History of Economic Analysis* (Oxford).

Skaggs, Neil (2005), 'Treating Schizophrenia: A Comment on Antoin Murphy's Diagnosis of Henry Thornton's Theoretical Condition', *European Journal of the History of Economic Thought*, 12/2 (June).

I. Closterman pinx:

William Petty Kn.t
Fellow of the Royall Society
Obijt 16. Dec.r 1687. Anno Ætat: 63.

I. Smith fec: et ex:

Sir William Petty

2

Sir William Petty: National Income Accounting

Imagine that we are back in the seventeenth century in an anatomical dissection room. In a way we do not need to imagine, for Rembrandt's portrait of the anatomical lesson presented by Dr Nicolaes Tulp (1632) provides a contemporary picture of the scene: a body stretched out on a table with the anatomist pointing his students to the incisions that he has made in the corpse's arm. Shift to Oxford, to an anatomy room in the university. William Petty (1623–87), dressed in anatomical black (see the portrait of Petty in his anatomical garb, holding a skull, in the National Portrait Gallery, London), arrives in the room to start his dissection lecture. A coffin is brought in by porters from the Oxford gallows. It contains the body of a young woman condemned to death for allegedly aborting her 18-week-old pregnancy. On the opening of the coffin, the corpse inside 'rattle[s] in the throate', whereupon one of the porters 'stamp[s] upon her breast and stomach severall tymes with his foot' in an effort to complete the work of the hangman (see Petty 1927: ii. 157–67). Though ready to plunge his anatomical scalpel into the corpse of the young woman, Anne Greene, who has been hanged on the gallows, Petty turns around and announces to his drowsy students, many of whom are probably recovering from a hard night on Oxford town (a hundred years later Adam Smith is complaining about the level of drunkenness in Oxford) that he believes he can resuscitate the corpse.

This was some variant on habeas corpus. Had Dr Petty lost the run of himself at the very start of his lecture? His opening lines would bring approval from modern-day educationalists. Try to attract the attention of your students from the beginning. But these were highly melodramatic opening lines. Petty was planning a resurrection. The students would have nudged each other. What was the mad professor up to? Of course he was not mad; professors never are. He had perceived some small signs of life in the wretched girl. In his own words, he found her to continue 'to rattle a little' despite the efforts of the 'lusty fellow' who had tried to stamp her into oblivion. Here was the opportunity to astound and amaze. Petty described his next actions:

We wrenched open her teeth which were fast sett, and putt in some strong waters. Whereupon shee seemeth obscurely to cough or spit. Wee then wrenched open her hands, the fingers being also stiffely bent down, and fell a rubbing her extreeme parts. While wee continued thus doing for a quarter of an hower, and while a fire was making, wee thought of letting her blood . . . When her arme was bound up . . . wee kept rubbing her in severall places, tickled her throate with a feather, and bound her thighs; afterwards gott her putt into a bed very well heated.   (Petty 1927: ii. 158)

So, with considerable medical skill and assistance from Dr Thomas Willis, he brought the young woman back to life: 'he bled her, put her to bed with a warm woman, and with spirits and other meanes restor'd her to life' (Petty 1927, vol. i, p. xiv). A contemporary pamphlet, *News from the Dead*, celebrated Petty's medical triumph.[1] Petty became famous for this resuscitation and within a year was made Vice-Principal of Brasenose College and Professor of Anatomy in Oxford.

Petty with his lively mind was able to use his knowledge of medicine and anatomy and later apply it to economic issues. He would even write a significant socio-economic analysis of the state of Ireland with the title *Political Anatomy of Ireland*. When this work was published posthumously in 1691, it also contained a work called *Verbum Sapienti*, which provided the first mould for the development of macroeconomic analysis.

Petty's Background

Petty was a man of many coats: anatomist, physician, professor of music, inventor, statistician, Member of Parliament, demographer, cartographer, founding member of the Royal Society, industrialist, and author. He was born in 1623 in Hampshire. He represented one of the best examples of a seventeenth-century rags-to-riches personality, for his father was a clothier in Romsey. Petty quickly showed his precocity. No man for hiding his talents, he explained in his will how he became a gifted mathematician, navigator, and Latin scholar at a young age: 'At the full age of fifteen years I had obtained the Latin, Greek and French tongues, the whole body of common arithmetick, the practical geometry and astronomy, conducing to navigation dialling, &c. with the knowledge of several mathematical trades' (Petty 1769, p. iv).

---

[1] Incidentally, Petty would not have been able to achieve such a result in the 19th century. In the Common Room in Trinity College Dublin there is a portrait of a cleric, the Revd Samuel Haughton, whose main claim to fame was to have devised the formula for ensuring the correct drop of a body on the gallows so that the condemned's neck was broken and death came instantly.

In an apparent effort to improve the family's clothing business, Petty travelled to France, earning his passage by acting as a ship's hand. His career as a sailor was cut short when, owing to short-sightedness, he failed to identify a sandbank, thereby endangering the ship off the coast of France. Apparently, the captain of the ship flogged Petty, breaking his arm in the process (see Bevan 1894). Put ashore in the Normandy town of Caen to recover, he was sufficiently precocious to impress the Jesuits who administered the University of Caen. He was admitted as a student and supported himself by teaching navigation and English. He also traded in low-cost jewellery. After a temporary return to England, he fled from the civil war and returned to the Continent to study medicine at Utrecht, Leiden, Amsterdam, and Paris. While in Paris studying anatomy, he mixed with members of the Mersenne circle and met Thomas Hobbes, a writer who was to have a formative influence on him.

On returning to England in 1646, Petty appears to have attempted to take up his father's business, but he moved quickly away from the cloth trade to inventing, making an instrument for 'double writing' described as 'A declaration concerning the newly invented art of double writing'. Being the enterprising individual that he was, Petty attempted to attract investors to subscribe in his scheme. A broadside folio invited investors 'to pay their money to the inventor at his lodging next door to the White Boar in Lothbury'. This enterprise failed, though it did not blunt his enthusiasm for inventing. At a later stage in his career he invented the equivalent of a modern catamaran: 'This vessel was flat-bottomed, of exceeding use to put into shallow ports and ride over small depths of water. It consisted of 2 distinct keels cramped together with huge timbers etc, so as that a violent stream ran between . . . ' (Petty 1899, vol. i, p. xiv). Petty spent a considerable amount of time trialling this boat and trying to convince people such as Charles II that it was the new method for sea travel. Unfortunately for Petty the boat, which he referred to as a 'sluice boat' and which outperformed the Holyhead packet in the Irish Sea, later sank in the Irish Channel during a storm.

In 1648 Petty, under the guidance of Milton's friend Samuel Hartlib, published *The Advice of W[illiam] P[etty] to Mr. Samuel Hartlib for the Advancement of Some Particular Parts of Learning*. In this pamphlet Petty recommended the establishment of a society for 'the advancement of the mechanical arts and manufactures'. This was to provide part of the impetus for the foundation of the Royal Society, of which he would become a founding member.

Another major shift in his vocational interest took place in 1648 when he moved to Oxford University as an assistant to the Professor of Anatomy, succeeding to the professorship in 1651. His friend the biographer John Aubrey described Petty's enthusiasm for anatomy:

He came to Oxon and entered himself of Brasen-nose College. Here he taught anatomy to the young scholars. Anatomy was then but little understood by the university, and I remember he kept a body that he brought by water from Reding a good while to read upon some way soused or pickled. About these times experimental philosophy first budded here and was first cultivated by these vertuosi in that dark time.   (Aubrey 1962: 303)

In 1650 Petty, the skilled anatomist, performed the reanimation described above. He later organized and wrote a petition on behalf of Anne Greene, contending that she had miscarried rather than aborted her baby. Abortion was a capital crime at the time and Petty's evidence enabled her to become a free woman (see Petty 1927: ii. 164–7). Apparently, the students were so impressed with the woman escaping from the gallows through Petty's skill that they clubbed together, 'made a little portion and married her to a man who had several children by her' (Petty 1899, vol. i, p. xiv).

In the same year Petty, through the assistance of his friend the haberdasher Captain John Graunt (1626–97), was also appointed Professor of Music at Gresham College, a more general post than its term implies, but at the same time showing Petty's great versatility. Graunt was a very close friend of Petty in the early part of his career, to the point where they jointly purchased the old town house of Lord Arundel in London (Strauss 1954: 159). Their common background in drapery may have been a factor in initiating the friendship. When Petty met Graunt, the latter was rich and successful (Aubrey described him as 'a very ingenious and studious person' who rose early in the morning to study before opening his shop), and Graunt promoted Petty's cause. The £40 annual income for the professorship of music at Gresham College was a very useful stipend for Petty at this stage of his career, and he repaid Graunt's favour by strongly supporting his admission to the Royal Society in 1663 (an admission that was greatly facilitated by the publication the previous year of the *Natural and Political Observations upon the Bills of Mortality*). In Aubrey's words: 'I believe, and partly know, that he had his hint from his intimate and familiar friend Sir William Petty.' This issue is discussed further below.

Like modern-day academics, Petty succeeded in obtaining a leave of absence from Oxford in 1651. This leave of absence was intended to be for two years, but although he was in fact abroad for seven years between 1652 and 1659 he managed to maintain his vice-principalship of Brasenose until 1659 and his professorship of music until 1660.

The reason for Petty's departure from Oxford was to become physician to Cromwell's army in Ireland. However, it was not as a physician that he was to make his mark there. Cromwell needed to pay his army in Ireland; the Exchequer was short of money and so, as often happens in wars, it was decided to appropriate the lands of the vanquished and award them to the soldiers in lieu of payment: when soldiers are not paid, they represent a potent threat to those in power. In order to pay the soldiers with lands it was necessary to carry out a survey of the lands available. Lands in areas that had 'rebelled' against the Cromwellians were confiscated, and the original Irish landowners, and indeed some earlier English owners, were to be transplanted to the barren, rock-strewn western province of Connacht. The Irish expression 'to hell or to Connacht' summarized the plight of those forced from their lands or threatened with such a sentence. To allocate the forfeited lands a detailed cartographical survey was needed. Speed's maps of Ireland, printed in 1610, show the extent to which the contemporary geographical representation of the country was totally inadequate. Ireland needed to be surveyed and mapped. Petty tendered for this survey, which had already been started, and with the help of some of his London friends such as Graunt was awarded the contract:

About September 1654, I perceiving that the admeasurement of the lands, forfeited by the aforementioned rebellion, and intended to regulate the satisfaction of the soldiers, who had suppressed the same, was most insufficiently and absurdly managed; I obtained a contract, dated 11th December 1654, for making the same admeasurement, and, by God's blessing, so performed the same... (Petty 1769, p. v)

Petty, who was 31 years old at the time, promised to produce the survey of the forfeited lands. He suggested that the soldiers pay for the survey through the deduction from their pay of 1 penny for every 3 acres surveyed. The organization of the survey necessitated assembling and training a large team of one thousand assistants to carry out a wide range of tasks ranging from drafting and mapping the complicated survey to the mundane task of carrying and pulling the measurement chains used in the survey. Petty signed the contract for the survey with the Surveyor-General on 11 December 1654. By 1 March 1656 he had completed the survey, which became known as the Down Survey, so-called because it was the first time that a survey of the country had been set 'down' in detailed maps. The Down Survey covered twenty-two out of the thirty-two Irish counties. Petty later described the logistics involved in measuring the land covered by the survey: 'This Survey was performed by measuring as much line by the chain (and measuring about 20 angles within every mile's space by the circumferenter) as would encompass the globe of the earth 8 times about in its greatest Circle' (Petty 1899: 615).

To understand Petty one needs to grasp the importance of the Down Survey to him. It was an incredible logistical achievement on his part to organize this survey at a time when the country was deemed to be still in a rebellious mood, a mood that would have deepened with the arrival of the surveyors, armed with their measuring tools in each and every townland and village in the country. 'Excuse me while I measure your land so that we may arrange to grant it to some of these accompanying English soldiers.' To allay their demands for immediate payment the soldiers were paid with debentures entitling them to purchase confiscated land. Short of money, many soldiers sold these debentures at considerable discounts to some of their officers, including Petty, who made sizeable fortunes on these transactions.

On the completion of the Down Survey, Petty continued to exploit his cartographical skills. Using his entrepreneurial instincts, he assembled all the data that he had collected and used it to produce a general map of Ireland, its provinces, and its counties, in *Hiberniae Delineatio*, which would be published in 1685. The royalties from this mapping and later editions of this work would have further increased Petty's income and wealth. The detail of his maps was so good that they remained the standard cartographical representations of Ireland until the establishment of the Ordnance Survey. By aggregating all the lands in twenty-two of the thirty-two Irish counties, presenting them in detailed maps in the Down Survey, and later producing an atlas of maps for all of Ireland, Petty had his first experience with aggregation, an experience that would serve him well later when it came to the aggregation of economic data.

With the money generated from the Down Survey, Petty was able to buy land all over Ireland. He showed himself to be very adept at purchasing choice lots of land in areas such as Meath and the city of Limerick, along with 50,000 acres of land around Mount Mangerton in County Kerry. In many cases he was able to buy the land very cheaply through his adroit acquisitions of debentures.

The Down Survey and his involvement in the distribution of the forfeited lands involved Petty in many acrimonious disputes. In one case a former Cromwellian knight, probably Sir Hierome Sankey, challenged him to a duel. John Aubrey described how Petty reacted to the challenge:

The knight had been a soldier, and challenged Sir William to a fight with him. Sir William is extremely short-sighted, and being the challengee it belonged to him to nominate place and weapon. He nominates for the place a dark cellar, and the weapon to be a great carpenter's axe. This turned the knight's challenge into ridicule, and so it came to nought.   (Aubrey 1962: 304)

Petty obviously had a keen sense of humour, his friend John Aubrey later describing him to be 'an excellent droll' capable of extemporizing sermons 'either the Presbyterian way, Independent, Capucine friar, or Jesuit'. Aubrey also provided a verbal portrait of Petty:

He is a proper handsome man, measured six foot high, good head of brown hair, moderately turning up: see his picture as Doctor of Physic. His eyes are a kind of goose-grey, but very short-sighted, and, as to aspect, beautiful, and promise sweetness of nature, and they do not deceive, for he is a marvellous good-natured person, and compassionate. Eyebrows thick, dark and straight (horizontal). His head is very large. He was in his youth very slender, but since these twenty years and more past he grew very plump, so that now (1680) he is abdomine tardus.   (Aubrey 1962: 305–6)

Despite Petty's support for the Cromwellians, the Restoration did not dramatically affect his fortunes, though he later contended that he lost a great part of his Irish lands through the Court of Innocents in 1663. The loss of these lands was counterbalanced by his elevation to a knighthood, in 1661 by Charles II, a monarch much bemused by Petty's bubbling mind for ideas and innovations. Petty would later turn down a peerage on two occasions, remarking that 'he had rather be a copper farthing of intrinsic value than a brass half-crown, how gaudily soever it be stamped and gilded' (Petty 1899, vol. i, p. xxix).

Over the next three years Petty, now a knight of the realm, would produce his two most important economics works: *A Treatise of Taxes and Contributions*, written and published in 1662, and *Verbum Sapienti*, written in 1664 but published posthumously in 1691.

Who were Petty's intellectual influences? In a letter to his cousin Sir Robert Southwell discussing Pascal's 'Différence entre l'esprit de géometrie et l'esprit de finesse', in which he argued that Pascal's distinction between geometricians and sagacious men was a false one in that he found that the best geometricians were the most sagacious men and the most sagacious men were the best geometricians, Petty classified the authors of 'great achievements' between the 'ancients' and the moderns (Petty 1927: 58). His 'ancient' authors consisted of the mathematician Archimedes, the man of medicine Hippocrates, the soldier and politician Julius Caesar, Aristotle, Cicero, Homer, Varro, and Tacitus. The 'modern' authors consisted of Molière, Francisco Suárez, Galileo, the philosopher and administrator Sir Thomas More, Francis Bacon, John Donne, Thomas Hobbes, and René Descartes. His judicious selection of men of letters interestingly excluded Shakespeare. Hobbes, who combined medicine with political philosophy, had taught Petty in Paris, and the inclusion of the Jesuitical philosopher Francisco Suárez no doubt resulted from the Jesuits' influence on Petty in Caen. Perhaps the two most interesting of the moderns in Petty's list were Bacon and Descartes. These were the philosopher–scientists who imposed method on Petty's approach to conceptualization. The empiricism of Sir Francis Bacon, combined with the logical orderliness of Descartes, greatly influenced Petty's methodological approach, which dictated that it was important to quantify and measure the world around him. He was not impressed by philosophers who reasoned in terms of big or small, better or worse. Petty wanted to know by exactly how much. In the letter to Southwell, Petty remarked, 'You know my virtue and vanity lies in prateing [talking] of numbers, weight, and measure' (Petty 1927: 51). More formally, he later wrote: 'The method I take to do this, is not yet very usual; for instead of using only comparative and superlative words, and intellectual arguments, I have taken the course (as a specimen of the Political Arithmetick I have long aimed at) to express myself in terms of number, weight or measure' (Petty 1899: i. 244).

Petty's coining of the term 'political arithmetic' was significant. He was to use it in the title of a number of his books, such as *Five Essays in Political Arithmetick* (1687) and *Political Arithmetick* (1690), believing that it was necessary to quantify the polity. For example, how could rulers govern if they did not know the size of the population? Thus, Petty attempted to measure the population in both England and Ireland. One approach he used was to calculate the number of people in towns and cities by counting the number of chimneys ('smoaks') per house and averaging the number of people that lived around the hearth represented by each chimney. He also used mortality bills to calculate tables of mortality. From these he was able to extrapolate the size and age of the population. His keen desire to establish a proper set of statistical data that could be used to develop inferences for economic policy made him the founding father of econometrics.

Petty's Macroeconomics

It must be remembered that Petty did not set out to write economic treatises *per se*. To understand him it is necessary to observe his obsession with his income and wealth and his desire to protect it from the hands of the taxing authorities. This may be clearly evidenced in his will, where he discussed incessantly the growth in his income and wealth. In the early part of the will Petty recalled his return to his birthplace in the 1640s:

I returned to Rumsey, where I was born, bringing back with me my brother Anthony, whom I had bred with about 10 l. more than I had carried out of England. With this 70 l. and my endeavours, in less than four years more I obtained my degree of M.D. in Oxford, and forthwith thereupon to be admitted into the college of physicians, London, and into several clubs of the virtuous; after all which expenses defrayed, I had left 28 l. and in the next two years, being made fellow of Brasenose, and anatomy professor in Oxford, and also reader at Gresham College, I advanced my said stock to about 400 l. and with 100 l. more advanced and given me to go for Ireland, unto full 500 l. (Petty 1769, p. iv)

Then, when discussing his contract for the Down Survey, Petty showed how his income and wealth had greatly increased:

. . . I gained about 9000 l. thereby; which with the 500 l. above mentioned, my salary of 20s. per diem, the benefit of my practice, together with 60 l. given me for directing an after-survey of the adventurers land and 800 l. more for two years salary, as clerk of the council, raised me an estate of about 13000 l. in ready and real money. (Petty 1769, p. v)

And so the will goes on and on, describing how he continued to build up his wealth. Having worked hard to make his fortune, he wanted to keep it. In the case of his two greatest economic works, *A Treatise of Taxes and Contributions* and *Verbum Sapienti*, he set out to show ways of reducing the burden of taxation on landowners and by implication the maintenance of his wealth. The by-product that emerged from these writings provided the basis of his economic reasoning.

In reading the collection of Petty's economic works entitled *The Economic Writings of Sir William Petty*, it should be borne in mind that Petty's head was teeming with so many ideas that he quickly moved from subject to subject. This means that there is a certain amount of *à la carte* searching to extract the full list of his economic ideas. Thus, for example, in the preface to the *Treatise of Taxes and Contributions* he made a strong appeal for what would later be termed a *laissez-faire* approach to the economy when he put forward the Latin phrase *vadere sicut vult* ('let things go as they will'). This one would regard as an intrinsically important statement of Petty's economic philosophy. It was fashioned by his medical training: just as it was often better for the physician not to tamper with a patient's body, so also the wise administrator did not interfere excessively in the economy: 'We must consider in general, that as wiser physicians tamper not excessively with their patients, rather observing and complying with the motions of nature than contradicting it with vehement administrations of their own; so in politicks and oconomicks the same must be used' (Petty 1899: i. 60). Note his use of the term 'oconomicks'. He was the first English writer to use this term, but unfortunately it would lie dormant in the *Treatise* and was not reintroduced into the English language until the late 1750s, when it was translated from French.

However, despite Petty's pleas for a *laissez-faire* approach to the economy, he also recommended a certain amount of government intervention. This intervention was needed to provide employment for the 'supernumeraries', i.e. the unemployed. Petty produced a rudimentary distribution of the labour force, which broke down as follows:

Food producers	100
Exporters	200
People employed in the ornaments, Pleasure and magnificence of the Whole	400
Governors, Divines, Lawyers, Physicians and Retailers	200
Supernumeraries (the unemployed)	100

Each food producer generated surplus product by providing food for nine other workers and their families. Petty was concerned about the unemployed, but this concern was not motivated by any social conscience on his part. He wanted to provide work for these people in England so that the additional demand created by their expenditure would increase the demand for goods from Ireland, which in turn would help relieve the burden of taxation on landowners in Ireland like him. Furthermore, he believed that the unemployed should provide some work in return for the food and other services produced by the employed sectors of the populace and by doing so be in a position to move into alternative, more profitable employment when the occasion arose. This has resonance with modern discussions on *hysteresis* effects: keep labour employed because once it becomes unemployed it can lose some of its skills and work ethic. Like Keynes,[2] Petty did not worry about

---

[2] 'Ancient Egypt was doubly fortunate, and doubtless owed to this its fabled wealth, in that it possessed two activities, namely, pyramid-building as well as the search for the precious metals the fruits of which, since they could not serve the needs of man by being consumed, did not stale with abundance. The Middle Ages built cathedrals and sang dirges. Two pyramids, two masses for the dead are twice as good as one...' (Keynes 1936: 131).

the exact type of work that the unemployed should perform, recommending, if necessary, the building of pyramids:

Now as to the work of these supernumeraries, let it be without expence of foreign commodities and then 'tis no matter if it be imployed to build a useless pyramid upon Salisbury Plain, bring the stones at Stonhenge to Towerhill, or the like; for at worst this would keep their minds to discipline and obedience, and their bodies to a patience of more profitable labours when need shall require it.   (Petty 1899: i. 31)

Additionally, Petty, like Keynes, in recommending public works programmes for the unemployed, hit upon the basic fundamentals of what would later be termed 'the Keynesian multiplier', namely that such expenditure would generate income that in turn would generate further expenditure:

Men repine much, if they think the money levied will be expended on entertainments, magnificent shews, triumphal arches, etc. To which I answer, that the same is refunding the said monies to the tradesmen who work upon those things; which trades, though they seem vain and only of ornament, yet they refund presently to the most useful; namely, to brewers, bakers, tailors, shoemakers, etc. Moreover the prince hath no more pleasure in these shews and entertainments than 100,000 others of his meanest subjects have, whom for all their grumbling, we see to travel many miles to be spectators of these mistaken and distasted vanities.   (Petty 1899: i. 33)

So Petty would have been quite happy with modern pop festivals and open-air musical concerts given the type of multiplier effects that he believed they were capable of generating for the economy.

The *Treatise* is regarded by many commentators as Petty's outstanding work on economics because they can find in it early insights into the theory of surplus product, insights that would inspire Karl Marx in the development of his theory of the exploitation of labour (see Aspromourgos 1988, 1996). However, for pure power-packed theorizing, his greatest contribution, in my opinion, has to be *Verbum Sapienti*. Published posthumously in 1691, alongside the *Political Anatomy of Ireland*, it looks as if it was tacked onto the latter work almost as an afterthought, for it contains only twenty-four pages of text. The 1691 editor was unable to see the sheer brilliance of this work. The same comment would apply to Charles Hull when he edited *The Economic Writings of Sir William Petty* in 1912. Again he missed the importance of *Verbum Sapienti*, an omission probably due to the fact that macroeconomics was still twenty years away from its formal rediscovery by the economists working on national income measurement and by John Maynard Keynes. Schumpeter recognized that 'modern income analysis' started with Petty, but prefaced this comment with his view that 'The superior quality of his mind shows in all his comments and suggestions, but there is nothing very striking or very original or very distinctive about them' (Schumpeter 1954: 213). It is only recently that researchers have started to look more closely at *Verbum Sapienti*. Richard Stone

(1984), in his Nobel Memorial Lecture, traced the origins of national economic accounting to this work. However, his analysis of it was rather cursory, quickly moving away from Petty's national income estimates to a discussion of Gregory King's contributions on the subject in *Natural and Political Observations and Conclusions upon the State and Condition of England*, which, alas, remained in obscurity until 1802, when it was published as an appendix to George Chalmers's *An Estimate of the Comparative Strength of Great Britain*. So, Stone notwithstanding, there is still a lack of awareness in the economics profession of the value of *Verbum Sapienti*, where Petty conceptualized the basics for the analysis and measurement of national income. Slack (2004) recently emphasized the importance of the first chapter of *Verbum Sapienti* from the point of view of national income accounting: 'The first five pages present in prose what is in effect a balance-sheet of national income and expenditure' (Slack 2004: 613). But Petty went far further than this because, not only did he measure national income, but, more importantly, he provided much of the template that initiated macroeconomic theory. Ironically, this was not his main objective. *Verbum Sapienti*, which essentially translates as 'A Word to the Wise', or, in modern terminology, 'A Message to the Government', was written from the perspective of Petty the harassed taxpayer. As shown earlier, he was close to his money. England was at war with Holland, wars need financing, and Petty feared that landowners would be taxed further to pay for it. He estimated that the landowners were already paying one-tenth of their estates (presumably revenue) in taxes but that by Christmas 1665 they would be paying one-third. The objective of the work was to show the government that the tax base was far wider than had hitherto been conceived and that landowners such as himself constituted only a part of the potential tax base. To show this he needed to demonstrate that the income from land was only part of the overall national income, and that the wealth of landowners was only a part of the overall wealth of the economy. He therefore needed to provide a measure of the national income and the national wealth of England.

We can imagine Petty glumly sitting down at his table and wondering how he might plead a case for shifting this tax to other sectors of the community. Beside him he had a copy of the recently published *Natural and Political Observations Mentioned in a Following Index and Made Upon the Bills of Mortality* (1662), written by his friend John Graunt. This book is regarded by many commentators as the first English book on statistics and certainly the first work on English medical statistics. During the great plague of 1592 every parish in the City of London was obliged to publish a weekly bill on the number of burials and christenings that took place within the parish. These bills of mortality provided details of the cause of death recorded by the 'searchers', generally old women who were paid a couple of pennies to undertake this work. The list of causes of death included 'bloudy flux', 'cancer', 'convulsion', 'griping in the guts', 'jaundies', 'meatles', 'plague', 'plague in the guts', 'rickets', 'small-pox', 'water in the head', 'worms', etc. Accounts were kept, according to Graunt, for 1592–4 but then fell into disuse. They were resumed again in 1603, most probably because of further fears of an outbreak of plague. The bills provided an early-warning system to the richer members of society on outbreaks of plague, one of the great fears of the time. On seeing such outbreaks in their parish, they could retreat to their country houses so as to avoid the possibility of contracting the disease. John Graunt decided that the information presented in the weekly bills, which were then aggregated to produce an annual account of birth and deaths in London, provided a rich base on which to make statistical demographic inferences.

The title page stated that the *Observations* had been written by Graunt. However, scholars are divided over whether he actually wrote this work. Friends and contemporaries of Petty, such as Aubrey, indicated that it was Petty rather than Graunt who had been the author. In 1927 Petty's descendant the marquess of Lansdowne furthered that view by his examination of some of Petty's unpublished manuscripts. However, Petty's bibliographer Geoffrey Keynes was not prepared to accept that Petty was the sole author of the *Observations* (Keynes 1971). Why would Petty not have claimed authorship? His partisans believe that he was returning a favour to Graunt, who had earlier been instrumental in having Petty appointed Professor of Music at Gresham College and later awarded the contract for the Down Survey. The argument goes that, by ensuring that Graunt was perceived as the author of the *Observations*, Petty was able to present him for election to the Royal Society.

This argument I find difficult to accept because it is evident that it was Graunt rather than Petty who collected all the parish bills of mortality, the necessary data for the *Observations*. Petty would not have had the time, or, indeed, the patience, to collect assiduously such material and then to aggregate the statistics from each parish. At best I believe Petty may have helped Graunt to draw up some of his conclusions but not to write the book.

That said, I believe it was the *Observations* that helped to encourage Petty to write *Verbum Sapienti*. Again let us imagine the scene. It may be surmised that Petty was cursing his luck because it appeared that the outbreak of war against Holland would lead to a considerable increase in his tax bill. He wanted to fight against this possibility. Suddenly the appearance of Graunt's book provided him with a key statistic to use for the base of his calculations. This was Graunt's estimate of the population of England and Wales:

There are about 100000 parishes in England and Wales, the which, although they should contain the ⅓ part of the Land, nor the ¼ of the people of that country-parish, which we have examined, yet may be supposed to contain about 600 people, one with another, according to which accompt there will be six millions of people in the nation.   (Graunt 1662: 45)

This estimate of 6 million was the base for Petty's calculations for measuring the national income of England and Wales. Petty's macroeconomic analysis starts with this estimate in the opening lines of chapter 1: 'There are of men, women, and children in England and Wales, about six millions' (Petty 1899: i. 105). Petty then estimated that the expenditure of each of these would be 4½*d.* per day, or £6 13*s.* 4*d.* per annum. Then, multiplying this latter by the population of 6 million, he arrived at an overall expenditure estimate of £40 million. Petty's analysis had been initiated thanks to the key population estimate of John Graunt.

Graunt's close contact with Petty when the latter was writing *Verbum Sapienti* is borne out in a privately held manuscript copy of the first part of the work, which Petty dictated for his friend. This manuscript which reproduces the contents of the introduction, chapter 1, and the first two paragraphs of chapter 2 of the published text pre-dated, in my opinion, the manuscript on which the published text was based. The reasons for believing this are as follows:

The manuscript, unlike the published text, has nineteen consecutively numbered paragraphs.

The manuscript does not have the introduction and chapter headings, which are found in the published text, and therefore gives the appearance of a work in progress.

It has the correct value that Petty imputed for the lands of England and Wales, namely £6 8*s.* per acre, rather than the mistaken value of £6 1*s.* 8*d.* per acre contained in the published text (1899: i. 105).

It has a different title from the running title of the printed text. The title 'A paper proposeing a way for the more equal Distribucion of the monthly taxe by Estimateing the nation's value etc' is far shorter than the running title of the printed text 'Verbum Sapienti; or, An Account of the Wealth and Expences of England and the Method of raising Taxes in the most Equal manner. Showing also, That the Nation can bear the Charge of Four Millions per Annum, when the occasions of the Government require it'. The shorter running title on the manuscript suggests that Petty, at the time of dictating the contents of the manuscript to his secretary, was concentrating on the tax issue of *Verbum Sapienti* and had not elaborated the longer running title that would accompany the printed text in 1691.

The manuscript, which finishes in mid-sentence, suggests that Petty had decided, after marshalling all the key arguments and statistics about the income and wealth of England and Wales, to send it immediately to his friend Graunt.

One can imagine Petty's excitement at this moment. He had started off concerned and irritable about the prospect of landlords such as himself paying more taxes to finance the Anglo-Dutch War. Suddenly, thanks to Graunt's population estimate and his own conceptual brilliance, he was able to estimate the wealth and income of England and Wales and to show the possibility of taxing the greatest component of national income, namely the income from labour. Petty had done this in the nineteen paragraphs of the manuscript. The rest of *Verbum Sapienti* would just be a further development of the analysis presented in these opening nineteen paragraphs. The template of *Verbum Sapienti*, found in these opening nineteen paragraphs, was of such importance that Petty would subsequently rework it in his private notes in 1685, 'A Gross Estimat of the Wealth of England considered in the particulars following' (Petty 1927: i. 181) and in the *Political Arithmetick* (Petty 1899: i. 310). So it is not unreasonable to surmise that Petty, excited by his discoveries in these nineteen paragraphs and acknowledging the influence of his friend Graunt, decided to send the paper to him immediately. At the top the manuscript one finds 'ffor Capt.a Graunt'. If my surmise is correct here, then the manuscript represents a vitally important part of the intellectual dialogue that arose between Graunt the demographer and statistician, and Petty the economist. Petty wanted to inform his very good friend of the immediate way he was thinking on the issue of how to measure the income and wealth of the nation.

The multiplication of Graunt's population estimate of 6 million inhabitants by his estimate of per capita expenditure of £6 13s. 4d. to produce a calculation of total national expenditure of £40 million was very much back-of-the-envelope economics. Petty had presented no data to support his estimate of per capita expenditure. However, it is Petty's method rather than his data that is important to observe for he went on to conceptualize some of the fundamentals of macroeconomics, starting from this estimate of national expenditure. These were:

the stock–flow distinction between wealth and income;
the national expenditure = national income identity;
an analysis of the different sources of income.

Keeping the £40 million national expenditure estimate in the back of readers' minds, Petty then calculated what would be termed today the 'non-human wealth' of England and Wales along with the income flows derived from each specific form of wealth. This may be summarized as in Figure 2.1. Using

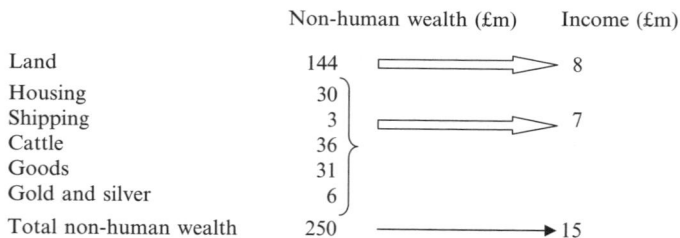

	Non-human wealth (£m)	Income (£m)
Land	144	8
Housing	30	
Shipping	3	7
Cattle	36	
Goods	31	
Gold and silver	6	
Total non-human wealth	250	15

Figure 2.1 Non-human wealth and associated flows of income

his calculation of the land of England and Wales, Petty estimated that the flow of income derived from such land was £8 million. But there were other wealth assets, besides land, such as housing, goods, shipping, cattle, and gold and silver. The income stream from these sources of wealth he estimated at £7 million. Adding them up, he derived an estimate of non-human wealth amounting to £250 million and the income arising from this wealth at £15 million. This raised a problem: if national expenditure amounted to £40 million and the flow of income from non-human wealth was only £15 million, then what was causing this inequality? The missing element was labour and the income it generated. So the income from labour was introduced as a residual in the manner illustrated in Figure 2.2.

It is important here not to focus excessively on Petty's estimates of wealth and income but on the way he conceptualized the whole process. Petty was the first writer to make the distinction between the stock of wealth and the flow of income that it generated. He was also the first to state that national income equalled national expenditure. These insights then enabled him to derive the income of labour once he hypothesized the amount of national expenditure and calculated the value of all the non-human wealth assets (land, housing, shipping, cattle, gold and silver, and personal estates). Then, by subtracting the income that he derived from non-human wealth from the estimate for national expenditure, he was able to derive the income of labour as amounting to £25 million: 'Now if the annual proceed of the stock, or wealth of the nation, yields but 15 millions, and the expense be 40 then the labour of the people must furnish the other 25' (Petty 1899: i. 108). Then, by capitalizing this income stream, he was able to estimate the value of human wealth. Add this to non-human wealth, and he had an estimate of the total wealth of England: 'Whereas the stock of the Kingdom, yielding but 15 millions of proceed, is worth 250 millions; then the people who yield 25 are worth 417 millions' (Petty 1899: i. 108).

Petty's approach is breathtaking. It is a virtuoso performance, for in a couple of pages he had demonstrated how it was possible to calculate the wealth of

National expenditure = national income
National expenditure = £40m
Income from non-human wealth = £15m

Income from human wealth = national expenditure − income from non-human wealth
    £25m   =   £40m   −   £15m

Income from human wealth = £25m
Capitalized human wealth = £417m

Figure 2.2 Deriving income from human wealth

the nation, national income, and how to relate national income to national expenditure. He had not only produced a measurement of the wealth and income of England and Wales but, more importantly, he had put in place the template for macroeconomic analysis.

However, notwithstanding the analytical brilliance of *Verbum Sapienti*, Petty was basically uninterested in the macroeconomic vistas that he had opened up. He did not call on his fellow members of the Royal Society to announce the breakthrough that he had made. Instead he wanted to drive the message home to the politicians that landowners had only a part of the wealth of the nation and that their land generated only one-fifth of the national income, and that therefore it was unfair to tax landowners excessively. The running title of the manuscript of *Verbum Sapienti*, discussed above, clearly spelt out his objective in writing the book. The message to his readers—Petty's manuscripts would have been directed to the men of power in London—was a tax message. Let the government look at the income of labour which produced three times more than the produce of the land and let it bring into the tax net this sizeable source of income. At this level Petty may be regarded as first advocate of income tax.

Petty's macroeconomic construction went largely undeveloped by the author, though there are echoes of it in the *Political Arithmetick* in his discussion of the link between money and the trade of the nation; and for the most part it was not understood by his contemporaries. It would take writers of the calibre of Cantillon, Law, and Quesnay to develop his skeletal outline further. However, it did serve to set down certain markers. One of the most notable of these was that gold and silver specie constituted only a very small part of the wealth of the nation. Petty calculated the specie money supply at £6 million and this represented less than 1 per cent of the total wealth of England. Mercantilist writers who had been stressing that money was the wealth of the nation would have to think again.

Additionally, almost as an *obiter dictum*, Petty discussed the velocity of circulation of money. Using the imagery of circles of expenditure Petty estimated that, if the circles were of short duration involving weekly wage payments, then the amount of money required to maintain these short circles of expenditure would be £40 million of expenditure divided by fifty-two weeks. However, if the expenditure circles were of a longer period involving only quarterly payments over the year for rents and tax payments, then the amount required would amount to £10 million. Assuming that half of the payments involved taxes and rents and the other half wages, Petty estimated that the average amount of money required in England, given these calculations of the velocity of money, was £5.5 million, very close to his calculation that the money supply equalled about £6 million.

This then enabled him to conclude, in what amounted to a rare purple passage, the following:

For money is but the fat of the body-politic, whereof too much does as often hinder its agility, as too little makes it sick. 'Tis true, that as fat lubricates the motion of the muscles, feeds in want of victuals, fills up uneven cavities, and beautifies the body, so does money in the state quicken its action, feeds from abroad in the time of dearth at home; even accounts by reason of its divisibility, and beautifies the whole, although more especially the particular persons that have it in plenty.   (Petty 1899: i. 113)

The problem with Petty's analysis of money is that it is very fleeting. He rarely applied his skills to analyse extensively the role of money. He had a basic understanding of the needs of the monetary system to meet what we would call the demand for money in an economy. One sees this in *Verbum Sapienti*, the *Political Arithmetick*, and the *Quantulumcunque Concerning Money* (1695). In the first, as has been shown, making certain assumptions with respect to the velocity of circulation of money through his use of two circulations (land rents plus wage payments), he estimated the overall demand for money in England to be £6 million. Later, in the *Political Arithmetick*, he elaborated three rather than two circulations, adding on the rent from housing to the rent from lands and the money needed for wage payments:

If there be six millions of souls in England, and that each spends 7 l. per annum, then the whole expense is forty two millions, or about eight hundred thousand pound per week; and consequently, if every man did pay his expense weekly, and that the money could circulate within the compass of a week, then less than one million would answer the ends proposed. But forasmuch as the rents of the lands in England (which are paid half yearly) are eight millions per annum, there must be four millions to pay them. And forasmuch as the rent of the housing of England, paid quarterly, are worth about four millions per annum there needs but one million to pay the said rents; wherefore six millions being enough to make good the three sorts of circulations above mentioned, I conceive what was proposed, is competently proved, at least until something better be held forth to the contrary.   (Petty 1899: i. 310)

In the *Quantulumcunque Concerning Money* he elaborated further on this issue when, in question 25, he answered the question whether there was any way to know how much money was required for a nation. Petty calculated that a further circle needed to be factored in when estimating the demand for money. This was money required to finance exports:

Answer. I think it may pretty well be guessed at; viz. I think that so much money as will pay half a year's rent for all the lands of England and a quarters rent of the housing, and a weeks expence of all the people and about a quarter of the value of all the exported commodities, is sufficient for that purpose. Now when the states will cause these things to be computed, and the quantity of their coins to be known, which the new coining of their old money will best do, then it may also be known whether we have too much or too little money.   (Petty 1899: ii. 446)

Despite Petty's successive additions of further circles of circulation to his initial demand for money function, his approach was still very much a back-of-the-envelope approach to quantifying the demand for money. However, behind this analysis he wanted to present a rudimentary method for measuring the demand for money. Once this is done, then if the money supply was less than the demand for money, it would be necessary to have banks meeting the shortfall. Petty had learnt from his stay in Holland the importance of the Dutch banks to the economic development of the Netherlands, and in the *Political Arithmetick* he cited a range of advantages that the Dutch had for promoting trade:

suppose a hundred thousand pounds will drive the trade of the nation, and suppose there be but sixty thousand pounds of ready money in the same; suppose also that twenty thousand pounds will drive on and answer all payments made of under 50 l. In this case forty of the sixty being put into the bank, will be equivalent to eighty, which eighty and twenty kept out of the bank do make up an hundred, (that is to say) enough to drive the trade as was proposed; where note that the bank keepers must be responsible for double the sum entrusted with them, and must have power to levy upon the general, what they happen to lose unto particular men. Upon which grounds, the bank may freely make use of the received forty thousand pounds, whereby the said sum with the like sum in credit makes eighty thousand pounds, and with the twenty reserved a hundred. (Petty 1899: i. 265–6)

In the above passage Petty assumes that the money supply of £60,000 is insufficient relative to the demand for money, which he assumes to be £100,000. He also assumes that the demand for currency is just £20,000. In this case there was the potential for the other £40,000 in coin to be deposited with the banking system, which in turn could expand credit, pushing up bank deposits to £80,000. When this happened the new money supply was as follows:

$$\text{Money supply } (\pounds 100,000) = \text{currency } (\pounds 20,000) + \text{deposits } (\pounds 80,000)$$

The expansion of bank credit and bank deposits enabled the shortage in the demand for money to be met and equilibrium to be restored. Petty recognized that this process meant that in some cases the bankers would make bad loans that would not be repaid. In a default-prone environment bankers would need to be able to operate their business so that the profits from other loans more than covered such capital losses when borrowers defaulted. Thus, in one short half-paragraph of the *Political Arithmetick*, Petty showed the importance of banks in ensuring that the money supply was kept in line with the demand for money, along with the requirement for bankers to be prudent in maintaining a balanced loan portfolio. But Petty wanted to go further than just having a banking system adapted to the needs of the English economy. Towards the end of the *Political Arithmetick* he unfolded a plan for creating a bank capable not only of meeting the demands of the English economy but also of financing the totality of world trade. For a normally conservative writer, this was quite a breathtaking proposal. Furthermore, Petty believed that it was not necessary to have specie as the backing for the extra money that would have to be created. Instead the credit could be expanded on the basis of the collateral of land. Petty, anticipating John Law, thus favoured the creation of a land bank to meet his plans for England taking over the financing of the totality of world trade.

by inbanking twenty millions worth of land, not being above a sixth or seventh of the whole territory of England; (that is to say) by making a fund of such value, to be security for all commodities bought and sold upon the accompt of that universal trade here mentioned ... and from what has been said in the last paragraph, about enlarging of stock, both of money, and land; that it is not impossible, nay a very feasible matter for the King of England's subjects, to gain the universal trade of the whole commercial world. (Petty 1899: i. 312)

It is typical of Petty that he devoted only two pages to the discussion of this proposal for England to take over the financing of world trade. The plan was so obvious to him that he did not devote excessive attention to it. With his bubbling mind there were plenty of other ideas in the pipeline to be developed. It was not a one-off proposal by Petty, for he returned to it in 1682, when he was writing the *Quantulumcunque Concerning Money*, arguing: 'We must erect a Bank, which well computed, does almost double the effect of our coined money: And we have in England materials for a bank which shall furnish stock enough to drive the trade of the whole commercial world' (Petty 1899: ii. 446). It was not until after the Glorious Revolution of 1688 that the English finally followed the Dutch model and established the Bank of England in 1694.

One would have liked to see Petty write a great deal more on this process, but his fertile mind wanted to describe other factors that he believed to be important when analysing the economic superiority of the Dutch over the English. This perceived Dutch superiority had also been the subject of part of Sir Joshua Child's *Brief Observations Concerning Trade, and Interest of Money* (1668). In this book Child stated that the *causa causans* of Dutch prosperity was their low rate of interest of 3 per cent: half the English rate. Petty did not accept this, contending that the low rate of interest was an effect rather than a cause of Dutch prosperity: 'as for lowness of interest, it is also a necessary effect of all the premises, and not the fruit of their contrivance' (Petty 1899: i. 261). In this way he dismissed Child's argument in half a sentence. In the *Quantulumcunque Concerning Money* he defined interest as 'a reward for forbearing the use of your own money for a term of time agreed upon'. He added to this definition a page later by inserting that interest incorporate an insurance premium besides that of the forbearance factor. He opposed the usury laws as well as restrictions on the export of money.

Shortly before his death in 1687 Petty wrote 'A Treatise of Ireland, 1687', which was presented to James II in September of that year. In it Petty proposed the transplantation of the Irish population to England. In this way he believed that Ireland would no longer constitute a hotbed of sedition to the Crown. Hull, when editing Petty's works in 1899, called this Petty's 'final solution of the perennial Irish Question' (Petty 1899: 547). Given his earlier implicit support of the transplantation of Irish natives to the rough terrain of the west of Ireland through his work for the Down Survey, it was perhaps just as well for the Irish that Petty's death prevented him from pushing his proposal for their enforced transplantation to England and Wales.

Sir William Petty died a rich man in his house in Piccadilly Street on 16 December 1687 'of a gangrene in his foot, occasioned by the swelling of the gout' (Petty 1769, p. xiii). His writings, most of which were published posthumously in the 1690s, had a profound and lasting effect on the eighteenth-century writers on economics. Petty would no doubt have been greatly pleased by his great-grandson the marquess of Lansdowne (a man whose name changed from William Fitzmaurice to William Petty, to Viscount Fitzmaurice, to the earl of Shelburne, and finally to the marquess of Lansdowne), who became prime minister of Great Britain for a brief period between July 1782 and April 1783. Shortly before he became prime minister, it was Shelburne, as Secretary for Colonial and Home Affairs, who effectively made the decision to terminate hostilities and acknowledge the establishment of the United States of America.

References

Aspromourgos, Tony (1988), 'The Life of William Petty in Relation to his Economics: A Tercentenary Interpretation', *History of Political Economy*, 20/3.

—— (1996), *On the Origins of Classical Economics: Distribution and Value from William Petty to Adam Smith* (New York).

Aubrey, John (1962), *Aubrey's Brief Lives*, ed. Oliver Lawson Dick (1949; Harmondsworth).

Bevan, Wilson Lloyd (1894), 'Sir William Petty: A Study in English Economic Literature', *American Economic Association*, 9/4.

Graunt, John (1662), *Natural and Political Observations Mentioned in a Following Index and Made Upon the Bills of Mortality* (London).

Keynes, Geoffrey (1971), *A Bibliography of Sir William Petty, F.R.S., and of the 'Observations on the Bills of Mortality' by John Graunt* (Oxford).

Keynes, John Maynard (1936), *The General Theory of Employment, Interest and Money* (London).

Lansdowne, marquess of (ed.) (1928), *The Petty–Southwell Correspondence 1670–1687* (London).

Petty, Sir William (1769), *Tracts Chiefly Relating to Ireland* (Dublin).

—— (1899), *The Economic Writings of Sir William Petty*, ed. Charles Henry Hull, 2 vols (Cambridge, 1986).

—— (1927), *The Petty Papers: Some Unpublished Writings of Sir William Petty*, ed. the marquess of Lansdowne, 2 vols (London).

Schumpeter, Joseph (1954), *History of Economic Analysis* (Oxford).

Slack, Paul (2004), 'Measuring the National Wealth in Seventeenth-Century England', *Economic History Review*, 57/4.

Stone, Sir Richard (1984), 'The Accounts of Society', Nobel Memorial Lecture, 8 Dec. 1984.

Strauss, E. (1954), *Sir William Petty: Portrait of a Genius* (London).

Mⁱᵉ JEAN LAW CONᵉʳ DU ROY EN TOUS CES CONˢⁱˡˢ CONTROLEUR
GNÁL DES FINANCES en 1720.

Sous l'Auguste et Sage Regence, | LAW consommé dans l'art de regir la finance
D'un Prince aimant la bonne foy: | Trouvé l'art d'enrichir les sujets et le Roy.

Loca Schenk Fecit | Pet. Schenk Exc. Amst.

John Law

3

John Law: A New Monetary System

Let us imagine that we are on Bloomsbury Heath, London, in 1694. The dawn is breaking and two carriages appear out of the darkness. Their occupants split into two groups. There is little talk. There is a flash of metal against the rising sun as blades are tested. A swordsman emerges from each group. A referee asks both swordsmen to draw their swords. *En garde*! There is a quick pass and one of the combatants drops to the ground mortally wounded. In the battle of the beaux on Bloomsbury Heath, John 'Beau' Law (1671–1729) has just killed Edward 'Beau' Wilson.

The ranks of the economists are not marked out by the inclusion of murderers—though Antoine de Montchrétien, author of the *Traicté de l'économie politique* (*c*.1615), had also killed a man in an earlier seventeenth-century duel. Many people would be very reluctant to allow Law into the pantheon of great economists because of his colourful past. How could a murderer, a rake, a philanderer, and a gambler be associated with serious-minded economists?

Born in Edinburgh, Law had left his home town in the early 1690s to sow some wild oats in London. At a time when his fellow countryman William Paterson was inspiring a consortium of merchants to establish the Bank of England, Law was mixing with the fops and dandies of London society. A debonair, handsome, and gregarious man, he was given nicknames such as Beau Law and Jessamine John by the ladies of his entourage. Excited by the gambling tables of London, Law quickly lost his inheritance and had to rely on his mother to bail him out of his gambling debts. Now, as he looked at the fallen body of Beau Wilson, he found himself surrounded by horsemen who arrested him for murder. Duelling was a capital crime and Law was brought before the courts, where he was convicted of murder and sentenced to death. The wheels of justice had turned and it appeared that Law was destined for a brief and not very illustrious career that would end on the gallows.

The duel with Wilson had been the talk of the beau monde of London. Some of these gossips maintained that Law and Wilson had been fighting for the favours of Betty Villiers, a mistress of King William of Orange. There was considerable speculation over how Wilson had managed to transform himself from a poor ensign fighting in Flanders to an apparently wealthy man about town driven around London in a splendid coach. It appeared that he was a kept man with a wealthy lover, and it was suggested that Betty Villiers had been keeping Wilson in this magnificent style. However, she was eminently more sensible than this and it is difficult to see this lady, who would later establish Middleton College in County Cork, wasting her money in this way. An alternative hypothesis regarding the source of Wilson's high style of living suggests that he was the homosexual lover of a prominent English lord and highly placed politician. If one accepts this particular story, parts of which may be gleaned from a pamphlet, *Love Letters of a Nobleman to the late Mr. Wilson*, published in the 1720s, it would appear that the nobleman wishing to rid himself of Wilson hired John Law to inveigle Wilson into a duel and kill him. If this interpretation is accepted, then Law's reputation sinks even further in that he was the equivalent of an eighteenth-century assassin.

This second interpretation of a duel arranged to ensure the removal of Wilson is given some credence by the speed with which plans were made for Law to escape from prison, plans which had been discussed at the highest political level (see Murphy 1997). Later a smokescreen was created suggesting that a friend had managed to slip a hacksaw to Law, enabling him to cut the bars of his prison cell. According to this story, he then jumped from the window onto a coach waiting below his cell, in the process injuring a leg. The reality was more prosaic in that the doors of his cell and the prison were secretly opened to enable him to leave. Law apparently did not believe this and had to be told twice that all he had to do was to walk out of the prison. By implication there were influential political leaders in London who had no wish for him to stand on the gallows and perhaps reveal the real reason behind the duel.

Law escaped to the Continent, and the English authorities probably felt that they would never hear any more about him. He appeared destined to end his life in oblivion. Former rake, bankrupted gambler, and murderer on the run were not the entries on a CV that would endear the 23-year-old Scotsman to European society. However, over the next twenty years Law became a very different man. This transformation involved him in metamorphosing into a highly successful gambler and a remarkable macroeconomist. By 1705 he had produced two brilliant works of economics, by 1714 he had become a multi-millionaire, by 1719 he was claiming that he was the richest man who had ever existed, and by 1720 he had introduced Europe's first great macroeconomic experiment, the Mississippi System, and had effectively been made the prime minister of France. So how did the convict on the run of 1694 manage such a remarkable transformation?

Law had a number of significant assets to assist in this transformation. The first was that he was a brilliant mathematician. Scottish contemporaries had noticed this talent when he had been in school in Edinburgh, where, incidentally, he had also acquired a reputation as a very good tennis player. Law, the failed gambler of the early 1690s, must have realized when he arrived on the Continent that he had been wasting his talents in making rash and uncalculated gambles. Fortunes are rarely made by relying on chance, and mathematics provided him with the tool to remove the chance element in gambling. By using his mathematical skills he was able to determine the odds of the different games of chance. The art of gambling is to make sure the odds are on your side, and Law was able to do this in a number of different ways. Faro was one of the most popular gambling games of the period, but Law quickly discovered that the odds were stacked in favour of the banker in this game, so he always assumed this position at the gambling table. As the banker he was the bookmaker at the table rather than the gambler. Another example of his use of mathematics was the way he relied on probability theory when gambling with a die. He would arrive in magnificent style at a gambling venue such as the Ridotto in Venice and proceed to spill a bag of 1,000 shining gold coins onto the table. He would then offer this cornucopia to anyone willing to bet a golden coin on throwing six consecutive sixes. The lure of the golden coins attracted many bidders. Law was offering odds of 1,000 to 1 to these punters, whereas the real odds were 46,656 to 1. By these stratagems Law had essentially shifted from acting as a punter–bettor to a bookmaker, all the time using probability theory to ensure that the odds were in his favour. He developed more sophisticated approaches to the application of probability theory by proposing new methods for running lotteries. At one stage he was involved in operating a lottery in Holland, and he also produced a range of proposals for the creation of a lottery in the Duchy of Savoy. Law's transformation from a mug punter to a sophisticated type of eighteenth-century bookmaker produced a significant change in his fortune. By 1714 he was able to bring 1.5 million *livres* into France, money which he would use to purchase shares in the companies that he created. But this profitable bookmaking activity, while it enabled him to live in a grand style, was only a partial backdrop to his new passion, his desire to change the world of money and banking.

This desire would lead to the activation of Law's second major asset, his hitherto dormant banking gene. Law was the son of a prominent Edinburgh goldsmith and at the end of the seventeenth century the Edinburgh goldsmiths were evolving into bankers. They had realized that taking specie and bullion on deposit, while a profitable activity, could be turned into an even more profitable source of revenue by lending the same specie and bullion out to borrowers at attractive interest rates. Edgar Faure, adopting the type of psychological profiling approach favoured by some French authors, surmised in *La Banqueroute de Law* (1977) that Law's championing of paper money was a Freudian reaction against his father: 'the enemy of gold born into a goldsmith's house'. This was not the case. The goldsmiths had realized that there was a far more attractive world ready for them to conquer, namely that of making money out of money, and the way to do this was to metamorphose into bankers.

The level at which Law wished to approach the world of money and banking was not confined to the establishment and management of a small bank. Law had a far more grandiose vision, conceiving his ideas at a macro level. This vision involved two essential elements. First of all, Law believed that it was possible to move the monetary system away from metallic money to a paper-based monetary system using as collateral assets such as land. From the very outset he made a crucial change in the definition of money. Other writers maintained that money was the value *for* which goods are exchanged; Law replaced the preposition 'for' with the preposition 'by'. This was no mere semantics; it was a major substantive change. Money did not have to be intrinsically valuable. The world could have a monetary system without relying on gold and silver. The second element in Law's vision was that the replacement of metallic money with paper money necessitated the creation of a giant bank that would be capable not only of substituting paper money for metallic money but of transforming the pattern of economic activity in the overall economy. Credit creation by the new bank would provide new financing for entrepreneurs to increase economic activity.

The scope of Law's vision became apparent when he made his first proposal to Lord Godolphin, a leading member of the government, for the establishment of a land bank in England. This proposal, 'Essay for a Land Bank', published as *John Law's Essay on a Land Bank* (1994), was submitted to Godolphin in 1704. Involving the creation of a paper money backed up by the collateral of land, it was not original in itself. Many other writers, ranging from William Potter and William Petty in the 1660s to a whole host of projectors including John Briscoe, Nicholas Barbon, John Cary, William Paterson, and Dr Hugh Chamberlen, in the 1690s and the first decade of the eighteenth century, had presented a variety of different land bank models. Law's proposals for land banks in both England ('Essay for a Land Bank') and later Scotland (*Money and Trade*) outshone all of these contemporary writings by the sheer scale of the macroeconomic vision and modernity of its economic conceptualization.

In the first part of this chapter Law's theoretical contributions to macroeconomics will be assessed. This will be followed by an analysis of the way in which Law attempted to implement his macroeconomic ideas as macroeconomic policy in France between 1716 and 1720. The structure of the first part of the chapter is as follows:

Law's theoretical contributions to macroeconomics
- Early contributions in the 'Essay for a Land Bank'
    Use of the term 'demand'
    Formulation of the concept of the demand for money

Analysis of inflation in a money supply–money demand framework
- Contributions in *Money and Trade* and the later writings
  The link between money and economic activity
  The circular flow of income
  The money-in-advance requirement
  The analysis of inflation in terms of money supply–money demand
  The law of one price.

Early Contributions in the 'Essay for a Land Bank'

Law's use of the term 'demand for money' derived from his use of the term 'demand'. Thweatt (1983) wrote that Law was the first writer on economics to use the term 'demand' in its proper economic sense. More recently Patrick Kelly pointed out that John Locke had used the term in its economic sense on two occasions in his economic writings (Locke 1991: i. 328, ii. 421). However, Locke confused the issue by using terms such as 'consumption' and 'vent' as synonyms for 'demand'. Law pointed out that vent was not an appropriate concept for Locke to equate with demand (Law 1934: i. 4).

By introducing demand into economic theory and then combining it with 'quantity' (supply), Law became the first writer to use supply and demand analysis. This arose when he presented the paradox of value in the context of water and diamonds; Law would later reproduce the water–diamonds paradox in *Money and Trade* and Adam Smith would borrow it, without acknowledgement, in the *Wealth of Nations*:

The value of goods is rated not as the uses they are applied to are more or less necessary but as they are in quantity in proportion to the demand for them. Water is of necessary use, yet of little value because the quantity of water is great in proportion to the demands of it. Diamonds are of less necessary use yet of great value because the demand for diamonds is great in proportion to the demand [quantity?] of them.   (Law 1994: 57)

Law stressed further the role of the market forces of supply and demand:

As the value of goods is rated according to the quality of them and the demand for them so their value changes from any change in their quality, in the quantity of them, or in the demand of them. If silver is coarser, i.e. has more alloy in it, it is of less value than when finer. If the quantity of silver is greater an ounce is of less value than an ounce of the same quality or fineness was when silver was in lesser quantity. If the demand for silver is greater an ounce is of more value than an ounce of the same quality or fineness was when the demand for silver was lesser.   (Law 1994: 57)

He reiterated this later: 'Everything receives a value from its uses and the value is rated according to the quality of it, the quantity of it and the demand of it' (Law 1994: 86). Law placed considerable emphasis on supply and demand analysis in the 'Essay', in *Money and Trade*, and in the many memorandums that he sent to the French authorities. It was supply and demand analysis that was used to present monetary theory in terms of the supply of money and the demand for money. He very clearly showed that if the supply of money was greater than the demand for it, then it would fall in value, i.e. prices would rise: 'If the quantity of money is greater than the demand for it the money'd man is wronged for money being less valuable £100 will not buy him the same quantity of goods £100 bought before' (Law 1994: 77). This he would reiterate a year later in *Money and Trade*, where he wrote: 'If money were given to a people in greater quantity than there was a demand for, money would fall in its value; but if only given equal to the demand it will not fall in value' (Law 1934: i. 160).

Law's development of the concept of the demand for money and his interlinking of the money supply with money demand in his 'Essay' suggest that he started his academic theorizing from what would later be deemed to be a monetarist perspective. This may be seen more clearly by moving forward in time to 1956, when Milton Friedman produced his seminal paper 'The Quantity Theory of Money: A Restatement' (1956). In this paper Friedman broke away from the old quantity theory approach by stipulating the importance of the demand for money. This he clearly stated in the opening lines of the article: 'the quantity theory is in the first instance a theory of the demand for money. It is not a theory of output, or of money income, or of the price level. Any statement about these variables requires combining the quantity theory with some specifications about the conditions of the supply of money' (Friedman 1956: 4). The basis for what would become the monetarist counterrevolution to the existing Keynesian orthodoxy of the 1950s was the concept of the demand for money. Friedman believed that his reformulation of the quantity theory of money within a framework of money demand and money supply was path-breaking. There appeared to be no antecedents. However, it has been shown that as early as 1704, in his 'Essay', Law not only produced for the first time the concept 'demand for money' but also showed how the price level would vary according as the supply of money went out of line with the demand for money. Does this imply that John Law was the first of the modern monetarists?

Macroeconomic Contributions in *Money and Trade*

Law was a great deal more eclectic than just a monetarist with concerns about inflation. His main work, *Money and Trade*, addressed to the Scottish Parliament in 1705, shows that his primary concern by then was the low level of output and employment in his native country of Scotland. *Money and Trade* incorporates many of the earlier themes raised in the 'Essay for a Land Bank' but goes further, much further, in its pursuit of a general macroeconomic framework along with an appropriate set of macroeconomic policy recommendations. The monetary environment that Law was addressing was an impoverished Scotland rather than the more prosperous England of the 'Essay'.

In *Money and Trade* he presented a very pessimistic appraisal of the economic affairs of Scotland:

This country is more capable of an extended trade than any other country of Europe, yet it is reduced to a very low state. Trade is ruined; the national stock is wasted; the people forsake the country; the rents of land are unpaid; houses in towns and farms in the country are thrown upon the owner's hands; the creditor cannot have the interest of his money to live upon; and the debtor's person and estate are exposed to the law.

(Law 1934: i. 152–4)

He paid particular attention to the unemployment problem as reflected in Scotland's inability to find work for its population:

But numbers of people, the greatest riches of other nations are a burden to us; the land is not improved, the product is not manufactured; the fishing and other advantages for foreign trade are neglected, and the reason generally given is, that laziness and want of honesty are natural to us.   (1705: i. 152)

This changed monetary environment meant that Law had to address not only the money–inflation issue, but, more importantly, the money–output issue. He wanted to show that money was not just linked to the price level. It was also linked to output, or trade as it was then called. The title of the book *Money and Trade* said it all. Law believed that money had a real role to play in the economy. For him, money drove trade:

Domestic trade depends on the money. A greater quantity employs more people than a lesser quantity. A limited sum can only set a number of people to work proportion'd to it and it is with little success laws are made for employing the poor or idle in countries where money is scarce; good laws may bring the money to the full circulation it is capable of, and force it to those employments that are most profitable to the country. But no laws can make it go further, nor can more people be set to work without more money to circulate, so as to pay the wages of a greater number. They may be brought to work on credit, and that is not practicable, unless the credit have a circulation, so as to supply the workman with necessaries; if that is supposed then that credit is money, and will have the same effects on home and foreign trade.   (1934: i. 14–16)

This passage merits considerable attention, for in it Law was expressing some of his fundamental beliefs; namely, that (1) trade depends on money; (2) there is some proportionate relationship between the amount of money in circulation and the number of people employed; (3) money is required because it is used to pay the wages of the workforce; (4) credit is not practicable unless it can be used to purchase goods and services demanded by the employed workers—credit used in such a way becomes money; (5) a greater quantity of money employs more people than a lesser quantity.

Law developed this theme on the relationship between the quantity of money and employment by asking what happens if 50 per cent of the public is unemployed while at the same time output is equal to expenditure and there is balance of payments equilibrium. In such an instance he contended that, if more money is injected into the economy, it will either increase employment or reduce the amount of underemployment, adding on a rider that the increased output generated will cause exports to expand, thereby generating a balance of payments surplus. On the other hand, if the money supply is reduced, employment and output fall, exports are reduced, and a balance of payments deficit will ensue:

> If one half of the people are employed, and the whole product and manufacture consumed; more money, by employing more people, will make an overplus to export: If then the goods imported balance the goods exported, a greater addition to the money will employ yet more people, or the same people employed to more advantage; which by making a greater, or more valuable export, will make a balance due. So if the money lessens, a part of the people then employed are set idle, or employed to less advantage; the product and manufacture is less, or less valuable, the export of consequence less, and a balance due to foreigners. (1934: i. 16–18)

For the moment let us leave aside Law's misguided belief that expansion of the money supply generates balance of payments surpluses and reduction in the money supply produces balance of payments deficits, so that we may concentrate on the theme linking money with employment and output. The importance of this theme is reinforced a couple of pages later when Law detailed the relationship between the money supply and employment in Scotland's manufacturing sector during a discussion in which he argued against prohibitions on woollen exports: 'if the product of Scotland cannot be manufactur'd with less than 50,000 people, and the money that can be spared to manufacture, be only capable to employ 25,000, one half of the product will be lost if it is not allowed to be exported' (1934: i. 20).

The importance that Law attached to the money–employment link is exemplified by his attempt to model a rudimentary circular flow of income theory in the penultimate chapter of his book—the first ever presented by an economist. Ironically, his former business colleague, and later one of the speculators against the Mississippi System, Richard Cantillon, has generally been credited with discovering the circular flow of income, while Quesnay has received the accolades for presenting Cantillon's ideas in a schematic form in the 'Tableau économique'.[1]

---

[1] R. V. Eagly has been the only writer who refers to the possibility of Law as the pioneer of the circular flow of income, though he did not develop this viewpoint (Eagly 1974: 17).

Law presented a hypothetical model of an island economy with a single landlord–proprietor where barter prevails. Initially he assumed a small and very rudimentary economy with a population of 1,300 people: 100 tenant farmers and their families (ten to a family), amounting to 1,000 people in all; the other 300 are 'poor or idle who live by charity'. The tenants pay their rents in kind and the surplus of the island is exported to import 'cloths and what other goods they want'. There is no indigenous manufacturing sector on the island: 'the people of this island know nothing of manufacture'. To all intents and purposes it is a barter economy with the island's surplus traded for goods manufactured elsewhere. Furthermore, the balance of payments is in equilibrium. It is proposed to the landlord–proprietor that money be introduced on the island so as to encourage employment among the unemployed and more intensive use of the underemployed:

> if a money is established to pay the wages of labour, the 300 poor might be employed in manufacturing such goods as before were exported in product; and as the 1,000 that labour the ground were idle one half of their time they might be employed so as their additional labour would be equal to that of 500 more, which lessen their import by providing them with a part of such goods as before they brought home from the Continent, and raise their export to 3 or 4 times the value it had.   (1934: i. 132–3)

Thus, key assumptions of the model are the existence of unemployment ('the 300 poor or idle'), underemployment (500 who are underemployed in the agricultural sector), and the absence of a manufacturing sector. The catalyst for increasing employment is the creation of money.

The circular process, shown in Figure 3.1, is initiated by the landlord–proprietor paying the labourers in the newly created manufacturing sector with paper money for their goods and services. The labourers use the paper money to purchase corn and other agricultural goods from the tenant farmers. This latter grouping uses the paper money to pay the landlord–proprietor his rent. Thus, the money flows between the three groups, financing the payment of goods and services as well as the payment of the rent, with the money returning to the landlord at the end of this process, thereby enabling him to start a further round of economic activity.

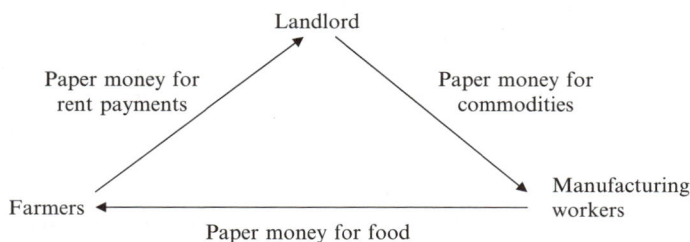

Landlord

Paper money for
rent payments

Paper money for
commodities

Farmers

Manufacturing
workers

Paper money for food

Figure 3.1 Law's elementary circular flow of income

The proprietor coins paper to the value of a year's rent, employs such as are willing to work, and gives them paper-money as the price of their labour. The tenant gives corn or any other goods he has to the labourer for paper-money, and the proprietor receives it for his rent. (1934: i. 134)

This is an analysis not of the actual status quo but of a desired economic situation produced by the creation of money. The status quo is represented by a barter economy in which there is a bilateral flow of commodities and rent payments between the agricultural tenants and the landlord–proprietor in an economy operating well within its production possibility frontier. By introducing money into the model, the system becomes a tripartite one allowing for the employment of the 'poor and idle' and the more intensive employment of the underemployed. More specifically, in Law's view, the introduction of money into the system facilitates the establishment and development of a manufacturing sector, which may be grafted onto the economy, enabling economic activity and employment to be greatly increased. It is important to stress this development, for in its initial barter state the island economy is deemed to be incapable of producing a manufacturing sector. It is the introduction of money to the island economy which permits the creation of a manufacturing sector. Law was stating that a shift to a money economy permitted the transformation of the island economy from a primitive agricultural barter system to a more progressive manufacturing-cum-agricultural economy.

Law then added a complication to this model. Suppose the labourers do not purchase enough agricultural goods to enable the tenant farmer to pay his rent, but use the money instead to purchase non-agricultural goods, thereby pushing up the price of the latter. In his model he assumed that the landlord issued money in the form of paper notes equivalent to the annual rent paid by the farmers to him. He also assumed that the workers in the manufacturing sector earned four units but only needed to consume two units of the products of the tenant farmers. In this case, 'the labouring men being masters of the remaining part of the paper, and having no occasion for more goods from the tenants, might raise the value of the paper' (1934: i. 134). He overcame this problem, not by analysing the dynamics of relative price movements as the prices of agricultural goods fall owing to excess supply and non-agricultural goods rise due to excess demand, but by recommending the further expansion of the money supply. He envisaged this further growth in the money supply increasing the demand for manufacturing labour, thereby attracting an inflow of labour, 'part of the poor and idle of the Continent to the island'. This rise in manufacturing employment increases the demand for agricultural output on the island. Law explained that it 'occasions a greater consumption, whereby the tenants are able to pay their rent in paper as contracted for' (1934: i. 134).

The island model showing Law's understanding of the circular flow of income appears in chapter 7, towards the end of *Money and Trade*. The demonstration of the circular flow of income was not, however, his primary concern. It was just an element of a larger design, for he wanted to show that money was an integral part of the circular flow of income. Without money, society could only exist at a primitive barter level of economic activity. With money, it could develop away from the rural agricultural model to incorporate a manufacturing sector producing a flow of goods and services between land-lords, farmers, and workers. The expansion of the circular flow required further injections of money.

Law was proposing what is currently termed the 'cash-in-advance require-ment model', which specifies that money needs to be acquired in advance before any transactions, and therefore expenditure, may take place. Long before such modern theorizing he was stating that money was needed to bring transactors (buyers and sellers, producers and employees) together. The quotations cited above clearly demonstrate his conviction that money was central to the employment- and income-generating process. Law was prepared to admit that his belief that there was a positive relationship between the growth in the money supply and income might have been deemed by some people as 'a supposition that's extravagant', but he went on to point out that such critics should have observed the example of other countries: 'As the money of England has increased, the yearly value [national income] has increased; and as the money has decreased, the yearly value has decreased' (1934: i. 144). It was a theme which Law returned to a year after the publica-tion of *Money and Trade*, when, in the 'Mémoire touchant les monoies et le commerce' (1706), he posed the question why employment was not generated in conditions where money was rare, unemployment was common, and employees were willing to work at low wage rates:

It will be asked if countries are well governed why they do not process their wools and other raw materials themselves, since, where money is rare, labourers work at cheap rates? *The answer is that work cannot be made without money*; and that where there is little, it scarcely meets the other needs of the country and one cannot employ the same coin in different places at the same time. (Law 1706, fo. 7; my emphasis)

This passage shows that Law was quite prepared to accept the possibility that, in the face of heavy unemployment, wages could be flexible. He was not prepared to accept that such flexibility would solve the unemployment prob-lem. Money was required to put the buyers of labour into contact with the sellers of labour. Without it Law saw little possibility of the unemployment problem being solved.

Law acknowledged that barter trading can take place without money but he asserted that barter limits the range of economic activity:

In this state of barter there was little trade, and few arts-men. The people depended on the landed-men. The landed-men laboured only so much of the land as served the occasions of their families, to barter for such necessaries as their land did not produce; and to lay up for seed and bad years. What remained was unlaboured; or gifted on condition of vassalage, and other services. The losses and difficulties that attended barter, would force the landed-men to a greater consumption of the goods of their own product, and a lesser consumption of other goods; or to supply themselves, they would turn the land to the product of the several goods they had occasion for; though only proper to produce of one kind. So, much of the land was unlaboured, what was laboured was not employed to that by which it would have turned to most advantage, nor the people to the labour they were most fit for. (1934: i. 4–6)

Here he was indicating that an economy can only stay at a primitive Robinson Crusoe level of development in its barter phase, and in particular cannot develop a manufacturing sector without money. He accepted that the use of specie money, particularly silver, had enabled society to evolve from a barter economy to a money economy, an evolution that helped reduce unemployment and increase output:

As money increased, the disadvantages and inconveniencies of barter were removed; the poor and idle were employed, more of the land was laboured, the product increased, manufactures and trade improved, the landed-men lived better, and people with less dependance on them. (1934: i. 14)

To Law, however, the evolution to a specie-using economy was only a partial solution to the unemployment problem. Supplies of silver were uncertain, being subject to the vagaries of discoveries in the Spanish Americas. There was an insufficient supply of silver money in Scotland at the time of his writing *Money and Trade*. A method had to be found of supplementing, if not supplanting, the monetary system based on silver.

Law believed that by increasing the money supply it was possible to increase economic activity, which in turn could increase the demand for money, thereby locking the increased money supply into the domestic economy without inflationary effects (the balance of payments effects will be discussed later).

It was shown above that Law was the first economic writer to use the concept of the demand for money in the 'Essay on a Land Bank'. In *Money and Trade*, which contains frequent use of the term, he specified the factors influencing the demand for money, saying that it was 'proportion'd to people, land or product', product being synonymous with what is defined as national income today. 'Money in Scotland is not above one 40th part of the money in England, proportioned to the people, land, or product; nor above a 10th part proportioned to the demand' (1934: i. 100). The juxtaposition of people and land with (national) product takes on a greater meaning later, for Law's concept of the optimum quantity of money involved a fully employed economy where people and land were fully utilized:

It cannot well be known what sum will serve the occasions of the nation, for as manufacture and trade advance, the demand for money will increase; but the many poor we have always had, is a great presumption we have never had money enough. (1934: i. 158)

Starting with a situation of unemployment disequilibrium, he argued that each increase in the money supply would, by generating an increase in economic activity and employment, thereby create an increase in the demand for money:

The paper money proposed being always equal in quantity to the demand, the people will be employed, the country improved, manufacture advanced, trade domestic and foreign will be carried on, and wealth and power attained (1934: i. 139)

and

At present perhaps 3 or 400,000 lib. is more than there is a demand for; but as trade and manufacture increase, the demand for money will be greater. (1934: i. 160)

He thus assumed that, with output expanding in line with the increase in the money supply, there was a potential non-inflationary demand for money up to that level of economic activity consistent with full employment. He was not advocating that the money supply be expanded ad infinitum, for he realized, and he had already written about this in the 'Essay', that if the money supply was expanded out of line with the demand for money, it would have inflationary repercussions: 'If money were given to a people in greater quantity than there was a demand for, money would fall in its value; but if only given equal to the demand it will not fall in value' (1934: i. 160).

As was the case with the 'Essay', Law continued to develop the importance of the money supply–money demand analysis for analysing inflation when he described how the global inflation rate would be influenced by changes in the money supply relative to the demand for money: 'As the quantity of money has increased . . . much more than the demand for it; and as the same quantity of silver has received a higher denomination, so of consequence money is of lesser value' (1934: i. 190). Law wanted to show that the quantity of silver had been over-expanded globally over the previous 200 years, resulting in a twenty-fold increase in international price. It is clear that, in this context, he was discussing the price of internationally traded goods, because he cited the increase in the prices of goods such as wheat, wine, meat, and malt. Furthermore, he cited the examples not only of Scotland, but also of France and England: 'In England 20 times the quantity of money is given for goods, that was given 200 years ago' (1934: i. 94). The reason for the over-expansion in silver was the influx of new silver from the Spanish Americas, which had pushed up European prices:

The reason is plain, why silver has increased more in quantity than in demand. The Spaniards bring as great quantities into Europe as they can get wrought out of the mines, for it is still valued though not so high. And though none of it came into Britain, yet it will be of less value in Britain, as it is in greater quantity in Europe.   (1934: i. 96)

These quotations show that Law consistently stated that inflation arose when the money supply increased out of line with the demand for money. Furthermore, he believed that the main culprit for the over-expansion of the European money supply had been Spanish silver:

If the money of any particular country should increase beyond the proportion that country bears to Europe; it would undervalue money there, or, according to the way of speaking, it would raise goods: But as money would be undervalued everywhere the same, or near to what it were there; it would be of great advantage to that country, though thereby money were less valuable; For that country would have the whole benefit of the greater quantity, and only bear a share of the lesser value, according to the proportion its money had to the money of Europe. When the Spaniards bring money or bullion into Europe, they lessen its value but gain by bringing it; because they have the whole benefit of the greater quantity and only bear a share of the lesser value.   (1934: i. 104)

Law's apparent pre-monetarist theorizing was further reinforced by his invocation of the law of one price. Having explained why European prices had risen as a result of an excessive increase in the quantity of silver, he faced the dilemma of reconciling the situation in his native Scotland with the overall European situation. Scotland was suffering from a shortage of money, whereas the European money supply had been over-expanded, causing the value of silver to fall. If this was the case, surely Scottish prices should have been a great deal lower than European prices?

Law even presented the case for this type of reasoning:

It may be objected that in Scotland the quantity of goods are proportioned to the demand as they have been some years ago; and money scarcer, the demand for it the same or greater. So if goods and money are higher or lower in value, from their greater or lesser quantity in proportion to the demand for them; money should by its great scarcity be more valuable, and equal to a greater quantity of goods. Yet goods differ little in price, from what they were when money was in greater quantity.   (1934: i. 100)

Law's answer to this type of reasoning showed that he understood two essential parts of the global monetarist approach. These were that (1) international, i.e. eighteenth-century European, inflation was caused by an excessive expansion of the money supply out of line with the demand for money; (2) prices for traded goods were determined by the international forces of supply and demand rather than the domestic forces of supply and demand:

The value of goods or money differs, as the quantity of them or demand for them changes in *Europe*; not as they change in any particular country. Goods in *Scotland* are at or near the same value with goods in *England*, being near the same in quantity in proportion to the demand as there: Money in *Scotland* is not above one 40th part of the money in *England*, proportioned to the people, land or product; nor above a 10th part proportioned to the demand. If *Scotland* was incapable of any commerce with other countries, and in the state it is now, money here would buy 10 times the quantity of goods it does in *England*, or more: But as *Scotland* has commerce with other countries, though money were much scarcer than now, or in much greater quantity than in *England*; if there were but 10,000 lib. in *Scotland*, or a million, the value of goods would not differ above 30 per cent from what they were abroad, because for that difference goods may be exported, or imported. Prohibitions may raise the difference higher. (1934: i. 102)

This passage shows that Law had a clear understanding of the way in which excessive expansions in the international money supply generated inflation and how such inflation was transmitted into a small open economy. He acknowledged that if the Scottish economy was a closed one, then the existing money supply could purchase ten times the amount that was currently possible. But this was not the case. The Scottish economy was an open one, so that its price level was determined by the international price level plus a mark-up of 30 per cent to meet what he had earlier called 'charges and profit' (1934: i. 30). Of course, if trade regulations (prohibitions) were put in place, then the Scottish price level could diverge even more from the European price level.

Law had earlier discussed the way in which international arbitrage kept prices in line across national frontiers:

If goods worth 100 lib. in Scotland, are worth 130 lib. in England, these goods will be exported, 30 per cent being supposed enough for the charges and profit. If the price of these goods lower in Scotland from a 100 lib. to 80, the price in England will not continue at a 130; It will lower proportionably, for either Scots merchants will undersell one another, or English merchants will export these goods themselves. So if they rise in Scotland from 100 lib. to 120; they will rise proportionably in England, unless the English can be served with these goods cheaper from other places, or can supply the use of them with goods of another kind. (1934: i. 30)

Thus, in Law's schema, prices in a small open economy are determined by international prices rather than by domestic money supply factors. He attacked William Petyt, who, when writing *Brittania Languens* (1680), had argued that prices are proportionately related to the money supply. In strikingly pre-Humean language, Petyt had asked what would have happened if the English money supply had been reduced to only £500. Would this not have caused oxen to be sold for a penny each? 'If there were but 500 l sterling in England, an ox could hardly be worth a penny, nor could the revenue of all England be 500 l per annum, or not above' (Petyt 1680: 12). Law disagreed, contending that, as oxen were internationally traded goods, their price would be determined by international rather than domestic factors. As oxen could be exported, their price would be determined by that potentially available on markets, such as the neighbouring Dutch market, rather than in a depressed English market: 'as the ox might be exported to Holland, it would give a price in England equal or near to that it would give in Holland' (1934: i. 102).

Weaknesses in Law's Theory

While Law's early writings in both the 'Essay on a Land Bank' and *Money and Trade* show considerable sophistication, they also contain the seed which was to lead to the excesses of 1720. This seed was germinating in Law's theoretical belief that an expansion in the money supply could generate not only an increase in output and employment, but also a balance of payments surplus. Although the early parts of *Money and Trade* seem to indicate a strong belief in a positive relationship between the money supply and exports, Law's position showed less certainty on this issue in the latter parts of the book.

Law was critical of the viewpoint that money was scarce as a result of a balance of payments deficit, believing that the shortage of money was the cause as well as the consequence:

Most people think scarcity of money is only the consequence of a balance due; but it is the cause as well as the consequence, and the effectual way to bring the balance to our side, is to add to the money. (1934: i. 115–16)

This was the implicit premiss which had enabled him earlier to specify a positive relationship between the money supply and exports:

The first branch of foreign trade, which is the export and import of goods, depends on the money. If one half of the people are employed, and the whole product and manufacture consumed; more money by employing more people, will make an overplus to export. If then the goods imported balance the goods exported, a greater addition to the money will employ yet more people, or the same people are employed to more advantage; which by making a greater, or more valuable export, will make a balance due. So if the money lessens, a part of the people then employed are set idle, or employed to less advantage; the product and manufacture is less, or less valuable, the export of consequence less, and a balance due to foreigners. (1934: i. 16–18)

In clear, unequivocal terms Law believed that expansions in the money supply could generate a balance of payments surplus, and a reduction in the money supply could produce a balance of payments deficit. This viewpoint is repeated as the book progresses: 'For without some addition to the money, it is not to be supposed next years export can be equal to the last: It will lessen as money has lessened' (1934: i. 46). Later he wrote that, if £100,000 was sufficient to carry on trade and produce a balance of payments surplus, 'the same measures, and a greater quantity of money, would make the balance greater' (1934: i. 56).

Law's views on this relationship between money and balance of payments become clearer in the context of the isolated island model with its circular flow of income process. The island economy is initially in equilibrium, exporting part of the raw materials it produces in return for cloth manufactured on the Continent. The introduction of money into the island economy is the catalyst which shifts the unemployed and underemployed agricultural workers into a new manufacturing sector which produces new manufactured exports and import substitutes. As has been shown above, this represents a significant technological transformation in the economy of the island, entailing the movement from this type of primitive agrarian economy to an agricultural-cum-manufacturing economy. However, Law presented no detail on how such a transformation would arise in practice. He was assuming that the economy could effortlessly achieve this transformation, that there was a latent range of manufacturing activities that could be implemented immediately, and that the only constraint was the lack of money. Incidentally, he would later attempt, in 1720, while expanding the money supply, to develop the French manufacturing sector, establishing a range of factories in Versailles and importing skilled foreign labour to train French workers.

Law expressed the view that in the island economy the quick responsiveness of output to an increase in the money supply would expand exports and reduce imports, thereby producing a balance of payments surplus:

And as the 1000 that labour the ground were idle one half of their time, they might be employed so as their additional labour would be equal to that of 500 more, which would lessen their import by providing them with a part of such goods as before they brought from the Continent, and raise their export to 3 or 4 times the value it had: The return of which would furnish them with greater quantities of foreign goods than they wanted for consumption, which might be laid up in magazines.   (1934: i. 134)

This passage shows Law's confidence in the responsiveness of output to an increase in the money supply, a responsiveness that not only solved the unemployment problem but also brought the bonus of a balance of payments surplus. There were two problems with Law's analysis. Was it naivety on his part to assume that output could respond so quickly to increases in the money supply and that a predominantly agricultural society could be transformed into a largely manufacturing society once entrepreneurs—and he uses the term in the 1706 'Mémoire touchant les monoies'—were relieved of their cash-in-advance requirement? It could be argued that, at the time he was writing, there had been a great surge of entrepreneurial ideas, as reflected in the number of companies floated on Change Alley, and that Law had seen on his travels the way in which nations such as Holland had developed a sophisticated manufacturing structure. These developments might have led him to think that the combination of surplus labour and entrepreneurial ideas would produce, once money was made available, a huge boost in output capable of pushing the balance of payments into surplus.

A second problem with his analysis was that he appeared to be unaware of its dynamically explosive implications, for if an increase in the money supply produced a balance of payments surplus, this surplus would in turn engender a further increase in the money supply, which in turn would generate a further balance of payments surplus, and so on.

59

It is only towards the end of the book, when dealing with the specific situation of Scotland, that Law recognized that he had introduced a highly restrictive assumption into his analysis; namely, that during the monetary expansion domestic consumption would not increase. Assuming output increased as a result of the monetary expansion, then it was easy to suggest that this would produce a balance of payments surplus if domestic consumption expenditure was assumed not to increase:

as this addition to the money, will employ the people [who] are now idle, and these now employed to more advantage: So the product will be increased, and manufactures advanced. *If the consumption of the nation continue as now*, the export will be greater and a balance due to us ...   (1934: i. 144; my emphasis)

Later on this same page he repeated that, if Scotland's low propensity to consume remained static, then there would be a considerable improvement in the balance of payments:

And our consumption not being half what the same number of people consume in England; *if the consumption continued as now*, the balance due to Scotland would be greater, than the balance due to England.   (1934: i. 144; my emphasis)

Law was sufficiently intelligent to recognize that this might be a highly stylized assumption and asked what would happen if he relaxed it and allowed the increase in consumption expenditure to outstrip the increase in domestic output 'if the consumption and expense increased equal to, or beyond the improvement' (1934: i. 146). Would this not cause the balance of payments to move into deficit?

Law offered two contrived solutions to this dilemma. In the first place, he contended that, if the paper money was only acceptable in Scotland, it would not be possible for such money to leave the country, 'so the people would not be set idle, nor the manufacture decay: that money being like an estate entailed' (1934: i. 146). In this scenario importers would be forced to reduce their imports into Scotland because the country could not offer any money, over and above that consistent with a balance of payments equilibrium, in payment for imports. In the second place, even if the country decided to pay for the balance of payments deficit ('credit given for the balance'), the deficit could be met, according to Law, by subsidizing certain types of exports so as to increase their growth: 'the revenue of the Commission will be a great help towards advancing our trade in its infancy' (1934: i. 108).

At this point in his analysis Law had belatedly acknowledged that his further conclusion that a growth in the money supply produced a balance of payments surplus was contingent on the assumption that consumption remained static in the face of such an increase in the money supply. In other words, he changed his approach as he came to analysing the particular way in which the policy might work in the Scottish economy, where trade was 'in its infancy'.

Indeed, a year later, when writing the 'Mémoire touchant les monoies', Law recommended restrictions on consumption expenditure in France, contending that, if this was not done, there would not be sufficient commodities to export and so to balance the foreign trade (1706, fo. 17). He was also prepared to envisage restrictions on international trade in order to shift the balance of payments from deficit to surplus: 'If a greater value of goods was imported than was exported . . . such restrictions may be put on consumption of our own and foreign goods, as may make a balance due' (1934: i. 146). Furthermore, he proposed that the profits of the land bank commission be used to subsidize exports by means of a draw-back: 'What encourages the export of goods, encourages the manufacture of them; And that money given as a draw-back, will not only encourage the export and manufacture; but likewise regain the reputation our goods have lost, and give them a better reputation than the goods of other nations' (1934: i. 146).

Thus, in the case of infant industries Law was prepared to recognize that there might be a need to bolster the profit margins of certain companies producing goods that did not 'yield a reasonable profit abroad' by means of a subsidy. He argued that such a subsidy was more necessary in Scotland than in other countries, 'for we do not manufacture so well as other nations: We are not able to sell for the same profit, our stocks being much smaller; and the goods of other nations will be preferred to ours, because our goods are suspected' (1934: i. 148). It should be noted, however, that Law dropped this subsidy suggestion in his other draft proposal on a land bank for Scotland, '1705 Act for a Land Mint'. In this latter proposal he envisaged profits from the bank accruing to shareholders rather than being used to subsidize infant industries.

It is paradoxical to note that a book which starts with a very clear statement of the way in which the forces of supply and demand operate finishes with a range of recommendations on ways of interfering with the price mechanism in Scotland through restrictions on consumption expenditure and subsidies for exports. Law attempted to reconcile the paradox by invoking the infant industry argument in the specific context of Scotland. Already, however, two important characteristics of his behaviour are evident, those of his interventionism and his improvisionism. Law was not prepared to sit back and wait for the market mechanism to produce full employment in Scotland. In his view it could not do this without the appropriate quantity of money being channelled into the economy. This was to be the consistent theme of his commentaries, not just on Scotland, but on all the other economies he examined. According as problems developed, as reality clashed with theory, as was the possible situation of Scotland's balance of payments being unable to cope with an expansion of the money supply, Law invoked a whole range of secondary policies to stem the undesirable effects flowing from the primary policy (i.e. the expansion of the money supply). His mind, so full of ideas, was capable of recommending a wide range of policies to plug emerging holes in the dyke, but such policies tended to distract him from analysing the implications of the primary policy. It was this improvisionism which was to cause him later, in 1720, to devote too much of his energy to producing secondary policy solutions for effects produced by the primary policy.

Law: Theorist Turned Policy-Maker

To understand the revolutionary nature of Law the policy-maker it is necessary to present some of the financial background. When Louis XIV, the Sun King, died, his financial legacy consisted of a bankrupted state. Continuous warfare had left France short of money and facing a very sizeable debt. Furthermore, the tax revenue collection system had been farmed out to the private sector leaving the financiers (*gens de finance*), such as Samuel Bernard, Antoine Crozat, and the Paris brothers, the veritable controllers of the financial system. They exerted control through management of the tax farms and lending money to the state. Effectively the state was heavily mortgaged to the financiers. These issues are discussed in Murphy (1997).

The change of monarchs provided the opportunity for the state to hit back at the financiers. At times like this in French history, popular opinion felt that there was a need for a *saignée* (bloodletting) of the financiers, who were regarded as *sangsues* (bloodsuckers). This led to the establishment of the Chamber of Justice, which had as its objectives the confiscation of the ill-gotten gains of the financiers along with their punishment through fines, sending them to the galleys, imprisonment, or even public execution. This was the theory. In practice the big financiers bribed their way out of their difficulties and paid fines that were small relative to the profits they had made. From the public viewpoint it looked as if justice had been done, but in reality the Chamber of Justice was more an inconvenience than a problem for the financiers. However, it did mean that, crucially, for a couple of years the financiers had to maintain a low profile. In the financial vacuum created by the Chamber of Justice's activities, John Law was finally able to push through his ideas.

France in 1716 was different from Scotland in 1705. Although both countries, in Law's opinion, suffered from a shortage of money and this shortage had created unemployment and underutilization of resources, France had a further crisis: a financial crisis. Over-borrowing had created a massive level of state indebtedness along with high interest rates as the state had to pay more for any securities it issued. Analysis of his writings between 1705 and 1716 indicates that Law increasingly realized that he needed to tackle both the monetary crisis and the financial crisis. He would later write that, if he had faced just the monetary crisis, the solution would have been easy to implement, but that he needed to tackle both if France was to move back to prosperity. Thus, while he started modestly with the establishment of the General Bank in May 1716, he viewed this as just the first building block in a series of interlocking blocks that would ultimately lead to the creation of the Mississippi Company.

The growing success of the General Bank enabled Law to address this second crisis: that of the management of the national debt. A new radical plan was necessary to restructure France's financial situation. He decided that the best way to accomplish this was to convert government debt into the equity of a huge conglomerate trading company. To do so he needed to establish a trading company on the lines of the British trading companies such as the East India Company and the South Sea Company.

The Chamber of Justice once again helped Law's case in that the financier Antoine Crozat had ceded his company's trading rights over Louisiana in part-payment of the tax exacted on him by the Chamber. In August 1717 Law took over the Company of the West (Compagnie d'Occident), which had been given monopoly trading rights over French Louisiana. The basis of this transaction involved the grant to the Company of the trading rights to Louisiana, in return for which the Company took over part of the state's short-term debt (*billets d'état*). The deal was advantageous to the Crown in that part of the short-term debt was taken off the market and the rate of interest on it reduced; this reduced rate of interest was also to constitute the revenue stream for the Company to finance its activities involving Louisiana. Thus, for the Crown it represented a way of reducing the interest burden of the state as well as funding it. From the Company's viewpoint it gave it the exclusive privilege of developing French Louisiana, a territory far larger than the state of Louisiana today. French Louisiana stretched from the Gulf of Mexico to Canada. It was bounded on the east by the British in the Carolinas and on the west by the Spanish in Texas. As such it constituted half of the land mass of the United States today (excluding Alaska). Law hoped that, by developing the agricultural and mineral wealth of this massive area, the Company would establish a strong income stream to increase the dividend payments on its shares. To subscribe, transactors handed over their *billets d'état* in return for shares in the Company. These first shares were called mothers (*mères*). Because of the heavy discount—around 70 per cent—on government debt in the market, transactors were able to purchase shares with a nominal value of 500 *livres* by parting with government securities that had a market value of around 150 *livres*.

The Company of the West represented a modest building block from a financial perspective for the creation of what later came to be known as the Mississippi Company. The income stream from the converted debt was very small relative to the financing needs for developing French Louisiana, and the shares were quoted at a sizeable discount relative to the nominal price for over a year from its establishment. Indeed, for over eighteen months the shares, though rising, remained quoted at below the par price of 500 *livres*.

Law's initial emphasis appeared to be one of growing the size of the Company by taking over the other trading companies and profitable monopoly ventures. In August 1718 the Company acquired the lease of the tobacco farm. In December it took over the Company of Senegal. In May and June of the following year the Company of the East Indies and the China Company were merged with the enlarged Company of the West. This new overall entity was named the Company of the Indies (Compagnie des Indes). A further company, the Company of Africa, was taken over later in June. This meant that the Company of the Indies, popularly referred to as the Mississippi Company, had become a giant holding company owning all of the overseas trading companies.

The takeovers of these companies helped grow the size of the Mississippi Company but Law was the first to recognize that such activity required financing and he began to use the General Bank (Banque Générale) as an instrument to facilitate his expansionist plans. On 4 December 1718, by a state Declaration, he succeeded in having the General Bank converted into the Royal Bank (Banque Royale). Private shareholders were bought out, and the ownership of the Bank reverted to the Crown. The crucial element in this conversion of the Bank was the decision, under Article 7 of the Declaration, to grant to the King's Council the power to determine the Bank's note issue. This meant that, other than the decisions of the King's Council, there was no constraint on the issue of banknotes. By this move France had moved to a fiduciary note issue, and a month later, on 5 January 1719, the first issue of the Royal Bank was sanctioned by the King's Council, permitting the creation of 36 million *livres* in banknotes. From this point on, Law could use banknote issues of the Royal Bank to provide liquidity in the market for the purchase of shares. The links with the Company of the West were further developed through the conversion of the Bank's holdings of the 6 million *livres* of *billets d'état* that had been subscribed by the original shareholders into shares in the Company. Assuming this conversion was made, this meant that the Bank owned 12,000 shares, or 6 per cent of the paid-up capital of the Company.

The Company's acquisitions and merger activities of 1718–19 required financing. Law arranged this through the issue of two tranches of shares known as the *filles* and *petites filles*. It has already been shown that the *mères*, issued in 1717 on the establishment of the Company of the West, were subscribed for in *billets d'état*, which were standing at a very sizeable discount. Effectively, as stated above, they cost around 150 *livres* in 1717, though issued at a nominal price of 500 *livres*. The second tranche of shares, the *filles*, was issued in June 1719 at 550 *livres*, a 50 *livres* premium, suggesting wider public interest in the shares after an interval of nearly two years. The share price jumped in July, enabling Law to issue a further batch of shares, the *petites filles*, this time at 1,000 *livres* each. Thus, for those who had bought the shares initially with the discounted *billets d'état* at an effective price of around 150 *livres*, considerable capital gains had been made. For those who stayed with the shares, there were even greater gains to be made.

By the end of July 1719 Law's Company had issued 300,000 shares with a nominal value of 150 million *livres*, which would have cost transactors, assuming the 70 per cent discount on *billets d'état* in 1717–18, around 108 million *livres*. The share price having jumped from 500 to over 1,000 *livres* in July 1719, the stage was set for a further sharp rise in Europe's first major stock market boom. This boom was linked to Law's wish to take over the totality of France's national debt by swapping shares for government securities. The sheer magnitude of this operation proved to be breathtaking.

On 26 August 1719 the Regent presented Law's proposal for the Mississippi Company to take over the tax farms and the remainder of the national debt. Writing in his diary, the duc d'Antin noted that this project had been under consideration by the Regent for a 'long time'. It was not a sudden flash of inspiration by Law, but represented a crucial part of a long-thought-out strategy.

This was corroborated by the author of the 'Histoire des finances', who must have been a member of Law's inner circle. He later commented that, despite the success of Law's operations up to the middle of July 1719, they had not cured the 'deep wounds' of the state, adding: 'What had been seen so far was more in the form of a preparation for the cure than a radical cure' (1934: iii. 344). Later he remarked: 'The object of the System did not stop with the establishment of a moderate credit . . . this would have sufficed in a state with a small debt burden' (iii. 378).

A far more ambitious plan was needed. Law's plan was to lend the king 1.2 billion *livres* at an interest rate of 3 per cent so as to repay the outstanding national debt. This money was to be used to repay the long-term state debts, the annuities (*rentes*), the remaining short-term floating debt (*billets d'état*), the cost of offices (*charges*) that had been or would be suppressed, and the shares of the tax farms. There were two main elements in Law's proposals. Firstly, the Company was given the right to borrow the 1.2 billion *livres* by creating shares. Secondly, the lease of the tax farms, which on 29 August 1718 had been granted for six years to a company fronted by Aymard Lambert, a straw man for the Paris brothers, was to be annulled and given to Law's Company for a period of nine years. In this way Law deprived the financiers of the use of the United Tax Farms and in the process took over the joint stock company that they had created to manage it.

Under the plan, holders of government securities were forced to give up government securities, bearing a 5 per cent rate of interest, while at the same time they were offered the possibility of acquiring shares of the Company that yielded less in terms of dividend but possessed the prospect of sizeable capital gains. With the share price jumping from 2,250 *livres* on 1 August to 2,940 on

14 August, to 5,000 and over in mid-September, capital gains rather than dividends occupied the minds of most transactors.

Through these measures Law proposed 'the radical cure' for the French economy. He aimed to transform the Company from a trading company to a trading-cum-financial conglomerate, controlling the state's finances, most notably tax collection and debt management. The writer Nicolas Du Tot, who would later (in 1720) work as an under-treasurer of the Royal Bank, said of this measure: 'This was a project which was big, elegant, and advantageous to the King and the people: but its principles were diametrically contrary to those of the old financial administration, so that its implementation was bound to encounter opposition' (Du Tot 2000).

On 1 August the original shares, the *mères*, which, as has been shown, could have been bought for around 150 *livres* in 1717, stood at 2,750. By 30 August they had risen to 4,100, and by 4 September they were at 5,000 *livres*, with the *filles* and *petites filles* rising *pari passu*. The debt holders, seeing the possibility of a capital gain, were quite happy to transfer their debt into shares rather than bonds. They needed the prospect of an expected capital gain to compensate for the interest reduction on their securities. Their difficulty in fact became one of converting quickly enough into the shares of the Company as the price of the shares rose very sharply during September.

On 13 September the Company announced a fourth issue involving the creation of 100,000 shares, with a nominal value of 500 *livres*, costing 5,000 *livres* per share, to be paid in ten monthly instalments of 500 *livres* per month. By this issue the Company aimed to raise 500 million *livres* from the public. Two further issues of these shares raising the same amount were made on 28 September and 2 October, along with a smaller issue of just 24,000 shares on 4 October; this last issue never actually sold to the public. Thus, within a three-week period the Company issued 324,000 shares, of which 300,000 were sold to the public at 5,000 *livres* a share, amounting in all to 1.5 billion *livres*. The Company had now started to operate in a different manner from that characterizing its operations between August 1717 and August 1719, when it had raised around 106 million *livres* through the first three share issues.

The four share issues of September–October 1719 were seventeen times greater in value than the first three share issues. This amount was never fully raised. Purchasers of the September–October issues, the *soumissions*, or *cinq-cents* as they were called, had only to put up 500 *livres* as an initial deposit for the shares and then repay the rest in nine monthly instalments. Payment by instalment was one of Law's favourite marketing ploys to increase the marketability of the shares to the general populace. Other marketing techniques used included making the shares bearer securities, thereby providing anonymity of ownership. Even when the maturing monthly payment dates caused problems for investors, and perhaps more importantly for the price of shares, Law softened the repayment terms by extending them from monthly to quarterly repayments. Small down-payments and an ever-increasing demand for shares pushed the price of fully paid-up shares to over 9,000 *livres* in the autumn of 1719.

The shares hit a high for 1719 of 10,000 *livres* on 2 December. At this point the market valuation of the Mississippi Company was 6.24 billion *livres*. Concomitant with these developments, the banknote issue of the Royal Bank had been increased from 160 million *livres* in June to 1 billion *livres* by the end of 1719 as money was lent to existing shareholders to purchase further shares.

France was awash with liquidity, particularly after the Company established a buying and selling agency, known as the *bureau d'achat et de vente*. Effectively, the workings of this agency monetized the shares. Share dealings were now reaching a frenzied level. Indeed, a week after Law's appointment as Contrô-leur Général des Finances in January 1720, the market went into another striking phase of speculative behaviour. Law had been worried by the emer-gence of private derivative markets in the Company's shares. Dealers on the rue Quincampoix had been offering options and futures contracts on the shares of the Mississippi Company. Law decided to rid the market of these private transactions by creating the Company's own options, which were called *les primes*. The *primes*, priced at 1,000 *livres*, offered transactors the possibility of having an option to purchase a share for 10,000 *livres* at a future date. Transactors rushed to sell their old shares and purchase the *primes*, believing that this gave them greater leverage to make future gains out of the Mississippi Company. For example, by selling one share at 10,000 *livres*, the transactor could acquire options to the equivalent of 100,000 of Mississippi stock. The *primes*, initially issued in a handwritten format, became the major financial instruments traded on the rue Quincampoix. Everyone now wanted to purchase them, and within a couple of days of their issue they were quoted at an 80 per cent premium. Law must have been horrified that the market had misinterpreted his signals with respect to the *primes*. He had meant to use them to dampen down speculation on the future price of the shares and to convince the market that the price would not go above 10,000 *livres*. Trans-actors, however, believed that this was an opportunity to make further gains on the shares. Law quickly restored order to the market by having the *primes* printed, thereby ensuring that enough were issued to meet demand, and the sizeable premiums on the *primes* quickly disappeared.

In the early months of 1720 Law appeared to have realized his vision. Economic activity was booming, the national debt seemed to be under con-trol, money was plentiful, and the interest rate had been driven down to 2 per cent. In January he wrote: 'One sees here a sequence of ideas which are interlinked and which reveal more and more the principle on which they are based' (iii. 98–9).

The Mississippi System, in all its unifying beauty, appeared to be working. Law was omnipresent, issuing instructions on a daily basis for the management of the companies within the huge holding conglomerate that he had put together. He even produced the equivalent of a management control chart, with a breakdown of the day-to-day management meetings for each of the companies and the executive directors who were to attend. The rue Quincampoix, a long, narrow, and sinuous street, was the centre of trading in the Company's shares. Such was the frenetic activity in trading the shares on the street that people barely had room to move, and the hump of a hunchback was frequently used as a table on which to write contracts. Goaded by the success of Law's System, the British quickly introduced a variant on it when the South Sea Company's proposal to take over most of the government debt was accepted by the government. Unfortunately for Law, and for the French economy, there were significant flaws in the Mississippi System, flaws that Richard Cantillon was quick to notice and exploit (see Murphy 1986).

Law had created a financial system the long-term viability of which was crucially dependent on the growth of the real economy. There had to be some equilibrium between the financial system and the real economy. For a brief period a temporary equilibrium existed, as transactors seemed content to remain within the financial circuit, trading money for shares and shares for money. However, once money started quickly spilling out of the financial circuit into the real economy, problems arose, problems that were exacerbated by the growing interdependence between the Royal Bank and the Company of the Indies. The linkage between the Bank and the Company had been growing, for the Bank's banknotes, printed in increasing quantities, were used as a prop to maintain the share price. In February 1720 the Bank and the Company were formally merged. The real economy proved to be incapable of generating sufficient growth in commodities to match the monetary expansion, so that the excess money created inflation and balance of payments problems. Law had always believed that the growth in the real economy, spurred on by monetary expansion, would be sufficient to mop up the newly created money. Indeed, he went further and argued, in *Money and Trade*, that monetary expansion would lead to a balance of payments surplus. For a period he tried to lock transactors into the financial circuit by a series of measures ranging from prohibitions on the holding of more than 500 *livres* of specie or bullion, to the demonetization of gold and a phased monthly devaluation of silver. Temporarily these measures worked. But there was still too much liquidity in the System. On 21 May 1720 an *arrêt* was published stipulating that shares were to be reduced by four-ninths (from 9,000 to 5,000) and banknotes by half between May and December.

This was an attempt to reduce the liquidity of the System, thereby bringing the financial circuit back into line with the real economy. Despite this, owing to public pressure, the revocation of the *arrêt* a couple of days later dented public confidence to such an extent that the System never recovered. Law's enemies the financiers were emboldened to criticize his policies openly. They realized that, if he succeeded, they would no longer be able to live in comfort off the financial system that they had created and he had replaced. They had every incentive to ensure that he failed. The tide had turned against Law. The price of shares and banknotes fell continuously during the summer (ironically, at the point when the shares in the South Sea Company were rising rapidly) and autumn of 1720. Ultimately, Law was forced to flee the country, with the aid of the Regent, in December. He spent the next three years attempting to persuade the Regent to invite him back: he had new plans and ideas on how to change the financial system. By 1723 his lobbying appeared to have succeeded, when he was invited by the Regent to return. Unfortunately, just as he was about to leave London for Paris, a messenger arrived with news that the Regent had died suddenly and the new Regent, Law's erstwhile friend the duc de Bourbon, did not want him to return. There were no further opportunities for Law to pursue his policies, though he did turn down an invitation from Peter the Great to travel to Moscow. He left London and travelled to Venice. There he spent his remaining years gambling in the Ridotto and building up a collection of fine art. See Venice and die. When he died in Venice in 1729, he left a sizeable collection of old masters (see Murphy 2006). However, many of these were ruined when the boat transporting them sank. In death, as in life, Law's attempts to grasp at wealth were transitory.

Nicolas Du Tot would later make the following comment on Law's System:

In this state, this construction was admired by everyone in France and was the envy of our neighbours who were really alarmed by it. Its beauty even surpassed all the hopes that had been placed in it since it made people despise and refuse gold and silver. It was a type of miracle which posterity will not believe; however, it is evident that there was a period, of many months, when no one wanted them [gold and silver]. (Du Tot 1738: i. 106)

Unlike many theorists, Law had been able to introduce many of his theoretical ideas as economic policies. He realized for a short period his dream of having paper rather than metallic money as the sole circulating medium of exchange.

Historians have for the most part been unkind to Law. Many of them have acquiesced in the eighteenth-century caricature of him as a quack and a charlatan. More recently Edgar Faure associated him with France's bankruptcy in La Banqueroute de Law (1977). However, in fairness to Law it was not he who made France bankrupt; this was the fault of the spendthrift Louis XIV. Law attempted to mitigate the consequences of this effective bankruptcy through his financial engineering, and it could even be argued that the enforced reduction of the national debt after the collapse of his System left France with a far lower amount of state indebtedness. Law's legacy was that financial innovation in the form of banking and capital market restructuring could succeed. However, his detractors used the failure of his financial innovation to fashion public opinion against paper money, banking, and financial innovation. By doing so they forced France back to the old financial system of the *ancien régime*, one that would greatly restrain France's economic performance relative to Great Britain's throughout the eighteenth century. Ultimately the French citizenry reacted against this financial system at the end of the century, a reaction that led to the French Revolution. Ironically, the success of the early part of the revolution was very much dependent on the creation of *assignats*, banknotes using the confiscated property of the Church and nobility as collateral, a proposal very similar to that which Law had recommended in *Money and Trade*. Yet another twist and turn between economic theory and policy.

At a theoretical level Law had been the first writer to introduce the circular flow of income and the money-in-advance requirement. He was also the first theorist to introduce the concept of the demand for money, the analysis of inflation in a money supply–money demand framework, and the law of one price.

At a policy level he had questioned the view that money needed to be an intrinsically valuable commodity, stressing that money is the value by which goods are exchanged and not the value for which goods are exchanged. Not only had he the vision to imagine a fiat monetary system, but he also had the technical ability to introduce one as part of his solution to France's monetary crisis. Further, at a corporate finance level, he had the vision to see the possibility of capital markets financing vast amount of investment expenditure.

References

Du Tot, Nicolas (1738), *Réflexions politiques sur les finances et le commerce*, ed. Paul Harsin, 2 vols (Paris, 1935).

—— (2000), *Histoire du systême de John Law*, ed. Antoin E. Murphy (Paris).

Eagly, R. V. (1974), *The Structure of Classical Economic Theory* (Oxford).

Faure, Edgar (1977), *La Banqueroute de Law* (Paris).

Friedman, Milton (1956), 'The Quantity Theory of Money: A Restatement', in Friedman (ed.), *Studies in the Quantity Theory of Money* (Chicago).

[Law, John] (1705), *Money and Trade Consider'd with a Proposal for Supplying the Nation with Money* (Edinburgh).

—— (1706), 'Mémoire touchant les monoies et le commerce', Archives Nationales, Paris, G7, 1468, MS 113.

—— (1934), *John Law: Œuvres complètes*, ed. Paul Harsin, 3 vols (Paris; repr. Vaduz, 1980).

—— (1994), *John Law's Essay on a Land Bank*, ed. Antoin E. Murphy (Dublin).

Locke, John (1991), *Locke on Money*, ed. Patrick Kelly, 2 vols (Oxford).

Murphy, Antoin E. (1986), *Richard Cantillon: Entrepreneur and Economist* (Oxford).

—— (1997), *John Law: Economic Theorist and Policy-Maker* (Oxford).

—— (2007), 'Death in Venice. John Law: Art Collector, Monetary Theorist and Corporate Financier', in A. Giacomin and M. Marcuzzo (eds), *Money and Markets* (Abingdon).

Petyt, William (1680), *Brittania Languens; or, A Discourse of Trade* (London).

Thweatt, W. O. (1983), 'Origins of the Terminology of Supply and Demand', *Scottish Journal of Political Economy*, 30/3.

Speculation on the rue Quincampoix in 1720

4

Richard Cantillon: Macroeconomic Modelling

Let us imagine that we are standing in the rue Quincampoix in Paris. It is the early spring of 1720 and this narrow street is packed with people pushing and shoving and shouting out prices. This is the French stock exchange of the day. We are standing beside a man who is watching all this frenetic activity impassively. He has just returned from Italy. The last time he was in Paris was in August 1719, when he observed similar scenes. Although a friend at the time of John Law, the person responsible for this stock market frenzy, he believed then that he was witnessing a financial bubble and had taken what he regarded as a prudent decision to sell all his shares and retire to Italy. His friend, meanwhile, was now the equivalent of prime minister of France. The man seems to have been wrong in his assessment of the market, for now the shares are trading at four times his selling price of August 1719, but as he witnesses the turbulent scenes of the rue Quincampoix, he believes more than ever that his initial analysis was correct. Circumstances have proved him wrong over the last six months, for the Mississippi System has not blown up; instead it has gathered strength. But now is the moment to strike and make a second fortune. Here is the occasion of occasions to use his economic theory to make a fortune out of the French financial markets. This is something many macroeconomists dream about, believing that some day the conditions will be right to use one's economic theory and to profit from some market imperfection.

This was the real-world scenario that the Irish-born economist Richard Cantillon (d. 1734) witnessed during the spring of 1720. Cantillon reckoned that it was impossible for John Law simultaneously to expand the money supply, reduce interest rates, and revalue paper money relative to silver and gold. Something had to give, and so he took a strong position against the French currency. Such was his success that, in the spring of 1720, John Law banished him from France because of the danger he posed to the Mississippi System. Later, in the summer of that year, Law attempted to cajole Cantillon back to France as his deputy, to assist him in shoring up the System. Belatedly

Law realized that he needed someone with the powerful analytical mind of Cantillon to stop the System from collapsing. Cantillon refused, and so we can only speculate on what the tandem of Law and Cantillon could have done for the French economy.

Cantillon's Background

Cantillon was born into a Hiberno-Norman family in Ballyheigue, County Kerry, in the south-west of Ireland (see Murphy 1986). His ancestors had come over to Ireland with the Normans in the thirteenth century and the name is believed to have been a corruption of the French *chant de loup*, 'the cry of the wolf'. There is no known date of birth for him, but it may be conjectured that he was born sometime between 1680 and 1690. As the local lords of the manor, the Cantillons had a good reputation in the area. However, they were dispossessed of their lands by the eighteenth-century confiscations, first under the Cromwellians and then under the Williamites. Many of the Catholic landowning classes were forced to flee Ireland after the signing of the Treaty of Limerick in 1691. This emigration became colourfully known as 'the flight of the wild geese'. There has been a tendency to think that most of these 'wild geese' ended up fighting, and ultimately dying, for Louis XIV and his allies in the continuing war with William of Orange. The reality was that many of them pursued careers other than the military, with a number of them leaving their mark in the vineyards of Bordeaux and Cognac. Names such as Barton, Dillon, Kirwan, and Lynch in the Bordelais, and Hennessy in Cognac, testify to the broader-based activities of part of the 'wild geese'. Cantillon's uncle Sir Daniel Arthur was a banker who had arranged the transfer of a substantial amount of capital out of Ireland before the final defeat of the Jacobites in Limerick. Arthur's banking connections may have been instrumental in Cantillon obtaining his first known job, that of acting as an assistant to James Brydges, the British Paymaster-General to the Forces Abroad in the Iberian peninsula during the War of the Spanish Succession (1702–13). It is surprising to find that Cantillon, with his strong Jacobite background, found employment with the British. However, money in those days flowed across the borders of warring belligerents. If the Huguenot bankers in Switzerland and Holland were prepared to lend to Louis XIV at a time when he was persecuting their fellow countrymen, it was not altogether surprising to find a young Irishman with Jacobite banking connections working for the British. Cantillon's employer, James Brydges, later ennobled as Lord Caernarvon and still later the duke of Chandos, turned out to be one of the biggest war profiteers of the eighteenth century. He made such a fortune from contracts to supply the troops that he was able to erect a magnificent house outside London called Canons, where he employed Handel as his *kapellmeister*, directing his private choir. Letters from

Chandos to Cantillon show that the Irishman was a very versatile bookkeeper for the former and helped him amass his fortune through astute foreign exchange transactions as money moved from London to pay the troops in the Iberian peninsula. At the end of the war Cantillon turned down a position offered by Chandos in London. Instead he moved to Paris and took over his cousin's bank in that city. The French banking and financial system was in a poor state because of the excessive expenditure of Louis XIV, but, on the death of the latter in the late summer of 1715, there was an air of change with the arrival of Philippe, duc d'Orléans, as Regent during the minority of Louis XV.

In the previous chapter it was shown how John Law was the main catalyst for this change. Cantillon met Law in Paris and, initially, they had a good working relationship. This was a meeting of two of the giants in the early history of macroeconomics. Law was a man of vision envisaging a society that operated without metallic money; Cantillon had a brilliant analytical mind capable of mentally constructing a model of the way he believed the economy worked. Law the System builder was pitted against Cantillon the model builder. Initially the two of them worked harmoniously together. Along with an Englishman, Joseph Edward Gage, they established a group of settlers to colonise land that they had been granted in French Louisiana. Cantillon's brother, Bernard, was made the leader of this early group of *colons* who sailed from La Rochelle to develop this settlement in 1719. Cantillon also invested in Law's joint stock company, the Company of the West (Compagnie d'Occident), which would later become the Mississippi Company. The shares in this Company rose from a low of about 150 *livres* to over 2,000 by the start of August 1719. Cantillon, at this stage, started to have doubts about Law's ability to keep the share price moving ahead, and, fearing a stock market crash, sold his shares and moved to Italy.

Cantillon mistimed the demise of the Company and the anticipated stock market crash did not take place in 1719. He must have been intrigued to read in the gazettes from Paris that the share price had reached over 10,000 *livres* in the first week of January 1720 and, furthermore, that Law had been made effective prime minister of France. Had he missed his opportunity to further enrich himself? Cantillon returned to Paris in the spring of 1720, even more convinced that the System was unsustainable. Through his Paris-based bank he took a position against the French currency in anticipation of the collapse, and Law, hearing about this, summoned Cantillon to his presence. He told Cantillon that he understood that he was speculating against the French currency and the System and that if he did not leave France within forty-eight hours he would have him locked up in the Bastille. Cantillon left France but continued to speculate against the Mississippi shares and the French currency. His letters to his banking agents in Paris show that he believed that it was impossible for Law to increase the money supply, lower the rate of interest, and revalue paper banknotes against gold and silver. There was an inherent contradiction. Cantillon's prophecy turned out to be correct, and from 21 May 1720 the System went into decline, with rapid falls in the value of both shares and the French currency. During the summer of 1720, when the System came under intensive pressure, Law tried to coax Cantillon back to France to assist him in restructuring the Company. Cantillon hesitated, but eventually, believing that the System was doomed, declined. By December 1720 Law was obliged to flee France and Cantillon had made a second fortune from his astute speculation against the System. The latter, moving quietly between London and Amsterdam during the summer of 1720, quickly recognized that the South Sea model was very closely related to the Mississippi System. Once again there were further opportunities to use his financial skills. As the South Sea stock soared in value, he arranged for a series of put options on South Sea stock with Dutch stockbrokers in the early summer of 1720. When the South Sea Bubble burst, Cantillon's put options were in the money and made him a further fortune. Thus, Cantillon amassed his wealth through (1) the early purchase and sale of Mississippi shares; (2) the bear position that he adopted on Mississippi shares and the French currency in the spring of 1720; and (3) the put options on the South Sea Company in the summer of 1720. A rich man, Cantillon married Mary Anne O'Mahony, a young beauty whose father, Count Daniel O'Mahony, one of the heroes of the battle of Cremona, came from Cantillon's home county, Kerry. Cantillon was sufficiently wealthy to have Largillière, one of the great portrait painters of the eighteenth century, paint his wife.

Cantillon's wealth—estimated at 20 million *livres* by the Visa inspectors who were appointed to examine and tax the Mississippi millionaires in 1721—was to cause him considerable distress. Clients of his bank, bankrupted by the System, initiated civil and criminal lawsuits against him. In many cases these lawsuits were defensive measures by these people to stave off prison for bankruptcy. By attempting to prove that Cantillon was the cause of their hardened circumstances, they were able to delay legal action by their own creditors to have them put in prison. Although their charges were never proven, the lawsuits weighed heavily on Cantillon. Cantillon was apparently murdered in his bed by his French cook in his house in Albemarle Street, London, in 1734. According to contemporary accounts, his body was burnt to ashes in the fire that engulfed the house after his murder. The politician Bolingbroke, who lived next door, searched in the burnt-out house the following day but could not find anything, such was the extent of the inferno that had engulfed Cantillon's house. Intriguingly, some six months after Cantillon's supposed demise, a certain chevalier de Louvigny arrived in the Dutch colony of Surinam in South America. This gentleman had plenty of money and was well armed. When the Dutch authorities sent some troops into the jungle, where he was based, to question him, the chevalier disappeared. However, they discovered freshly dug earth. On digging up this earth they located a chest of documents all relating to Richard Cantillon of Albemarle Street, London. So how had these documents arrived in Surinam? Had the French cook carried these highly incriminating documents all the way from London to Surinam? Or, was the chevalier de Louvigny in reality Richard Cantillon, who had decided to fabricate his death and leave London so as to escape from the numerous lawsuits that he faced both there and in Paris?

Some twenty-one years later, in 1755, the *Essai sur la nature du commerce en général*, probably written by Cantillon between 1728 and 1730, was posthumously published in Paris. The title page indicated that it had been published by a certain Fletcher Gyles in Holborn, London. However, Gyles had died of apoplexy many years before and his publishing imprint had been borrowed by the Paris publishing house of Guillyn, who used it as a smokescreen to overcome the French censorship laws.

The *Essai* was widely read by the French *économistes* and went into a number of editions. A vastly inferior and bowdlerized English version of it was produced by Cantillon's cousin Philippe de Cantillon. A full English translation was not published until 1931, when Henry Higgs performed this task for the Royal Economics Society. Great care needs to be exercised in reading Higgs's English translation, which is a hybrid, for Higgs included a considerable part of the eighteenth-century translation made by Malachy Postlethwayt for the *Universal Dictionary of Trade and Commerce* (1751–5). Postlethwayt had a manuscript copy of the *Essai* and translated large chunks of it for inclusion, without acknowledgement to Cantillon, in the *Dictionary* in sections dealing with banking, cash, circulation, money, interest, etc. Higgs obviously produced a more modern translation than Postlethwayt, and readers need to be careful when analysing certain words from the 1931 translation because their meaning was not the same in the first half of the eighteenth century. The term *capital* is a case in point. Cantillon used the terms *capital* and *capitaux* in the financial sense of the term as money held by depositors or lent out to borrowers. He also used terms such as *avances* and *fonds*, which have been translated by Higgs as 'capital'. This is confusing to the English reader, for it was not until Turgot wrote the *Réflexions sur la formation et la distribution des richesses* in 1769–70 that the term 'capital' in its economic sense, i.e. a stock of tools and raw materials etc. constituting a separate factor of production, came into usage. However, Cantillon's use of the terms *fond* (see e.g. Cantillon 1931: 193, 199) and *les avances* (p. 225) show that he had started to grasp the concept of capital that Turgot would later launch. It also works the other way, because Higgs translated *entrepreneur* as 'undertaker', whereas today this term has none of its eighteenth-century meaning and is only associated with the person who arranges funerals.

Cantillon's Macroeconomics

The *Essai sur la nature du commerce en général*, Cantillon's only known work, is divided into three books. Unfortunately, it is not complete because it does not incorporate the statistical supplement, which Cantillon referred to on a number of occasions in Book I. The book is written in a clear, crisp, and clinical style. Although the collapse of Law's System lurks ominously in the background, references to contemporary issues were minimized. Even though neither Law, nor the System, was directly mentioned, it may be contended that the *Essai* represented Cantillon's intellectual refutation of Law's theories and policies.

The *Essai* is remarkable on many fronts, and economists have found in it a wide range of issues which are of considerable appeal; see authors such as Bordo (1983), Brewer (1992), Cesarano (1983), Hayek (1936), Hébert (1981), Prendergast (1991), Spengler (1954), and the contributors to the INED edition of Cantillon's *Essai* (2002). From the perspective of this book the following contributions are emphasized:

1. the model-building approach;
2. the description of the role of the entrepreneur;
3. the analysis of market forces;
4. the outline of the circular flow of income;
5. the monetary theory.

Cantillon had an ambitious objective, as the title of his work shows. He wanted to produce an essay on the nature of trade in general. The term 'economics', first discovered by the Greeks, used in the title of Montchrétien's *Traicté de l'œconomie politique* (1615), and fleetingly referred to by Petty in the preface of the *Treatise of Taxes and Contributions* (1662), was still waiting to be rediscovered by the French *économistes.* Prior to this rediscovery in the late 1750s, 'trade' and 'commerce' were terms that acted as synonyms for what we call economics today. So Cantillon's objective, as may be seen from the title of his book, was to produce an essay on the nature of economics in general. This was a highly ambitious objective because there was very little in terms of the foundations of the subject on which to build, aside from Petty, Boisguilbert, and Law's contributions.

To meet his objective, Cantillon needed to produce an economic model. The modelling of an economy requires considerable abstraction so that the complexity of human behaviour may be reduced to manageable proportions. Cantillon's method was to isolate the key elements working in the economy. In Cartesian style he first of all stripped the economy down to its bare essentials in order to identify the fundamental forces at work. His tabula rasa was the abstraction of the single large landed estate, 'a large estate that I wish to consider as if it was the only one in the world' (1931: 33). Let us assume—the catch cry of all economic model builders—that there exists just this one single large landed estate. This initial abstraction presented a very bleak existentialist stage for his play in which three types of economic actor appear:

1. the landlord,
2. the overseers (inspectors),
3. the workers.

The landlord is omnipotent because he owns all of the land of the large estate and employs the overseers to direct the workers to produce whatever he fancies. The play at this stage is rather uninteresting, for it deals with a command barter economy in which the landlord passes on his dictates to his overseers, who, in turn, ensure that his commands are implemented. It is a Hobbesian world, where life is nasty, brutish, and short, with the main acting role confined to the landlord. At a whim he may decide to turn the landed estate into a hunting estate where tillage is minimized. Few workers are required for such an activity, so employment and, ultimately, population fall. Alternatively, if he fancied himself as an aesthete and decided to transform the landed estate into beautiful ornamental gardens, his overseers would need to employ many workers for the creation and maintenance of such. This change in tastes would increase employment and expand the population.

Cantillon's reduction of economic life to this type of a primitive set-up sets the stage for the progressive transformation of the single landed estate by the stages shown in Figure 4.1. Thus, building on the abstraction of the single landed estate, Cantillon was able to transform progressively this primitive structure from a command economy to a market economy, from a barter system to a monetary system, and from a closed to an open economy.

Act II in the model-building process sees the replacement of the command economy by the market economy. The stage setting is changed, for now the market produces crowds of buyers and sellers moving across the stage seeking to exchange goods and services. This transformation involves the introduction

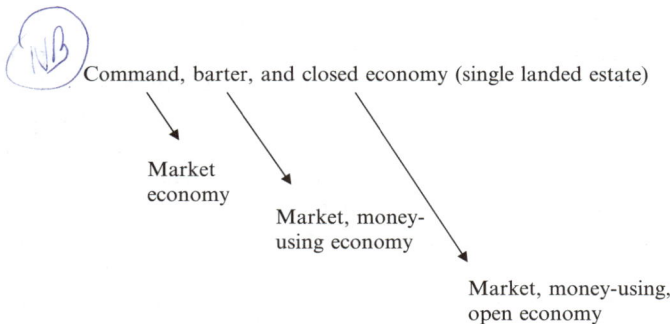

Command, barter, and closed economy (single landed estate)

Market economy

Market, money-using economy

Market, money-using, open economy

Figure 4.1 Cantillon's three-tiered transformation function

of a new series of principal actors, the entrepreneurs, who are called on stage to replace the overseers. The three classes of economic actors are now:

1. the landlord,
2. the entrepreneurs,
3. the workers.

Despite the continuing power of the proprietor of the landed estate to influence economic activity through his expenditure decisions, he is now a mute actor, expressing his views through the prices that he is prepared to pay for commodities on the market. He can no longer dictate to the overseers. He can only express his purchasing decisions via expenditure in the market. His speaking role has been transferred to the entrepreneurs, who have to determine the range of commodities that they believe the proprietor wishes to acquire and the prices that he would be willing to pay for such commodities. Modern interpreters would not allow the play to progress in this way. A *deus ex machina* in the form of the Walrasian auctioneer would be introduced. Entrepreneurs, so remarkably absent from modern textbooks on economics, would be discarded and a divine voice would present, without charge or delay, the market-clearing vector of prices. End of action, end of the play.

Cantillon's choreography did not permit the closure of the play in this peremptory manner. There is still a great deal of human action—economic action—that needs to be presented. The entrepreneurs—there are many of them, ranging from entrepreneur producers to entrepreneur wholesalers, to entrepreneur retailers and even entrepreneur beggars—have a key role to play in the price-making process.

Cantillon summarized their *raison d'être* in one pithy sentence. They buy at a known price (*un prix certain*) to sell an unknown price (*un prix incertain*). In other words, the entrepreneur knows the price of factors of production that he uses in the form of wages for labour, rent for land, profits for capital. Combining these inputs, he produces output at a known price. However, he cannot guarantee that his selling price will cover his costs of production. The entrepreneur faces uncertainty. If he assesses the purchasing decisions of buyers correctly, and prices his commodities appropriately, he will make a profit. If he prices his commodities at excessively high prices and is unable to sell them, he will be forced off-stage and out of business. Cantillon was a real-life entrepreneur. He had been a banker, a cloth merchant, and a wine dealer during his varied career. As such he was well versed in the gyrations of prices and realized the importance of the entrepreneur as a catalyst in the market. In his structure there was no mechanism for market transactors to be presented with the market-clearing vector of prices without cost or delay. There was no invisible hand, or auctioneer, to assist the entrepreneur when it came to price-making. Instead the entrepreneur had to use his own expertise to assess the state of the market. Entrepreneurs, if they are also producers, need to form expectations of what buyers are likely to purchase, or, if they are also wholesalers or retailers, learn what purchasers are actually buying. Markets work because of the activities of entrepreneurs. They work badly if the entrepreneur is short-sighted, unimaginative, lazy, or excessively risk-averse. They work more efficiently if entrepreneurs are alert, creative, hard-working, and prepared to take measured risks. While Cantillon at times invoked the laws of nature, he was sufficient of a pragmatist to recognize that markets do not work in a vacuum but rely very much on the skill and acumen of the entrepreneur. Cantillon gave a prime role to the entrepreneur in his model of the economy, which few of his successors, aside from the Austrians, developed.

Situating the entrepreneur centre stage, Cantillon examined the way in which resources were allocated according as prices diverged. This necessitated producing a price to which other prices could be related. He termed this price 'intrinsic value'. Following on the work of Petty, he attempted to determine the intrinsic value of a good in terms of one factor, land inputs. This led him to present a cost of production approach to determining the intrinsic value of a good. In this schema, intrinsic value consisted of the costs of production (land and labour inputs) plus normal profit. He was also aware of demand-side factors. This enabled him to have the market price determined by demand and supply factors. According as supply and demand changed, the market price could diverge from the intrinsic value of the good.

If the market price became greater than the intrinsic value, the gap between the two acted as a signal to entrepreneurs to allocate more resources to the production of this commodity. Alternatively, if the market price was below intrinsic value, then this acted as a signal to entrepreneurs to remove resources from the production of this commodity:

If there are too many hatters in a city or in a street for the number of people who buy hats there, some who are least patronized must become bankrupt: if they be too few it will be a profitable enterprise which will encourage new hatters to open shops there and so it is that the entrepreneurs of all kinds adjust themselves to risks in a state.   (Cantillon 1931: 53)

Adam Smith, in Book I chapter vii of the *Wealth of Nations*, borrowed, without acknowledgement, Cantillon's theory of the allocation of resources. He did this by changing 'intrinsic value' into 'natural price' and then distinguishing between 'market price' and 'natural price'. So perhaps the greatest chapter of the *Wealth of Nations* should be intellectually recognized for its dual authorship, that of Cantillon alongside Smith. Notwithstanding Smith's use of his work, Cantillon maintained the dominant hand in his analysis of the allocative effects of the market in that he identified the key role for the entrepreneur in this allocation process, whereas Smith used the quasi-mystical concept of the 'invisible hand' to ensure that overall harmony was achieved in markets. In other words, Cantillon recognized that there was a person, the entrepreneur, to initiate and develop the market mechanisms. Smith, on the other hand, was content to consider that the whole process was worked out in some invisible manner by the competitive forces of the market. Here we see the difference between Cantillon, the market practitioner, and Smith, the phil-osopher–observer of markets. Cantillon, with his considerable experience as an entrepreneur in wine, textiles, and banking, knew that markets without entrepreneurs would not work. Smith, who showed considerable hostility to the merchant class in the *Wealth of Nations*, was content to demonstrate that, as long as there was competition, the system worked. Although he recognized man's innate entrepreneurial psyche in his disposition 'to truck, barter and exchange', his neglect of the entrepreneur was disappointing. This neglect was continued in the nineteenth century through Walras's use of the auctioneer to coordinate all buying and selling decisions in the market. Through this ficti-tious personality of the auctioneer, economists were able to omit entrepre-neurs from their analysis. How were prices to be determined? By the invisible hand or by the auctioneer if we are to follow Smith or Walras. The sheer grind of the entrepreneur working to find an equilibrium clearing price for his products was masked by the metaphor of the invisible hand that would do credit to Jesuit theologians attempting to explain doctrinal problems in terms of church mysteries. So how do we teach economics to business-oriented students while neglecting the key role the entrepreneur plays in markets? Only Cantillon, Quesnay, who focused exclusively on the entrepreneur farmer, Turgot, Jean-Baptiste Say in the early nineteenth century, and Joseph Schumpeter in the twentieth, were prepared to highlight the fundamental importance of entrepreneurs in the market economy.

Cantillon was not only interested in the way entrepreneurs ensured the flow of goods and services between markets, he was also concerned with analysing the aggregated flow of goods and services in the economy. Once Cantillon expanded his model from the command economy to the market economy the reciprocity of exchange between different economic groups became a key issue to develop: 'All these entrepreneurs become consumers and customers one in regard to the other, draper of the wine merchant and vice versa. They propor-tion themselves in a state to the customers or consumption' (Cantillon 1931: 53). This reciprocity in exchange between entrepreneurs enabled him to en-visage a circular flow process whereby income, output, and expenditure were all interrelated. The earlier socio-economic grouping of landlords, entrepre-neurs, and workers was changed to landlords, farmers, and workers, with entrepreneurship implicitly assumed to pertain to the latter two groupings. Cantillon envisaged a process whereby agricultural output was divided up into three rents:

It is the general idea in England that a farmer must make three rents. (1) The principal and true rent which he pays to the proprietor, supposed equal in value to the produce of one third of his farm, a second rent for his maintenance and that of the men and horses he employs to cultivate the farm, and a third which ought to remain with him to make his undertaking profitable.   (Cantillon 1931: 121)

I had thought that my setting of Cantillon's analysis on a stage with actors involved in changing roles was original until I read Malachy Postlethwayt's plagiarized account of the circular flow of income process in the *Universal Dictionary of Trade and Commerce*. Postlethwayt had a manuscript copy of Cantillon's *Essai*, though we do not know whether it was in English or French. He borrowed copiously from Cantillon without any acknowledgement. However, his presentation of the circular flow process appears so seamless, as may be seen from the extract given below, that one wonders whether in fact Cantillon had written an English version of the *Essai* which was even more complete than that produced in the French version of the *Essai* and that Postlethwayt borrowed from this English rather than the French version. This extract appears under the heading 'Cash' in the *Universal Dictionary*:

It is the general opinion in England, that a farmer makes three rents; viz. the principal rent he pays the proprietor; a second rent for the charge of his farm, and the wages of his servants; and a third rent for himself and family, whereon to subsist, and for the education of his children. This opinion is founded on experience, which shews, that, of a farm of 300 acres, of equal goodness, the produce of 100 acres sold at market is sufficient to pay the principal rent to the landlord, or proprietor...

In this oeconomy the tradesmen, who have set up for undertakers [entrepreneurs], buy of the farmers, etc. their materials; the clothier buys wool of the farmer, the tanner hides, the baker wheat, the butcher oxen, sheep, etc. the land-proprietor, for the use of his family, buys what he wants of all these, who are supposed to have each of them a portion of the 2000 ounces of silver, to set up.—And, as the land-proprietor is paid 1000 ounces of silver by his farmer once a year, he pays the said quantity of money to them for that wherewith they supply him, by which they are reimbursed the sums they had advanced in their undertakings, and find also a maintenance for themselves and children.

The actors in regard to the second rent, viz. the tradesmen and undertakers, smiths, carpenters, etc. so far as they are assistant to the farmer; the labourers, servants, etc. belonging to the farmer; pay and receive of the farmer, and of one another reciprocally, 1000 ounces *per annum*, according to the supposition.

The farmers themselves, who are the actors in regard to the third rent, and have a third part of the produce of the estate free supposing they save and lay up nothing, create also for extraordinary expences for the education of their children, or for the better conveniency of living, a circulation also of 1000 ounces of silver per annum, according to this supposition: and so, upon the whole, if the estate be let for 1000 ounces of silver per annum, it seems to require 3000 ounces of silver to carry on the circulation of the three rents, if the payments be made once a year.   (Postlethwayt 1751–5: i. 463–4)

Cantillon's analysis of the circular flow of income is to be found in the section of his work dealing with money. It starts in chapter iii of Book II, 'Of the Circulation of Money'. This chapter heading helps put in perspective Cantillon's objective. The doctrine of the three rents serves to introduce the circular flow of income process. However, the circular flow of income process was not an end in itself. Cantillon only examined it in order to determine the equilibrium quantity of money required in the economy. Thus, one of Cantillon's major contributions to macroeconomics, the circular flow of income process, was envisaged as only an indirect part of his more ambitious objective, the analysis of the equilibrium quantity of money required in the economy.

Using the doctrine of the three rents, Cantillon visualized absentee landlords spending all the income they derived from the first rent in the city, with farmers spending more than one-half of the third rent (that is one-sixth of agricultural income) on urban-produced commodities. This meant that more than one-half of the agricultural income was destined for expenditure in the cities. He further assumed that half of the population lived in cities and consequently consumed more than half the produce of the land. Thus, the farmers exported more than half of the agricultural output to the cities and, with the income so earned, paid the landlord's rent and bought urban commodities equal to one-sixth of agricultural output. The expenditure of the landlords enabled them to purchase agricultural output sent from the country. One person's expenditure forms another person's income, which was derived from the production of commodities. Furthermore, by making certain assumptions with regard to the location of population, and in the absence of savings, Cantillon was able to show that this process could reproduce itself. In this way, he furnished one of the first macroeconomic analyses of the circular flow of income, output, and expenditure. It has been shown in Chapter 2 that Petty had set in motion the macroeconomic analysis of the economy in *Verbum Sapienti* (1691), where he produced the national income identity that income equals expenditure and then clearly distinguished between the stock of wealth of the nation and the human and non-human flows of income derived from this stock. John Law, in chapter 7 of *Money and Trade*, using the model of the island economy, had provided further insights into the circular flow process. Cantillon's tripartite socio-economic grouping consisting of landlords, farmers, and workers is similar to Law's triad of landlords, farmers, and manufacturers. The income–expenditure–output-generating process is similar in both models.

However, it was undoubtedly Cantillon's analysis that inspired François Quesnay to encapsulate the circular flow process in the 'Tableau économique'. Cantillon and Quesnay differed in terms of their view on the consequences arising from the net product in agriculture. Quesnay was able to envisage the agricultural surplus producing economic growth. Cantillon believed that any expansion in agricultural production would just increase population. Quesnay was more interested in the dynamic income-generating process and the implications that it had for fiscal policy, that is the possibility of the net product in agriculture supporting the full weight of taxation through the imposition of a single tax. Cantillon had a different objective in mind when analysing the circular flow, for he believed that it would enable him to determine the amount of money required in the economy. He needed to compile an estimate of the output of the economy and then, making allowances for the velocity of circulation of money, derive an estimate of the amount of money required to drive this level of output. In his estimate, the amount of money required in a state, modified by his analysis of the velocity of circulation of money, was one-third of the landlord's rent. As the landlord's rent was one-third of overall output, this meant that he estimated the demand for money at one-ninth of output, which, as he wrote, was near enough to Petty's estimate that 'the money in circulation is equal to one tenth of the produce of the soil' (Cantillon 1931: 131).

Having estimated the demand for money, Cantillon then wished to show what would happen when the money supply moved out of line with the demand for money. He was not prepared to accept a crude monetarist view that, if the money supply increased, prices would rise proportionately. Instead he likened the process of monetary expansion to the pressure of water in a river: 'From all this I conclude that by doubling the quantity of money in a state the prices of products and merchandise are not always doubled. A river which runs and winds about in its bed will not flow with double the speed when the amount of water is doubled' (Cantillon 1931: 177). There was therefore a need to examine the channels through which monetary expansion may influence expenditure. Cantillon was critical of John Locke for not detailing the monetary transmission mechanisms: '[Locke] has clearly seen that the abundance of money makes everything dear, but he has not considered how it does so. The great difficulty of this question consists in knowing in what way and in what proportion the increase of money raises prices' (Cantillon 1931: 161).

Cantillon was prepared to take up this challenge, and he provided an in-depth examination of what are currently termed 'monetary transmission mechanisms'. He provided a detailed taxonomy of these mechanisms as may be seen from Table 4.1. This table shows that he considered four potential sources of monetary expansion: (*a*) the mining of gold and silver; (*b*) a balance

TABLE **4.1** *Taxonomy of monetary transmission mechanisms in the* Essai

Sources of monetary expansion	Decisions by money-holders	Markets	Market supply conditions	Consequences
Mining of gold and silver	Expenditure		Openness of the economy	Employment and output
		Commodity		
Balance of trade surplus	Saving			Inflation
		Financial		
Capital inflows	Hoarding		Degree of spare capacity	Balance of payments
Invisible earnings				

of trade surplus; (*c*) capital inflows; (*d*) invisible earnings. It is evident that Cantillon was not prepared to assume an increase in the money supply. He wished to identify specific sources of the monetary expansion because he believed that different monetary sources would have different consequences. He then proceeded to show that, depending on the sources of the monetary expansion, the money might be spent, saved, or hoarded. Arising from these decisions, the money could flow either into the commodity market or into the financial market. There were two further elements in the chain linking changes in the money supply to changes in expenditure. First of all, it was necessary to consider the openness of the economy, and, secondly, the degree of spare capacity in it. Depending on these factors, the increased money supply might affect employment and output, or inflation, or the balance of payments. Blaug termed the differential effect on prices of an increase in the money supply, arising from different monetary injections, the 'Cantillon Effect' (1962: 21). Cantillon, though he acknowledged that an increase in the money could push up prices, was not prepared to accept that there was a proportionate relationship between the money supply and prices. It all depended on what was happening to what is now referred to as the 'black box' of the transmission mechanism (see, for example, Bernanke and Getler 1995). Cantillon posed the question of the way in which money was introduced into the 'black box', asking who would be the first recipients of the expanded money supply.

To show the way in which he developed his theory of the different transmission mechanisms it is useful to show the types of effects he envisaged resulting from increases in the money supply that originated from (1) gold or silver mining, (2) capital inflows, (3) a balance of trade surplus, (4) other monetary inflows resulting from tourist expenditure, subsidies paid by foreign states, and financial capital accompanying new immigrants into the economy.

Gold or silver mining. Cantillon envisaged the increased money supply from the mines augmenting the expenditure of the gold and silver producers as well as serving to increase the supply of money destined for lending. The increase in expenditure raised both prices and employment. The fall in the purchasing power of those on fixed incomes might force some workers in this situation to emigrate. The process continued, with inflationary pressures making domestically produced goods less competitive, thereby allowing imports to increase and a balance of payments deficit to emerge, which would reduce the money supply. Cantillon cited Spain and Portugal as examples of this process, for neither country had been able to retain permanently the specie that it had taken from South America.

Capital inflows. Cantillon recognized that foreign borrowing could increase the money supply and lower the rate of interest, which in turn could expand manufacturing investment: 'By means of this money the entrepreneurs in the state find it possible to borrow more cheaply to set people on work and to establish manufactures in the hope of profit' (Cantillon 1931: 191). He acknowledged that one of the beneficial side-effects of the increased expenditure was that it increased the amount of indirect taxation accruing to the state, but he pointed out that external borrowing was costly because of the outflow of interest payments to non-residents and, more importantly, potentially destabilizing because foreign debt holders might want to withdraw their funds at a time when the state most needed them.

A balance of trade surplus. In analysing the consequences of a balance of trade surplus, Cantillon suggested that the first consequence of an increase in the money supply generated through a trade surplus was to increase output and employment: 'This annual increase of money will enrich a great number of merchants and entrepreneurs in the state who will give employment to numerous mechanics and workmen who furnish the commodities sent to the foreigner from whom the money is drawn' (Cantillon 1931: 167). The positive output and employment effects would in turn be followed by higher prices of land and labour as domestic consumption expenditure increased. The increase in prices would reduce exports and increase imports, though he admitted that this development could take a long time to emerge because of the technical advantages that the exporting country initially possessed. Ultimately prices would rise so that the benefit of the increase in the money supply was only transitory and would disappear in a balance of payments deficit: 'Moreover it is usual in states which acquired a considerable abundance of money to draw many things from neighbouring countries where money is rare and consequently everything is cheap: but as money must be sent for this the balance of trade will become smaller' (Cantillon 1931: 169).

Other monetary inflows. In his discussion of the consequences arising from monetary expansions caused by these other monetary inflows, Cantillon challenged the notion that prices would rise proportionately with the increase in the money supply:

The proportion of the dearness which the increased quantity of money brings about in the State will depend on the turn which this money will impart to consumption and circulation. Through whatever hands the money which is introduced may pass it will naturally increase the consumption; but this consumption will be more or less great according to circumstances. It will be directed more or less to certain kinds of products or merchandise according to the idea of those who acquire the money. Market prices will rise more for certain things than for others however abundant the money may be. In England the price of meat might be tripled while the price of corn went up only one fourth. (Cantillon 1931: 179)

This quotation shows Cantillon introducing an important qualification to the analysis of how prices changed in an economy. It was the qualification that distinguished between traded and non-traded goods. It has already been shown that John Law made a similar qualification in his analysis. In the above quotation Cantillon was contending that corn was a traded good, that is, a good bought and sold across national frontiers, whereas meat was a non-traded good. Corn, at his time of writing, could be imported freely into Britain, but legislation prevented the importation of cattle: 'But what generally causes meat to become dearer in proportion than bread is that ordinarily the free import of foreign corn is permitted while the import of cattle is absolutely forbidden' (1931: 173). The price of corn was therefore determined by the price prevailing on the international market plus transportation costs. Any increase in the domestic money supply would not cause any significant increase in the price of corn. On the other hand, the price of meat would be directly affected by the increase in the domestic money supply because meat was a non-traded good: 'An ox weighing 800 pounds sells in Poland and Hungary for two or three ounces of silver, but commonly sells in the London market for more than 40. Yet the bushel of flour does not sell in London for double the price in Poland and Hungary' (Cantillon 1931: 179). He provided other examples of non-traded goods, such as timber because of its high transportation costs, and perishable items such as butter and milk.

The distinction that Cantillon made between traded and non-traded goods assumes greater importance when it is considered in the context of his analysis of the self-adjusting specie flow mechanism. By making this distinction, he was able to produce a more eclectic approach to the self-adjusting specie mechanism. In the long-run he believed that it was not possible for a country to retain excess money balances. There was a self-equilibrating process at work whereby the excess money balances spilled out of the economy through a balance of payments deficit. He described the process as follows:

If more money continues to be drawn from the mines all prices will owing to this abundance rise to such a point that . . . the mechanics and workmen will raise the prices of their articles so high that there will be a considerable profit in buying them from the foreigner who makes them much more cheaply. This will naturally induce several people to import many manufactured articles made in the foreign countries, where they will be found very cheap: this will gradually ruin the mechanics and manufacturers of the state who will not be able to maintain themselves there by working at such low prices owing to the dearness of living . . . The great circulation of money, which was general at the beginning, ceases: poverty and misery follow and the labour of the mines appears to be only to the advantage of those employed upon them and the foreigners who profit thereby. This is approximately what has happened to Spain since the discovery of the Indies. (Cantillon 1931: 165–7)

This passage represents a clear statement of the self-adjusting price specie flow mechanism developed in the following stages. An expansion in the money supply increases expenditure, which raises prices. The increase in prices makes exports less competitive and imports more competitive, which in turn causes a balance of payments deficit. The balance of payments deficit causes the money supply to fall back to that point where the demand for money equals the money supply. See Figure 4.2. The process is self-adjusting, indicating that a country cannot retain an increased money supply that is out of line with the demand for money. The key element in the process is the relative price effect arising when the money supply pushes domestic prices up and makes domestic goods less competitive on the international markets. Cantillon introduced this discussion of the self-adjusting price specie flow mechanism when analysing the effects of an increase in the money supply produced through gold and silver mining discoveries. It was his way of explaining why Spain and Portugal had not been able to retain the benefits originating from the inflows of gold and silver that they had exploited from the mineral wealth of South America.

However, the price specie flow mechanism, with its reliance on the relative price effect, was only one part of the self-adjusting mechanism. By the time Cantillon came to discuss the fourth method of increasing the money supply, he had introduced a further analytical sophistication. What would happen to the self-adjusting mechanism if domestic prices did not increase consistently with the increase in the money supply? As shown above, Cantillon made the distinction between traded and non-traded goods. If the good was a traded good, its price would not increase: 'An increase of money only increases the price or products and merchandise by the difference of the costs of transport when this transport is allowed' (1931: 179). In such an instance the increase in the money supply would have a direct cash balance effect, with the increased money supply increasing expenditure on imports and goods originally destined for the export markets. So Cantillon had an eclectic approach to the self-adjusting specie flow mechanism incorporating both a relative price effect and a cash balance effect. This, it must be emphasized, was considerably more sophisticated than the approach of David Hume, who has been credited as the originator of the self-adjusting price specie flow mechanism.

In analysing the effects of an increase in the money supply on economic activity in Book II, Cantillon opened up the economy to international influences by his inclusion of the distinction between traded and non-traded goods. The stage had become more cosmopolitan, with international goods and services flowing into and out of the economy. Consistently with his

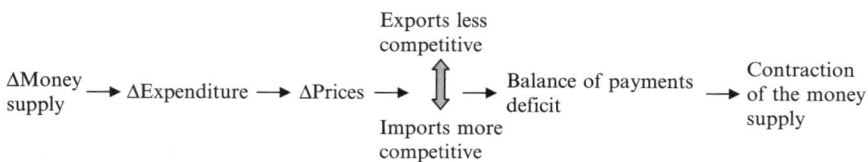

Figure 4.2 Self-adjusting price specie flow mechanism

gradual model-building approach, there were further refinements to be added; namely, the influence of exchange rates and the role of the banks. On one level, Book III may be interpreted as a refined exposition of the nature of foreign exchange and the role of the banking system, with Cantillon display-ing many of the sophisticated tricks of the trade that he had learnt as a banker and foreign exchange expert. At this level, these banking and foreign exchange modules serve to complete his model of the economy, a model that had been assembled in the following sequence:

> The evolution of society from the centralized command economy to an entrepreneur-activated market economy (Book I).
> The transformation from a barter economy to a money economy (Book II).
> The move from a closed economy to an open economy (Book II).
> The shift from a simple domestic specie system to a more complex inter-national system with foreign exchange rates (Book III).
> The addition of a paper money system to the specie system (Book III).

The fifth element, the addition of a paper money system, provides a further level at which to consider the arguments advanced in Book III. At this level there is a systematic undercurrent of criticism directed at Law's System, with which he had had such a chequered history. For the rest of his life, following his business relationship with Law and subsequent speculation against the System, he would be dogged by the consequences of his earlier activities. His major creditors, Lady Mary Herbert and her partner Joseph Gage, along with the Carol brothers, brought civil and criminal proceedings against him, al-leging that he had defrauded them through his lending activities during the System. All this meant that, when he was writing the *Essai* sometime between 1728 and 1730, Cantillon was still immersed in the fallout. Indeed, the memo-randums produced by his lawyer, Maître Cochin, reflect passages from the *Essai*, indicating that Cantillon used his analysis of money and banking to help prepare his lawyer's brief. More than this, I believe, Cantillon wanted to produce an intellectual refutation of Law's System to show why Law was wrong in his approach. To do this, he needed to produce his model of the way the real economy operated. Then, towards the end of Book III, he grafted onto this model elements of Law's System, most notably a note-issuing bank and a minister (unnamed, of course) intent on using monetary policy to lower the rate of interest. While careful to recognize that some national banks, such as those in Amsterdam, London, and Venice, were of benefit in facilitating the exchange process, he was highly critical of such banks when they over-expanded the money supply:

An abundance of fictitious and imaginary money causes the same disadvantages as an increase of real money in circulation, by raising the price of land and labour, or

by making works and manufactures more expensive at the risk of subsequent loss. But this furtive abundance vanishes at the first gust of discredit and precipitates disorder.
(Cantillon 1931: 311)

This passage is code for his attack on Law, who had produced too much 'fictitious and imaginary money'. For Cantillon, the transformation of the economy from a depersonalized specie-using system to a paper money–credit-creating system under the personalized control of a 'minister of state' such as John Law had been an excessively risky strategy. The problem arose when a strong wealth effect, generated by the very considerable increase in the price of shares, kicked in and the public attempted to use its paper gains to purchase commodities. In analysing the consequences of the South Sea Bubble in London, it is obvious that he was also discussing developments in Paris:

In 1720 the capital of public stock and of bubbles which were snares and enterprises of private companies at London, rose to the value of 800 millions sterling, yet the purchases and sales of such pestilential stocks were carried on without difficulty through the quantity of notes of all kinds which were issued, while the same paper money was accepted in payment of interest. But as soon as the idea of great fortunes induced many individuals to increase their expenses, to buy carriages, foreign linen and silk, cash was needed for all that, I mean for the expenditure of the interest and this broke up all the systems.   (Cantillon 1931: 317–19)

Cantillon's final word here, 'systems', was highly significant, for it was only contemporaneously used by reference to the Mississippi System. Cantillon further stressed this link with Law's System in the final paragraph of the *Essai* when he attacked the policy of a minister using the bank to lower the rate of interest. This was a direct attack on John Law in all but name:

It is then undoubted that a Bank with the complicity of a Minister is able to raise and support the price of public stock and to lower the rate of interest in the State at the pleasure of this Minister when the steps are taken discreetly, and thus pay off the State debt. But these refinements which open the door to making large fortunes are rarely carried out for the sole advantage of the State, and those who take part in them are generally corrupted. The excess banknotes, made and issued on these occasions, do not upset the circulation, because being used for the buying and selling of stock they do not serve for household expenses and are not changed into silver. But if some panic or unforeseen crisis drove the holders to demand silver from the Bank the bomb would burst and it would be seen that these are dangerous operations.   (Cantillon 1931: 323)

Here Cantillon was stressing the policy message of his model-building approach. By analysing the equilibrium amount of money required in a money-using, internationally open, market-driven economy, he aimed to demonstrate how the economy would reject any financial innovation which caused an excessive increase in the money supply.

The *Essai* transcends the particular financial episodes of the Mississippi System and the South Sea Bubble, and Cantillon's legacy was to leave to future generations a model-building framework for analysing the economy. This was an outstanding contribution. Inspired by it, François Quesnay developed the circular flow of income through the 'Tableau économique' and Smith borrowed the allocative role of the price mechanism.

References

Bernanke, Ben S., and Mark Getler (1995), 'Inside the Black Box: The Credit Channel of Monetary Policy Transmission', *Journal of Economic Perspectives*, 9 (Fall).

Blaug, Mark (1962), *Economic Theory in Retrospect* (Homewood, Ill.).

Bordo, Michael (1983), 'Some Aspects of the Monetary Economics of Richard Cantillon', *Journal of Monetary Economics*, 12.

Brewer, Anthony (1992), *Richard Cantillon: Pioneer of Economic Theory* (London).

Cantillon, Richard (1931), *Essai sur la nature du commerce en général* (1755), ed. Henry Higgs for the Royal Economics Society (London).

Cesarano, Filippo (1983), 'The Rational Expectations Hypothesis in Retrospect', *American Economic Review*, 73/1 (Mar.).

Hayek, Friedrich von (1936), 'Richard Cantillon: Sa vie, son œuvres', *Revue des sciences économiques* (Apr., June, Oct.).

Hébert, Robert F. (1981), 'Richard Cantillon's Early Contributions to Spatial Economics', *Economica*, 48/148 (Feb.).

Murphy, Antoin (1986), *Richard Cantillon: Entrepreneur and Economist* (Oxford).

Postlethwayt, Malachy (1751–5), *The Universal Dictionary of Trade and Commerce*, 2 vols (London).

Prendergast, Renée (1991), 'Cantillon and the Emergence of the Theory of Profit', *History of Political Economy*, 23/3.

Spengler, Joseph (1954), 'Richard Cantillon: First of the Moderns', *Journal of Political Economy*, 62/4, pt 1 (Aug., Oct.).

Sold at Mr. Martin's Great Scotland Yard Whitehall.

David Hume

5
David Hume: The Classical Theory of Money

Let us imagine a young man of 28 who has just written one of the greatest works of British philosophy. The book, *A Treatise of Human Nature* (1739–40), has been published and the author is nervously awaiting the judgement of his peers. His state of expectation is great and he has not even dared to put his name on the title. Very few read the two volumes, and those who do are for the most part extremely critical of their content. Desperate, the young man prepares an abstract of the work to make it more comprehensible and to bring it to the attention of the reading public. All in vain: the work falls 'dead-born from the press'. The author, like many before and since, discovers that it is one thing to have written a great work; it is another to have it recognized as such. Undeterred, the young man produces another volume of the *Treatise*, and within two years has a further work, *Essays: Moral and Political*, published. This latter work provides a structure for the critical analysis of contemporary British politics. It is somewhat more successful than the *Treatise*.

One might think that, with these two works to his name, the young man is a more than eminent candidate for the professorship of moral philosophy in his home town of Edinburgh. But chairs do not always go to the most suitable candidate, as many academics know to their cost. Committees and cabals are formed in many cases, not to find the best candidate, but to ensure that someone not of a similar mind to them is blocked from the chair. This is the case in Edinburgh in the 1740s. Philosophers who cast doubt on the existence of God are deemed inappropriate for the chair of moral philosophy. In this specific instance, the whiff of his irreligiosity is too great for the upstanding clergy of Edinburgh. David Hume (1711–76), Britain's greatest philosopher of the eighteenth century, discovers to his great dismay that his appointment has been vetoed. He will undergo further disappointment when he is turned down for the chair of logic at Glasgow University in the early 1750s.

Even though he never actually graduated from university, even with a primary degree, David Hume completed his own particular philosophy, politics, and economics 'degree' with the publication of the *Political Discourses* in 1752. As this book was largely devoted to economics, Hume had produced an intellectual triad starting with philosophy, extending to politics, and finishing with economics over the short space of some fifteen years. Even with this brilliant self-made PPE, Hume would still be deemed unacceptable for a major position in academia.

Hume's Background

David Hume was born on 26 April 1711 in Edinburgh. He started life as David Home, but he later changed the spelling to Hume, the way in which the name is pronounced. Shortly before he died, fearing the end was nigh, Hume penned a short autobiography, which was published posthumously as *My Own Life* (1776). This short work provides us with considerable insights into Hume the man. His description of his family background shows the type of social position that he favoured:

I was of a good family both by father and mother. My father's family is a branch of the Earl of Home's or Hume's; and my ancestors had been proprietors of the estate, which my brother possesses, for several generations. My mother was daughter of Sir David Falconer, President of the College of Justice. The title of Lord Halkerton came by succession to her brother. My family, however, was not rich; and being myself a younger brother, my patrimony, according to the mode of my country, was of course very slender.

(Hume 1776: 2)

So Hume was happy to have links with the Scottish nobility and to impress on his readers that, owing to the laws of primogeniture, he had had to fend for himself; family circumstances dictated that he was destined to be a self-starter. Although Hume maintained that his family was not rich, it was relatively comfortable. His father, Joseph, a lawyer by profession, was also the laird of the family estate in Berwickshire on land that maintained twenty-eight shearers, and the Hume family had a place in Edinburgh society. However, his father died in 1713, when David Hume was 2, and Hume's mother, Katherine, then aged 30, reared David, his elder brother, John, and his sister, Katherine. Hume appears to have had great affection for his mother, whom he described as 'a woman of singular merit' who devoted herself to rearing her children and did not marry again.

David Hume started at Edinburgh University, alongside his brother John, in 1723. The attendance of a 12-year-old boy at university suggests that Hume was a precocious youngster; however, the type of collegiate education at the university was, according to Mossner, 'more akin to that of a modern classical high-school than a modern college' (1980: 41). Hume appears to have spent around three to four years at the university and never graduated. This was standard practice for many students of the time—neither his father nor his brother had graduated—so nothing deeper needs to be investigated in regard to the possibility of Hume not sitting for degree examinations or failing them. Hume wrote, in *My Own Life*, that he 'passed through the ordinary course of education with success'. He made no mention of the types of subject that he had studied, but, revealingly, indicated that he 'was seized very early with a passion for literature, which has been my ruling passion of my life, and the great source of my enjoyments'.

Hume craved above all the life of a bookish man, but his family had a different plan for him. Books did not make money, and young David did not have the luxury of an independent income. He needed to become a professional man, and the family wished to turn the second son into a lawyer. The tension between the man of letters and the apprentice lawyer soon came to the fore, with Hume writing: 'I found an insurmountable aversion to every thing but the pursuits of philosophy and general learning; while they fancied I was poring upon Voet and Vinius, Cicero and Virgil were the authors which I was secretly devouring' (Hume 1776: 4–5).

This tension, created by his desire to excel as a writer and his antipathy towards the law, pushed Hume into a nervous breakdown, 'my health being a little broken by my ardent application'. He had a further problem in that he had not the income to support his literary ambitions. In 1734 he even tried to become a merchant in Bristol but 'found that scene totally unsuitable to me'. So, by the age of 23, Hume had shown that he was unable to cope with a career in either law or business. Where could he go?

Still burning with the desire to become a man of letters, Hume decided to leave Britain and to travel to France. There, living a life of thrifty independence—his father had left him an income of £50 a year—he planned for his future life in a country retreat: 'I resolved to make a very rigid frugality supply my deficiency of fortune, to maintain unimpaired my independency, and to regard every object as contemptible, except the improvements of my talents in literature' (Hume 1776: 6).

Living initially in the champagne town of Rheims, and later in the 'douceur angevine' of La Flèche, Hume showed iron discipline in writing *The Treatise of Human Nature* over the next three years. One can imagine the new author travelling back to London with the finished draft of this work, visiting his publisher, checking the proofs, and waiting with excitement for the public judgement of his work. Many a young man (Hume was only 27 when the *Treatise* was published) would have been crushed by its poor reception: 'Never literary attempt was more unfortunate than my Treatise of Human Nature. It fell dead-born from the press, without reaching such distinction as even to excite a murmur among the zealots' (Hume 1776: 7–8). But by now Hume had learnt to be philosophical about the fickleness of his literary fate. Battle-scarred but not defeated, he described himself as being 'naturally of a cheerful and sanguine temper'. This new mood enabled him to write the first part of his *Essays: Moral and Political*, published in 1742. This book was better received than the *Treatise*, encouraging Hume to pursue further his literary work.

In 1744 Hume was presented with the opportunity to succeed Dr John Pringle in the chair of ethics and pneumatical philosophy at Edinburgh University. Despite the pre-eminence of his scholarship, Hume quickly learnt that, because of his 'skepticism and heterodoxy', opposition was building up against his possible selection (letter to Matthew Sharpe of Hoddam, Hume 1932: i. 59). When Pringle resigned, in March 1745, Hume must have been greatly disappointed to discover that the Glasgow-based philosopher Francis Hutcheson, who had opposed Hume, had been appointed to the chair. However, Hutcheson refused the position. This appeared to offer another chance for Hume, but the mixture of political and religious opposition to him meant that he was defeated, in his own words 'by a pack of scoundrels' (Hume 1954: 17). His disappointment must have been very great, and his moroseness was undoubtedly increased by the death of his beloved mother that same year.

The paths that men of letters pursue have many side roads. While waiting for the decision on the professorship, Hume had become the tutor of the young marquess of Annandale, with a salary that 'made a considerable accession to my small fortune'. Hume did not keep the position for long as the marquess's eccentricity moved towards depression and madness and some years later he was certified as a lunatic. By the middle of April 1746 Hume had resigned his tutorship. He then accepted an invitation to become the secretary to General St Clair for a military expedition to Canada. This expedition was aborted and rerouted to the coast of France. From tutorship, followed by secretaryship, Hume moved on to the world of diplomacy, becoming General St Clair's aide-de-camp in the courts of Vienna and Turin. These positions enabled him to become more financially independent, 'now master of near a thousand pounds'. While in Turin, in 1748, Hume's *Enquiry Concerning Human Understanding* was published. He had high hopes for this work, but this time interest in Middleton's *Free Inquiry* meant that 'my performance was overlooked and neglected'.

Unperturbed, Hume retired to the quiet of the family's country home in 1749. There, living with his brother over the next two years, he set about writing the second part of the *Essays: Moral and Political*. This work would be published in Edinburgh as the *Political Discourses* in 1752. Prior to the publication of the *Political Discourses* Hume had a second opportunity to obtain a university chair. This arose when Adam Smith was transferred from the chair of logic at Glasgow University to the chair of moral philosophy on the death of the former professor of moral philosophy, Thomas Craigie. With the chair of logic needing to be filled, Hume was again a candidate. By this stage of his career it is highly likely that he had met Adam Smith, whose cherished friend he would later become. However, at the time Smith's support for Hume was somewhat equivocal, and he wrote that, though he would have preferred 'David Hume to any man for a colleague', he still believed 'that the public would not be of my opinion; and the interest of the society will oblige me to have some regard to the opinion of the public' (Mossner 1980: 248). Without the support of the influential duke of Argyll, Hume had little chance of countering the adverse public opinion of him. And so it was to be. Glasgow University turned down the opportunity to employ Hume, and thus the golden opportunity to have Hume and Smith working in the same university was lost. Instead, Hume was elected Librarian to the Faculty of Advocates in January 1752, a position which was not well paid—Hume apparently gave his income from this position to the blind and indigent Scottish poet Blacklock—but which gave Hume access to a very well-stocked library, a prerequisite for the research that he needed to carry out later for the writing of the *History of England*.

These then are the background circumstances to Hume's career prior to the publication of the *Political Discourses*. It is conjectured that his financial circumstances may have been influential in encouraging him to write on commercial issues—here it must be remembered that the terms 'economics' and 'political economics' were waiting to be coined by the French *économistes* and that 'commerce' was a synonym for what would later be termed 'economics'. His philosophical and political works had not been literary successes, and Hume, by now a professional writer, needed a book that would find favour with the reading public. So he switched to writing on commerce and related issues, such as money and the rate of interest. The *Political Discourses* would constitute a one-off for Hume. Although the book was his first literary success—it went into many editions and was the subject of two translations into French—he never again published a book on economics. However, the book served to bring him to the attention of the commercially minded publishers, who offered him attractive advances to start writing a multi-volume *History of England*. Ironically, then, Hume's success as an economic writer led to his transformation into an historian. Economics' loss would be history's gain.

Hume's Macroeconomics

In retrospect the title of the *Political Discourses* is a misnomer. It should have been, if the term had been coined at the time, the *Economic Discourses*, for the book consists of a majority of essays—seven out of the twelve—on economic issues. To these we can add one further economics essay, 'Of the Jealousy of Trade', which first appeared in the second edition in 1758. The other five deal with a variety of issues, 'Of the Balance of Power', 'Of Some Remarkable Customs', 'Of the Populousness of Antient Nations', 'Of the Protestant Succession', and Discourse XII, 'Idea of a Perfect Commonwealth'. Some writers, such as Rotwein (Hume 1955), believe that 'Of the Populousness of Antient Nations' should also be included in the economics essays. The economics-oriented essays are:

    I. Of Commerce
    II. Of Luxury
    III. Of Money
    IV. Of Interest
    V. Of the Balance of Trade
   VII. Of Taxes
  VIII. Of Public Credit
2nd edition (1758): Of the Jealousy of Trade

More particularly, it may be noted that, with the possible exception of the essay 'Of Luxury', all of the above essays deal with macroeconomic issues. With some slight modifications of translation into the modern idiom of economics, it may be seen that Hume was writing on the general economic model ('Of Commerce', 'Of the Jealousy of Trade'), the role of money and the rate of interest ('Of Money', 'Of Interest'), the balance of payments ('Of the Balance of Trade'), fiscal issues ('Of Taxes'), and public sector debt management ('Of Public Credit'). Hume was therefore very much a macroeconomist at work. Maybe, with the benefit of hindsight, the even more precise title of the book should have been the *Macroeconomic Discourses*. 'Discourse' is also a key term in the title, for Hume applied a philosopher's approach to the issues that he discussed, using the discursive approach attacking views that appeared to be eminently plausible through the use of his relentless logic. This approach led to his implicitly posing a multiplicity of questions. Is it true, he asked in philosophical fashion, that the accumulation of money is beneficial to the nation? Is money wealth? Is it possible to accumulate balance of payments surpluses indefinitely? Is it the case that money has a real role to play in influencing economic activity? Will an increase in the money supply lower the rate of interest? Is it desirable to control international trade with other nations? Challenging questions abound in the *Political Discourses*, but so also do the Humean answers.

From the macroeconomics perspective it is proposed to highlight four significant Humean contributions. These relate to:

    the neutrality of money,
    the self-adjusting price specie flow mechanism of the balance of payments,
    the determination of the rate of interest,
    the issue of free trade.

It will be shown that Hume had strong views on the neutrality of money, particularly in the long term. He challenged the view that increases in the money supply could influence output in the long term. He was not prepared to accept the mercantilist view that the accumulation of bullion was an appropriate policy for the nation. Instead he outlined the self-adjusting price specie flow mechanism to show how a nation could not accumulate excessive stocks of gold and silver. He disagreed with the view that the rate of interest was determined by the demand and supply of money. In his final writing on economics, 'Of the Jealousy of Trade', Hume argued strongly in favour of free international trade. The core of theory that he constructed in some of the central essays of the *Political Discourses* is now regarded by many writers as the core of pre-monetarist theorizing.

However, despite the lucidity of his style and the simplicity of his presentation, there are problems with Hume. His brilliant insights are marred on too many occasions by hesitancies and equivocations. It could be argued that problems arose from doubts, a natural part of the philosopher's reasoning. It could also be maintained that the search for a balanced position led to his desire to take all viewpoints into consideration. However, I believe there was another factor at work; namely, that Hume did not understand the pace at which the financial society around him was changing. The emphasis here is on financial society, for Britain was in the throes of a major financial revolution, one that would establish the base for its later industrial revolution in the nineteenth century. He was not alone. His great friend Adam Smith, as will be shown, suffered from a similar financial myopia. Although Hume noted the liquidity of East India stock and the daily interest paid by Scottish banks, this disconnection from the financial society that he lived in may be seen in his equivocations with respect to the influence of money in the economy and the role of paper money and bank credit. It manifests itself in 'Of Public Credit', where Hume lost a large part of the plot with his critique of the financial innovations which were to provide the very basis for the growth of one of the key parts of the British economy, the financial services sector, and his rash prediction that the growing public debt would end in the bankruptcy of Great Britain. Humean enthusiasts will, no doubt, react strongly against such criticism, but it is important to show not just the discoveries of the great macro-economists that are surveyed in this book, but also their flaws.

There have been many attempts to reconcile Hume's equivocations by distinguishing between short-term versus long-term effects, or more recently in terms of endogenous versus exogenous money changes (see Wennerlind 2005). These explanations have not been convincing because, in my opinion, they do not take into consideration the gap between theorists' understanding of the economy and the underlying financial reality of the world they lived in. Both Hume and Smith suffered from this disability, one that Henry Thornton would later show in his *Enquiry into the Nature and Effects of the Paper Credit of Great Britain* (1802).

The Neutrality of Money

The opening lines of the essay 'Of Money' present what appears to be the central core of the Humean view of money:

> Money is not, properly speaking, one of the subjects of commerce; but only the instrument which men have agreed upon to facilitate the exchange of one commodity for another. It is none of the wheels of trade: It is the oil which renders the motion of the wheels more smooth and easy. If we consider any one kingdom by itself, it is evident, that the greater or less plenty of money is of no consequence.   (Hume 1752: 41)

These are striking lines in that they appear to suggest that Hume attached no great importance to money. He acknowledged that money acted as a unit of account, but did not believe that it was central to the process of economic activity. Unwilling to accept the Lockean metaphor that money was the wheels of trade, Hume demoted it to the role of a lubricant of the wheels of trade. He quickly reiterated this view a few pages later:

> It is indeed evident, that money is nothing but the representation of labour and commodities, and serves only as a method of rating or estimating them. Where coin is in greater plenty; as a greater quantity of it is required to represent the same quantity of goods; it can have no effect, either good or bad, taking a nation within itself; any more than it would make an alteration on a merchant's books, if, instead of the Arabian method of notation, which requires few characters, he should make use of the Roman, which requires a great many.   (Hume 1752: 46)

Once again Hume stressed the unit of account role of money and insisted that a change in the money supply could have no real effect on economic activity. In this he was advancing what would become known as the classical theory on the neutrality of money, i.e. that money has no real role to play in influencing economic activity. However, having made this presentation, Hume proceeded to equivocate:

> But notwithstanding this conclusion which must be allowed just, it is certain, that, since the discovery of the mines in America, industry has encreased in all the nations of Europe, except in the possessors of those mines; and this may justly be ascribed, amongst other reasons, to the encrease of gold and silver.   (Hume 1752: 46)

Hume had now allowed that money had a role in increasing industry in Europe, except in the case of Spain and Portugal, the original beneficiaries of the newly exploited and gold and silver. How did it happen that an increase in the money supply money had a positive effect on output?

> Accordingly we find, that in every kingdom, into which money begins to flow in greater abundance than formerly, every thing takes a new face: labour and industry gain life; the merchant becomes more enterprising, the manufacturer more diligent and skilful, and even the farmer follows his plough with greater alacrity and attention. This is not easily

to be accounted for, if we consider only the influence which a greater abundance of coin has in the kingdom itself, by heightening the price of commodities, and obliging every one to pay a greater number of these little yellow or white pieces for every thing he purchases. And as to foreign trade, it appears, that great plenty of money is rather disadvantageous, by raising the price of every kind of labour.   (Hume 1752: 47)

Hume's dilemma was to explain how he could stress in his opening lines that money had no effect on real output, and then, a few pages later, apparently allow for money to have an effect on real output. Hume adroitly solved this dilemma through the introduction of a time dimension into the analysis. This allowed for the increase in the money supply to have an effect on output in the short run, but not in the long run:

But some time is required before the money circulates through the whole state, and makes its effect be felt on all ranks of people. At first, no alteration is perceived; by degrees the price rises, first of one commodity, then of another; till the whole at last reaches a just proportion with the new quantity of specie which is in the kingdom. In my opinion, it is only in this interval or intermediate situation, between the acquisition of money and rise of prices, that the encreasing quantity of gold and silver is favourable to industry.   (Hume 1752: 47)

Hume's explanation of the short-run effects of the increased money supply on output has close parallels with that of Cantillon (see Chapter 4). Initially, the new money finds its way into the hands of a few people, such as merchants or manufacturers, 'who seek to employ it to advantage'. They hire additional labour, and this extra supply of labour is prepared to accept the old wage rate, 'being glad of employment from such good paymasters'. Even when labour starts to become scarce, Hume maintained that the initial impact will be an increase of output:

If workmen become scarce, the manufacturer gives higher wages, but at first requires an encrease of labour; and this is willingly submitted to by the artisan, who can now eat and drink better, to compensate his additional toil and fatigue. He carries his money to market, where he finds every thing at the same price as formerly, but returns with a greater quantity and of better kinds, for the use of his family... 'Tis easy to trace the money in its progress through the whole commonwealth; where we shall find, that it must first quicken the diligence of every individual before it encrease the price of labour.
(Hume 1752: 48)

To support his argument Hume quoted from the work of Nicolas Du Tot, the under-treasurer of the Royal Bank in France during John Law's Mississippi System. Du Tot had attempted to show that a debasement of the currency did not produce a proportional rise in prices. Hume agreed with his analysis, adding in a footnote:

By the by, this seems to be one of the best reasons which can be given for a gradual and universal encrease of the denomination of money... Were all our money, for instance, recoined, and a penny's worth of silver taken from every shilling the new shilling would probably purchase every thing that could have been bought by the old; the prices of everything would thereby be insensibly diminished; foreign trade enlivened; and domestic industry, by the circulation of a great number of pounds and shillings, would receive some encrease and encouragement. In executing such a project, it would be better to make the new shilling pass for 24 halfpence, in order to preserve the *illusion*, and make it be taken for the same. (Hume 1752: 49; my emphasis)

I have italicized the word 'illusion' in this quotation because it indicates the extent to which Hume's analysis has close parallels with the monetarist line of thinking. Hume believed that the reason why output could temporarily increase as a result of an increase in the money supply was that workers suffered from the illusion that they were earning more. Once this illusion disappeared, the long-term effects rolled in and money was neutral in the long run. Over 200 years later Milton Friedman, a Humean enthusiast, in 'The Role of Monetary Policy' (1968), relied on money illusion to explain why an increase in the money supply might have a beneficial effect on output in the short run but not in the long run. Hume's invocation of the long-term neutrality of money, his allowance that money could have a real effect in the short run, his introduction of a time dimension to explain why this happened, and his use of the term 'illusion' to show how workers would be fooled in the short run to produce more labour, have all strong pre-monetarist chords (for further links between Hume and monetarism, see Mayer 1980).

Hume concluded from all of this that the level of the money stock did not matter but that it was important to keep it increasing, albeit at a respectable rate:

From the whole of this reasoning we may conclude, that it is of no manner of consequence, with regard to the domestic happiness of a state, whether money be in a greater or less quantity. The good policy of the magistrate consists only in keeping it, if possible, still encreasing; because, by that means, he keeps alive a spirit of industry in the nation, and encreases the stock of labour, in which consists all real power and riches. A nation, whose money decreases, is actually, at that time, weaker and more miserable than another nation, which possesses no more money, but is on the encreasing hand. This will be easily accounted for, if we consider, that the alterations in the quantity of money, either on one side or the other, are not immediately attended with proportionable alterations in the price of commodities. There is always an interval before matters be adjusted to their new situation, and this interval is as pernicious to industry, when gold and silver are diminishing, as it is advantageous when these metals are encreasing. (Hume 1752: 50)

This extract shows clearly that Hume favoured expansion in the money supply, albeit small expansions, and feared the deflationary consequences that a reduction in the money supply might entail.

The Self-Adjusting Price Specie Flow Mechanism of the Balance of Payments

Although Hume could envisage society benefiting from a slowly increasing money supply, he was not prepared to accept the mercantilist belief that the state should set out to accumulate sizeable money stocks through protectionist trade policies. He demonstrated that this policy was self-defeating, in the essay 'Of the Balance of Trade', through his invocation of the self-adjusting price specie flow mechanism (on this issue, see Cesarano 1998; Fausten 1979). From the start of this essay Hume was in attack mode, equating specie accumulation, through a policy of trade restrictions, with ignorance:

'Tis very usual, amongst nations ignorant of the nature of commerce, to prohibit the exportation of commodities, and to preserve amongst themselves, whatever they think valuable and useful. They consider not, that, in this prohibition, they act directly contrary to their intentions, and that the more is exported of any commodity, the more will be rais'd at home, of which they themselves will always have the first offer.
(Hume 1752: 79)

Hume asked the question, what would happen if a nation was successful in building up its money stock fourfold:

Must not all labour and commodities rise to such an exorbitant height, that no neighbouring nations could afford to buy from us; while their commodities, on the other hand became so cheap in comparison, that, in spite of all the laws, which could be formed, they would be run in upon us, and our money would flow out; 'till we fall to a level with foreigners, and lose that great superiority of riches, which had laid us under such disadvantages?   (Hume 1752: 83)

This was brilliant theorizing by Hume, for in one paragraph (he had earlier shown how a contraction of the money supply would have a reverse effect) he exposed the fallacy that the accumulation of an excessive supply of money would be beneficial to the nation. He showed that, if the money supply increased, then this increased expenditure in turn pushed up prices. The increase in prices made exports less competitive and imports more competitive. The fall in exports and the increase in imports created a balance of payments deficit. The balance of payments deficit in turn caused the money supply to fall back to its old level. The whole process was self-adjusting. In one power-packed paragraph he had produced the self-adjusting price specie flow mechanism.

For this, Hume has been credited with being the founder of the monetary approach to the balance of payments, that is, monetarism applied to an open economy. However, when discussing Richard Cantillon's contributions in Chapter 4, it was shown that Cantillon has a prior claim to this title. Indeed, Hayek (1936) believed that the similarities between Cantillon's and Hume's approaches were so close that Hume must have had access to a manuscript copy of the *Essai* before writing the *Political Discourses*. It is known that there were at least four copies of the *Essai* in circulation in advance of publication. However, in my opinion, Hayek's suggestion may be rejected because, if Hume had read Cantillon's work, he would have found two transmission processes between changes in the money supply and the balance of payments rather than the one he presented. Cantillon, as noted, had a relative price effect, similar to that outlined by Hume, where the source of the change comes from changes in the relative prices of imports and exports: imports become relatively less expensive and exports become more expensive because of the effect of the increased money supply on domestic prices. However, Cantillon outlined a further transmission process whereby the increased money supply did not change domestic prices because of the law of one price for internationally traded goods. Nevertheless, the increased money supply did cause a balance of payments deficit because of the effect that the excess cash balances had in increasing expenditure on imports and reducing the amount of exports owing to increased internal consumption. Thus, Cantillon had not only the relative price effect in operation but also the cash balance effect, whereas Hume relied on the former.

Indeed, Hume was given the opportunity to incorporate into his analysis the cash balance effect, and also an employment effect, by his friend James Oswald of Dunnikier, a Scottish Member of Parliament at the time for the constituency of Fife. Oswald would later become a Commissioner of Trade and a Lord of the Treasury. He had a brilliant mind and had quickly impressed both Hume and Adam Smith (he was born in Kirkcaldy, also Adam Smith's birthplace). In a letter written in August 1744 Hume remarked that he had spent a week visiting Oswald at Kirkcaldy: 'He has shown me the whole oeconomy of the navy, the sources of the navy debt; with many other branches of public business. He seems to have a great genius for these affairs; & I fancy will go far in that way, if he perseveres' (Hume 1932: i. 58).

Apparently as a result of Oswald's persistence in these naval matters in the House of Commons, the government of the day appointed him Scottish Commissioner of the Navy. Not only was Oswald capable of marshalling complicated matters relating to the government of Britain, but he also had remarkable insights on economics. This may be seen by his analysis of some of the key sections of Hume's 'Of the Balance of Trade', where, in my opinion, Oswald produced a more insightful assessment of the transmission mechanism of monetary forces in an open economy than Hume himself. Hume had sent a draft of the *Political Discourses* to Oswald, who criticized Hume's argument in a letter to him dated 10 October 1749:

Your argument seems to be this: The price of all things, depending necessarily on their quantity and the quantity of money to purchase them, alters the quantity of money, whether by increasing or diminishing it, and the price of all things is altered in the same proportion. An overbalance in trade is only acquired, and can only be preserved, by the low price of labour and commodities. Whenever, therefore, the overbalance creates a greater quantity of money in any one country than is in the neighbouring countries, and consequently raises the price of labour and commodities, the balance will turn in favour of the others...Now this proposition is so far from being universally true, that in a country which has a free communication with its neighbours, it is, I think evidently false. For, in such a country, suppose the quantity of money to be annihilated in any given proportion, it will not necessarily follow that the price of all labour and commodities will sink in the same proportion; because these objects not being confined to the mere quantity of money in that country, may, and unless obstructions of a foreign nation interfered, necessarily would be purchased by money of other neighbouring countries with which there is a supposed communication, and where a like diminution of money had not taken place. (Hume 1955: 191)

Oswald was outlining the law of one price—one that John Law and Richard Cantillon had earlier presented—as an argument against Hume's viewpoint that the increase in the money supply would push up prices proportionately. Oswald contended that this would not happen if the economy was an open one and traded goods along with labour could be imported from foreign countries:

The increased quantity of money would not necessarily increase the price of all labour and commodities; because the increased quantity not being confined to the home labour and commodities, might, and certainly would, be sent to purchase both from foreign countries, which importation, unless obstructed by arbitrary and absurd laws, would keep down the price of commodities to the level of foreign countries; and if the price of labour still continued for a short time at a higher rate than that level, it would only serve, by attracting foreigners, to increase the number of useful inhabitants in proportion to the increased quantity of money. (Hume 1955: 191–2)

Hume replied to Oswald a year later, but his answer avoided the main issue that Oswald had raised. Unfortunately, he would never incorporate Oswald's reservations on the Humean self-adjusting price specie flow mechanism in the context of an open economy. The nub of Hume's answer was as follows:

You allow, that if all the money in England were increased four-fold in one night, there would be a sudden rise of prices; but then, say you, the importation of foreign commodities would soon lower the prices. Here, then, is the flowing out of the money already begun. But, say you, a small part of this stock of money would suffice to buy foreign commodities, and lower the prices. I grant it would for one year, till the imported commodities be consumed. But must not the same thing be renewed next year? No, say you; the additional stock of money, may in this interval, so increase the people and industry, as to enable them to retain their money. Here I am extremely pleased with your reasoning. I agree with you, that the increase of money, if not too sudden, naturally increases people and industry, and by that means may retain itself; but if it do not produce such an increase, nothing will happen except hoarding. (Hume 1955: 197–8)

Hume's response shows that he did not really grasp the importance of Oswald's analysis of the law of one price. Instead Hume changed tack and agreed with Oswald that an increase in the money supply would have a real effect on output, increasing 'people and industry'. Furthermore, as a result of output increasing, the demand for money would increase, and this would lead to the retention of part of the increased money supply in the domestic economy. This admission by Hume that money could have a real effect on output demonstrates the extent to which he was still unclear about what happened after the money supply increased. Oswald, with his very acute mind, had forced Hume into a corner where (1) he did not reply to Oswald's very reasoned exposition of the law of one price to show why prices would not necessarily increase in an open economy consequent on a money supply increase, and (2) he accepted that money could have a real effect on output and this could lead to a retention of at least part of the increased money supply in the domestic economy.

Despite the clarity of his attack on the mercantilistic policy of specie accumulation, the equivocations that one finds in Hume's essay 'Of Money' over whether there is a real role for money to play in the economy reappear in another shape in this essay. The equivocations are not the same, but, again, come under the rubric of whether money has a real effect on economic activity. In this case the equivocation related to the role of paper credit, banknotes, and other financial instruments in the economy. One moment Hume was railing against paper money and the next instance praising it. One has the impression that Hume, based in Scotland, where the banking system through its introduction of the overdraft system appeared to be more dynamic than that south of the border, was having difficulties grasping the extent of the financial revolution that was happening around him. He was not prepared to give banks any significant role in the economy. In a letter to Montesquieu in 1749, he had written, 'Banks are convenient, but it may be questioned whether they are of very much value' (Hume 1955: 188). He could see certain benefits accruing from the use of paper money and credit, but he still stressed his belief that metallic money was the base on which the system revolved and that 'it is impossible to heap up money, more than any fluid, beyond its proper level' (Hume 1752: 84).

Hume was careful to emphasize that his concept of level (equivalent to the equilibrium demand for money) meant 'the proportion of the labour and commodities which are in each province' (1752: 86). This he repeated in a footnote a page later: 'wherever I speak of the level of money, I mean always its proportional level to the commodities, labour, industry, and skill, which is in the several states' (Hume 1752: 87). This point was one that Hume wanted to ingrain on his readers. Earlier he had stressed it in a letter to Oswald: 'I never meant to say that money, in all countries which communicate, must necessarily be on a level, but only a level proportioned to their people, industry and commodities.'

Now, how can this money sink below this 'level'? Hume blamed banks and paper money for money going out of line with its level: 'I scarcely know any method of sinking money below its level, but those institutions of banks, funds, and paper-credit with which we are in this kingdom so much infatuated' (Hume 1752: 89–90). He elaborated by explaining that the problem was caused by this excess money supply pushing up prices, thereby causing a balance of payments deficit, leading to a loss of money: 'These render paper equivalent to money, circulate it throughout the whole state, make it supply the place of gold and silver, raise proportionably the price of labour and commodities, and by that means either banish a great part of those precious metals, or prevent their farther increase' (Hume 1752: 89–90). Here Hume invoked his self-adjusting price specie flow mechanism and used a variant of Gresham's Law, that paper money chases gold and silver out of the kingdom. 'By our present politics, we are as careful to stuff the nation with this fine commodity of bank-bills and exchequer notes, as if we were afraid of being overburthened with the precious metals' (Hume 1752: 91).

In the next paragraph Hume appeared to be praising France for having 'a great plenty of bullion . . . owing to the want of paper-credit'. Furthermore, the French hoarded gold and silver bullion through the use of silver and gold plate in their houses. This, he believed, enabled them to keep their prices down and to have a stock of bullion, in the form of such domestic plate, available for emergencies. Hume praised this situation:

> Great quantities of plate are used in private houses; and all the churches are full of it. By this means, provisions and labour still remain cheaper among them, than in nations that are not half so rich in gold and silver. The advantages of this situation, in point of trade as well as in great public emergencies, are too evident to be disputed.   (Hume 1752: 91)

Having given Genoa as a further example of the benefit of the quasi-hoarding of gold and silver through the use of plate, and criticizing the British tax on plate, Hume attacked 'our darling projects of paper credit', describing them as 'pernicious'. Intriguingly, by 1764, in the later editions of the *Political Discourses*, then incorporated as *Essays and Treatises on Several Subjects*, he appears to have had some second thoughts on the issue. He deleted the highly ironic 'darling' from 'our darling projects' and incorporated two long paragraphs analysing in greater depth banks and paper credit. In these paragraphs he showed that he was aware of the way in which banks in his home town of Edinburgh had recently pioneered the introduction of overdrafts, 'one of the most ingenious ideas that has been executed in commerce' (Hume 1955: 70). But, having shown that at least he was aware of the financial innovations that had been driven by the introduction of overdrafts by the Edinburgh banks and later followed by their Glasgow counterparts, Hume once again equivocated:

'But whatever other advantages result from these inventions it must still be allowed that, besides giving too great facility to credit, which is dangerous, they banish the precious metals' (Hume 1955: 71–2). Note these words 'they banish the precious metals'. So ultimately Hume's position was against the use of paper credit: 'Our modern politics embrace the only method of banishing money, the using of paper-credit' (Hume 1752: 98).

Hume's continued emphasis on metallic money showed a deep streak of conservatism on monetary issues. While prepared to acknowledge that paper credit may have provided some benefits, he was altogether suspicious of it, fearing the consequences of an over-expansion of banknotes. Though acknowledging the innovation of the Scottish banks in providing overdrafts and small-denomination notes, he appeared to believe that these innovations could potentially be very destabilizing.

So was Hume unable to grasp fully the underlying changes occurring in the Scottish banking system, changes which would ultimately greatly help the process of industrialization? This possibility becomes clearer when it comes to analysing his essay 'Of Public Credit', where Hume, perhaps influenced by his reading of Montesquieu's *De l'esprit des lois* (1748) (there are close parallels between Hume's ideas in 'Of Public Credit' and those earlier expressed by Montesquieu in Book XXII chapter xvii of *De l'esprit des lois*), reinforced this image of a conservative prepared to find fault with any type of financial innovation such as the creation of the public debt. Paradoxically for someone who had been critical of a state policy of accumulating specie and bullion, Hume appeared, at the start of this essay, to admire governments that put aside funds to meet the contingencies of greater expenditure arising from war or exceptional circumstances. Such funds would ensure that the state did not have to resort to borrowing, with the attendant increase in the public debt.

The corollary to this was a deep suspicion of government borrowing in the capital market, along with an intense hostility towards the practitioners in this market. Hume believed that the activities of these people in Change Alley, the stock exchange of the day, produced nothing: 'But what production we owe to Change-alley, or even what consumption, except that of coffee, and pen, ink and paper, I have not yet learn'd; nor can one foresee the loss or decay of any one beneficial commerce or commodity, tho' that place and all its inhabitants were for ever bury'd in the ocean' (Hume 1752: 127). These were strong words. On the next page he observed that 'Public securities are with use become a kind of money' (Hume 1752: 128). He wrote that 'public stock' was similar to 'being a kind of paper-credit', having 'all the disadvantages attending that species of money. They banish gold and silver from the most considerable commerce of the state, reduce them to common circulation, and by that means render all provisions and labour dearer than otherwise they would be' (Hume 1752: 131).

Part of Hume's opposition to borrowing arose from the evidence that he had collected about the collapse of Law's System. Hume had read Law and the commentators on his System: Melon, Du Tot, and Paris-Duverney. He had not been impressed by Law's attempts to solve France's national debt problems:

'tis not altogether improbable, that, when the nation become heartily sick of their debts, and are cruelly opprest by them, some daring projector may arise, with visionary schemes for their discharge. And as public credit will begin, by that time, to be a little frail, the least touch will destroy it, as happen'd in France; and in this manner, it will *dye of the doctor.* (Hume 1752: 136)

Terms such as 'daring projector' and 'visionary schemes' were direct allusions to Law and his System and were intentionally hostile to Law. Hume believed Law had been a failure in his understanding of money and credit and in his policy of attempting to correct the problem of the French national debt. Implicitly he was highly critical of someone who demonetized gold and silver, expanded the money supply, and was involved in debt management. Hume was a metallist, critical of expansionary monetary policy, and believed that the national debt was a bad development.

So government securities were added to paper credit in Hume's list of financial instruments that would lead to the banishment of metallic money from the economy. If Hume had been in Law's position, his writings indicate, he would have shut down the banking system, abolished government securities, and closed the stock exchange.

Hume went so far as to predict that the accumulation of the British public debt would inevitably lead to state bankruptcy, with the state defaulting on its debts and the interest payments on them. Although he believed this bankruptcy was inevitable, he was coy about predicting an actual date for this eventuality:

One would incline to assign to this event a very near period, such as half a century, had not our fathers prophesies of this kind been already found fallacious, by the duration of our public credit, so much beyond all reasonable expectation. When the astrologers in France were every year foretelling the death of *Harry* the IV. *These fellows*, says he, *must be right at last.* We shall, therefore, be more cautious than to assign any precise date; and shall content ourselves with pointing out the event in general. (Hume 1752: 140)

Showing his insistence on the inevitability of Great Britain's eventual bankruptcy, Hume stressed in his final sentence of this essay: 'One may safely affirm, that, in order to deliver such prophecies as these, no more is necessary, than merely to be in one's senses, free from the influence of popular madness and delusion' (Hume 1752: 141). He was insistent that there could be no coexistence between the nation and public credit: 'either the nation must destroy public credit, or public credit will destroy the nation' (Hume 1752: 135).

Of course, Hume's Cassandra-style warning never came to pass. The national debt was handled in a very competent manner by the British authorities, and the City of London, the centre for dealing in the various financial instruments of which Hume disapproved, grew to become the world's largest financial centre, in the process generating enormous wealth and employment, not just for the City but for the British economy over the following centuries. Hume's lack of vision on Britain's future financial strength exemplified his innate conservatism on money and financial issues. Instead of being enlightened by the monetary and financial developments around him, he stuck his head in the sand and uttered dirge-like warnings about the danger of banks and paper credit, of borrowing and national debt, of financial projectors and the brokers and jobbers of the City, interspersing these warnings with the occasional howler, such as his assertion that 'the more the government borrows, the cheaper may they expect to borrow' (Hume 1752: 130).

The Determination of the Rate of Interest

Flawed / inaccurate :

In 'Of Interest' Hume attacked as fallacious the view that it was the supply and demand for money that determined the interest rate. According to Hume, an increase in the money supply would just increase prices: 'The lowness of interest is generally ascrib'd to the plenty of money. But money, however plentiful, has no other effect, if fixed, than to raise the price of labour' (Hume 1752: 61).

Hume believed that there were three factors that caused high interest rates: (1) a great demand for borrowing, (2) little riches to supply that demand, and (3) great profits arising from commerce (Hume 1752: 54). In showing this and presenting the factors that he believed were the determinants of the interest rate, Hume also presented his skeletal outline of the macroeconomy. Analogously to the penultimate chapter of John Law's *Money and Trade*, Hume described a primitive pastoral economy inhabited by landlords on one side and peasant farmers on the other. Because of their prodigality, the landlords saved nothing, and the peasant farmers did not have the means to put aside funds as savings.

Hume then advanced his analysis from this dualistic primitive economy to a tripartite classification incorporating merchants alongside the landlords and the peasant farmers. He deemed the merchants to be 'one of the most useful race of men in the whole society'. The merchants hired labour and provided commodities to consumers. The merchants, in similar style to Cantillon's entrepreneurs, dynamized the economic society by increasing trade and industry. Furthermore, the merchants, unlike the prodigal landlords, learnt the merits of frugality—they became savers also. By pooling their savings and lending them, the merchants pushed down the rate of interest: 'Thus an increase of commerce, by a necessary consequence, raises a great number of lenders, and by that means produces lowness of interest' (Hume 1752: 71).

The growth of commerce and industry, resulting from the activities of the merchants, unleashed two major forces: (1) the increased savings made by the merchants lowered the rate of interest; (2) the increased economic activity catalysed further competition among merchants, which drove profits down. As a result of these two forces, both the interest rate and the rate of profit fell. Hume took the view that the interest rate and the profit rate equalized:

> No man will accept of low profits, where he can have high interest; and no man will accept of low interest where he can have high profits. An extensive commerce, by producing large stocks, diminishes both interest and profits; and is always assisted, in its diminution of the one, by the proportional sinking of the other.   (Hume 1752: 72–3)

In linking the rate of interest with profits Hume was following the views already developed by Joseph Massie in his *Essay on the Governing Causes of the Natural Rate of Interest* (1750).

Hume further contended that the lower interest rate was a consequence of the growth of trade rather than a cause of it: 'interest is the barometer of the state, and its lowness is a sign almost infallible of the flourishing condition of a people' (Hume 1752: 73). This contention enabled him to attack the prevailing view that it was an increase in the money supply that lowered interest rates. He asserted that the advocates of this view had taken 'a collateral effect for a cause' because 'the same industry, which sinks the industry, commonly acquires great abundance of precious metals'. In other words, increased economic activity, which lowers the interest rate, also increases the money supply.

This presented the issue of the coexistence of a low interest rate and an increased money supply. The two were in fact, according to Hume, 'almost inseparable'. But he was still left with the problem of explaining why interest rates fell in Spain and Portugal consequent on the increase in the money supply resulting from the importation of gold and silver from the Spanish Americas. Furthermore, this increased money supply had been accompanied by a reduction of interest rates across Europe. Hume maintained that in neither country 'can we justly ascribe that effect merely to the increase of gold and silver'. He repeated this when dealing with the fall in European interest rates:

> As to the reduction of interest, which has followed in England, France, and other kingdoms of Europe, that have no mines, it has been gradual; and has not proceeded from the increase of money, *considered merely in itself*; but from that of industry, which is the natural effect of the former increase, in that interval, before it raises the price of labour and provisions.   (Hume 1752: 77–8; my emphasis)

The phrase 'considered merely in itself' shows Hume's partial equivocation over whether an increase of the money supply could drive interest rates down. Earlier he had admitted that, in the Spanish and Portuguese cases, the

113

increased money supply augmented the number of lenders above those of borrowers in these countries. This in turn led to a fall in the interest rate, which would be 'so much the faster if those, who have acquired those large sums, find no industry or commerce in the state, and no method of employing their money but by lending it at interest' (Hume 1752: 76–7). This, he admitted, would be the short-term effect, but in the long run the increase in the money supply would just lead to higher prices. Hume had a very clear view that the interest rate was determined by real economic activity, though the above quotations show that he was prepared to allow for at least a short-run effect emanating from an increased money supply to lower interest rates in certain cases.

The Issue of Free Trade

At this stage in the middle of the eighteenth century there were few advocates of free trade. Sir Dudley North had been a rare exception, advocating a policy of free trade in the *Discourses upon Trade* (1691) at the end of the seventeenth century, but his work had a very limited circulation. The abbé Castel de Saint-Pierre, a member of the French delegation involved in the negotiation of the Treaty of Utrecht in 1713, had attempted to focus attention on the possibility of a free-trading European union of states, in his prescient *Projet pour render la paix perpétuelle en Europe* (1717), when he wrote, 'Neither the balance of power nor treaties are sufficient to maintain peace; the only way is by European Union' (Brown et al. 2002: 398).

Few turned out to be interested in these views. Continuous warfare between the European nations did not engender hopeful prospects for free trade. The French *économistes* had started to investigate the possible gains from having a policy of *laissez-faire, laissez-passer* (freedom to manufacture and freedom to trade) at the time that Hume's final economics essay, 'Of the Jealousy of Trade', was published, six years after the publication of the original *Political Discourses*.

Already in 'Of the Balance of Trade' Hume had shown the self-defeating nature of one nation attempting to accumulate specie and bullion at the expense of another through prohibitions on trade. Now he aimed to go further and show that international trade was not a zero sum game. He wished to demonstrate that trade could produce mutual benefits for all: 'that where an open communication is preserved among nations, it is impossible but the domestic industry of every one must receive an increase from the improvements of the others' (Hume 1955: 78). So we find a more confident Hume extolling the virtues of free trade and condemning the utter stupidity of envious enmity between nations:

Nothing is more usual, among states which have made some advances in commerce, than to look on the progress of their neighbours with a suspicious eye, to consider all trading states as their rivals, and to suppose that it is impossible for any of them to flourish but at their expense. In opposition to this narrow and malignant opinion, I will venture to assert, that the increase of riches and commerce in any one nation, instead of hurting commonly promotes the riches and commerce of all its neighbours; and that a state can scarcely carry its trade and industry very far, where all the surrounding states are buried in ignorance, sloth, and barbarism. (Hume 1955: 78)

Hume understood that trading nations mutually benefited from the growth in economic activity of their neighbours. There was a need for politicians across the world to cooperate rather than to be involved in continual feuding:

Were our narrow and malignant politics to meet with success, we should reduce all our neighbouring nations to the same state of sloth and ignorance that prevails in Morocco and the coast of Barbary. But what would be the consequence? They could send us no commodities: They could take none from us: Our domestic commerce itself would languish for want of emulation, example and instruction: And we ourselves should soon fall into the same abject condition to which we had reduced them. I shall therefore venture to acknowledge that, not only as a man, but as a British subject, I pray for the flourishing commerce of Germany, Spain, Italy and even France itself. I am at least certain, that Great Britain, and all those nations, would flourish more, did their sovereigns and ministers adopt such enlarged and benevolent sentiments towards each other.
(Hume 1955: 81–2)

Hume did not go a great deal further in advancing the case for international free trade. This final essay of the *Political Discourses* was his last incursion into writing on economic issues. He had by this time turned to writing a history of England, which engaged all his attention. The success of the multi-volume *History of England* enabled Hume to feel financially free. He would later try his hand at diplomacy, and worked for two and a half years as the private secretary to the earl of Hertford and later as Chargé d'Affaires in the British Embassy in Paris between 1763 and 1765. During this stay in Paris, Hume was involved in negotiating the settlement of the outstanding paper money (including card money) of New France that arose after the British takeover of Canada (see Dimand 2005).

In the spring of 1775 Hume was 'struck with a disorder in my bowels'. He realized that this cancer was incurable and calmly settled down to write his own brief autobiography. In this he wrote: 'I was, I say, a man of mild disposition, of command of temper, of an open, social, and cheerful humour, capable of attachment, but little susceptible of enmity, and of great moderation in all my passions' (Hume 1776: 32–3). He died in Edinburgh on 25 August 1776, the year of publication of the *Wealth of Nations* by his great friend Adam Smith. Smith's enormous admiration for Hume comes through in the final lines of the eulogy of Hume that he wrote to accompany the publication of the *Life of David Hume*: 'Upon the whole, I have always considered him, both in his lifetime and since his death, as approaching as nearly to the idea of a perfectly wise and virtuous man, as perhaps the nature of human frailty will permit' (Hume 1776: 62).

One of the great benefits of Hume's *Political Discourses* is that of reading one of the most elegant essayists of the English language at work. Hume had the ability to present difficult ideas and concepts in brilliantly simple prose. He is an economic writer whom one reads with considerable pleasure, not simply for his economic ideas but for the manner in which he presents them. It is a gift that few writers on economics have possessed, and Hume ranks alongside more recent writers, such as John Maynard Keynes and John Kenneth Galbraith, in the challenging lucidity of his economic discourse. The man who was turned down for two chairs by Scottish academia ultimately trumped his detractors by becoming one of the beacons, not only of the Scottish, but more importantly of the European, Enlightenment (see Robertson 2005).

References

Brown, John, Terry Nardin, and Nicholas Rengger (eds) (2002), *International Relations in Political Thought* (Cambridge).

Cesarano, Filippo (1998), 'Hume's Specie-Flow Mechanism and Classical Monetary Theory: An Alternative Interpretation', *Journal of International Economics*, 45 (June).

Dimand, Robert W. (2005), 'David Hume on Canadian Paper Money: An Overlooked Contribution', *Journal of Money, Credit and Banking*, 37/4 (Aug.).

Fausten, Dietrich K. (1979), 'The Humean Origin of the Contemporary Monetary Approach to the Balance of Payments', *Quarterly Journal of Economics*, 93 (Nov.).

Friedman, Milton (1968), 'The Role of Monetary Policy', *American Economic Review*, 58 (Mar.).

Hayek, Friedrich von (1936), 'Richard Cantillon: Sa vie, son œuvre', *Revue des sciences économiques* (Apr., June, Oct.).

Hume, David (1752), *Political Discourses* (Edinburgh).

—— (1776), *The Life of David Hume, Esq., Written by Himself* (London).

—— (1932), *Letters of David Hume*, ed. J. Y. T. Grieg, 2 vols (Oxford).

—— (1954), *New Letters of David Hume*, ed. Raymond Klibansky and Ernest Mossner (Oxford).

—— (1955), *David Hume Writing on Economics*, ed. Eugene Rotwein (Madison; repr. 1970).

Mayer, Thomas (1980), 'David Hume and Monetarism', *Quarterly Journal of Economics*, 95 (Aug.).

Mossner, Ernest Campbell (1980), *The Life of David Hume* (1954; 2nd edn, Oxford).

Robertson, John (2005), *The Case for Enlightenment Scotland and Naples 1680–1760* (Cambridge).

Wennerlind, Carl (2005), 'David Hume's Monetary Theory Revisited: Was he Really a Quantity Theorist and an Inflationist?', *Journal of Political Economy*, 113/1.

Franciscus Quesnay

in utrique Medicinâ Magister, Academiæ Reg. Chirurg. Paris. Secretarius, et Scholæ Profess. Regius,
Reg. Scientiar. et liberal. art. Academ. Lugdun.et Medicus Celsiss. et Potentiss. Ducis de VILLEROY.

François Quesnay

6

François Quesnay: The Circular Flow of Income

Let us imagine that we are in France in December 1758. In fact we are in the magnificent Château de Versailles, observing Louis XV, the king of France, fascinated by typography, experimenting with his new printing set. At his side sits Dr François Quesnay (1694–1774), the private physician of his mistress, Madame de Pompadour. Quesnay has a page of figures, which he is encouraging the king to set in type. There are lines and zigzags between these figures, which add to the complication of the printing process. Quesnay urges the king on, stressing the importance of what he is calling the 'Tableau économique', the 'Economic Picture'. Once the king has set all the type, he decides to print the page, but he does so with a regal flourish. The quarto page will be printed in gold leaf. Louis XV's flourish is an important one, for Quesnay's page of figures, lines, and zigzags represents the first ever presentation of the macro-economy in a diagrammatic format. It is Quesnay's conceptualization of the macroeconomic picture of France as he understands it. Given its importance, though one suspects the king is more interested in the typography than the economics, it is totally appropriate for it to be printed in gold.

Du Pont de Nemours, in his *Mémoires*, indicated that he had been the source for circulating this story about Quesnay's involvement of the king in the first printing of the 'Tableau', and there were many subsequent allusions to this in the *Éphémérides*, which Du Pont edited (see Quesnay 2005: i. 393).

Kuczynski and Meek (1972) have provided a detailed account of the early editions of the 'Tableau économique'. Their work shows that there is no known extant printed copy of the 'first edition', but there is a manuscript version of this work written in December 1758. Only three copies of the 'second edition' were printed and, fortunately, two of these are still extant. Kuczynski and Meek have published the 'third edition'—again very few copies of this were printed by Quesnay—based on a copy of this work found by Kuczynski in the papers of Du Pont de Nemours in the Eleutherian Mills Historical Library, Delaware. Intriguingly, a number of years ago a bookseller that I know in Paris asked if I would like to see a copy of the 'Tableau économique' printed in gold: the owners of this work were considering putting it up for sale. Drawing a large gasp of air, I said I would be more than delighted to see it and arranged to meet him the next day. Alas, in the intervening period the owners drew back on their decision to sell and would not show us this remarkable document. At a later stage I was informed that it had been sold to a purchaser in Germany. So all I can say is that, as far as I can ascertain, there is a copy of the 'Tableau économique', printed in gold, in private hands in Germany, which would appear to confirm the story that Louis XV was actively involved in producing the first printing of Quesnay's manuscript version of the 'Tableau économique'. Furthermore, it may be the first edition in a printed format. For this reason I have assumed that Louis XV was printing it in December 1758.

Quesnay's Background

François Quesnay was born on 4 June 1694 in a small village called Méré, near Montfort-l'Amaury, in the Yveslines, about 45 kilometres from the centre of Paris. His origins and career as both a surgeon and an economist have been excellently outlined by Jacqueline Hecht in 'La Vie de Quesnay' (Quesnay 2005). His father was a small farmer and merchant who also collected the tithes for the local abbey. Quesnay's parents had thirteen children, nine daughters and four sons, of whom only six were still living by 1710—a stark reminder of the high rate of infant mortality at the time; Quesnay was the eighth child.

From a young age Quesnay appeared to be interested in medicine, reading intensively on the subject. His father died in 1707, when Quesnay was 13 years old, and some four years later his mother allowed him to learn the rudiments of bloodletting from a local surgeon, Jean de La Vigne. Quesnay was not over-impressed by this surgeon and pleaded with his mother that he be allowed to study surgery in Paris. Surgery did not rate very highly at the time. The surgeons were still in the same guild as barbers, and were categorized, despite their skills, at a level considerably beneath doctor physicians. A measure of this low level of recognition for their work may be gleaned from the fact that Quesnay's mother insisted that he become an apprentice engraver in Paris to have something to fall back on if his career as a surgeon did not blossom. While apprenticed to a master engraver and living in the Latin Quarter, Quesnay enrolled in lectures at the Faculty of Medicine as well as lectures in surgery at the Collège de Saint-Côme. On finishing his engraving apprenticeship, Quesnay commenced working as a surgeon at Orgerus, near Montfort. Having married Jeanne-Catherine Dauphin, on 30 January 1717, Quesnay attempted to become a surgeon at Mantes, but the restrictive practices of the local surgeons ensured that he had to move back to Paris, where he graduated from the Collège de Saint-Côme in August 1718. He returned to Mantes and soon established a reputation as an excellent surgeon for births, bloodletting, and operations.

Quesnay's talent soon came to the notice of the duc de Villeroy. One day the comtesse d'Estrades fell ill when in the company of the duc de Villeroy. Quesnay was called and immediately recognized that the comtesse was suffering from a fit of epilepsy. Such was the care and attention that he administered to the comtesse that she recommended him to her relative the marquise de Pompadour, popularly known as Madame de Pompadour. Thus, Quesnay became the official doctor to the king's mistress and was invited to live in Versailles in the spring of 1749. When he accompanied Madame de Pompadour to her residence in Paris, he stayed with her at the Élysée, now the residence of the president of France.

Despite his closeness to the centre of power, Quesnay kept out of the intrigues of the court, even refusing to join a group plotting to have Madame de Pompadour replaced in the king's favour by the comtesse de Choiseul-Romanet. When the plotters thought that the latter lady had won over the king with her charms, and claimed that Madame de Pompadour was to be ousted as the royal mistress, Quesnay was asked if he wished to join in with the apparent new favourite. With great dignity he replied, 'I was attached to Madame de Pompadour in her prosperity, and I shall be in her disgrace' (Butler 1980: 931). Madame de Pompadour survived this courtesan putsch, and thereafter regarded Quesnay with great affection for such loyalty and for his great professionalism, leaving him a pension for life on her death. He was also very well regarded by the king, who referred to him as his 'thinker' (*penseur*).

Quesnay was in his mid-fifties when he moved to Versailles. By this stage of his career he had already written extensively on medicine through works such as *Essai physique sur l'œconomie animale* (1736), *Traité de la suppuration* (1749), *Traité de la gangrene* (1749), and *Traité des effets de l'usage de la saignée* (1750), as well as editing the *Mémoires de l'Académie royale de chirurgie* (1743). The titles of these works indicate there was nothing to suggest that Quesnay had any interest in economics at this stage of his career. This was soon to change.

Quesnay and the Enlightenment

As France moved into the second half of the eighteenth century, a new movement was developing which was to transform profoundly the nature of French society. This was the Enlightenment, an intellectual movement attempting to capture the progress that had been achieved in the arts and sciences. In presenting this progress, it questioned the prevailing ideas and dogmas. This led to a questioning of the basis of royal authority as well as of the Catholic Church. The initial great work that launched this revolution of ideas was Montesquieu's *De l'esprit des lois* (1749), which proposed a system of political power based on a system of checks and balances between the legislature, the executive, and the judiciary. Montesquieu's views, along with those of John Locke, would form the backbone of the United States Constitution when it was later drafted in the 1770s. Following closely on Montesquieu's book, the publication of the first part of the *Encyclopédie*, edited by Diderot and d'Alembert in 1751, represented a further challenge to the authority of the old institutions. The *Encyclopédie* gave intellectuals the opportunity to provide the most up-to-date assessments of their subjects, new knowledge which corroded the legitimacy of the power base of the old institutions, a corrosion that would ultimately lead to the French Revolution. Paralleling these political and social developments, the French Enlightenment nurtured another incipient revolution, an economic revolution, one that would reach its apogee in the eighteenth century with the publication of Adam Smith's *Wealth of Nations*, a work extolling the virtues of the economic liberalism.

The credit for launching this economic revolution may be attributed to two figures: Vincent de Gournay and François Quesnay. But prior to them a lesser-known figure, Pierre de Boisguilbert, had provided part of the intellectual template that Gournay, Quesnay, and even Adam Smith would use. Consider the following passage and guess who wrote it:

All the commerce of the land, both wholesale and retail, and even agriculture, are governed by nothing other than the self-interest of the entrepreneurs, who have never considered rendering service nor obligating those with whom they contract through their commerce; and any innkeeper who sells wine to passers-by never intended to be useful to them, nor did the passers-by who stop with him ever travel for fear that his provisions would be wasted. It is this reciprocal utility which makes for the harmony of the world and maintains states; each man thinks of procuring the greatest degree of individual interest with the greatest ease possible, and when he travels to purchase a commodity four leagues from his home, it is because it is not sold three leagues away, or else that it is cheaper, which compensates for the longer journey.   (Boisguilbert 1705: 748–9)

This passage is quite amazing, containing key words such as 'self-interest', 'entrepreneurs', 'reciprocal utility', 'harmony of the world', 'the greatest degree of individual interest with the greatest ease possible'. As Faccarello (1999: 168) has pointed out, parts of the above quotation read suspiciously like Adam Smith's famous passage:

It is not from the benevolence of the butcher, the brewer, or the baker, that we expect our dinner, but from their regard to their own interest. We address ourselves, not to their humanity but to their self-love, and never talk to them of our own necessities but of their advantages.   (Smith 1976: i. 26–7)

In this passage Smith wanted to show how the pursuit of self-interest generated a harmonious outcome for economic society. However, Boisguilbert had already worked this out more than three-quarters of a century before Smith. Boisguilbert's emphasis on self-interest as a catalyst behind economic activity, along with his strong advocacy of a system of *laissez-faire* (he was, along with d'Argenson, the first economic writer to use the term), made him an influential predecessor of Gournay and Quesnay.

Although some writers tend to categorize together the French economic writers of the 1750s and 1760s into a collective homogeneous group, tagged as the Physiocrats, this was not the case. When economics as a new science was emerging in the 1750s in France, there was not this uniformity of approach because Quesnay and the Physiocrats had been preceded by the highly important personality of Vincent de Gournay (1712–59), the man who inspired a group of young writers prior to Quesnay's taking up the subject. Gournay's influence on these writers will be discussed in the next chapter, dealing with Turgot, as he was the latter's mentor.

By 1757 Quesnay, with time on his hands in Versailles, had started to think seriously about economic issues. He wrote two articles for the *Encyclopédie*, which appeared in November 1757, one with the title 'Fermiers' (Farmers) and the other with the title 'Grains' (Cereals). These articles had no immediate impact on readers of the *Encyclopédie*, but they did show the importance that Quesnay attached to capital intensity in farming. In the same year he met Victor Riquetti, marquis de Mirabeau, whose son H. G. Riquetti, comte de Mirabeau, was later to play such an important role in the early stages of the French Revolution. Mirabeau at this stage was a celebrated man of letters, for the first part of his book *L'Ami des hommes* (The Friend of Mankind, 1756), a work that became an eighteenth-century bestseller, had just been published. This work had been inspired in part by Cantillon's *Essai* and there is a considerable suspicion that Mirabeau intended incorporating Cantillon's *Essai* in his book until the publication of the *Essai* in 1755 effectively stopped this potential piece of plagiarism. The meeting between Mirabeau and Quesnay was described in detail by the former in a letter to Rousseau:

I had like him [Cantillon] and so many others, concluded, according to the superficial appearance of things, that, since when I put my hand in front of my eyes it hides the sun from me, my hand is bigger than the sun. I had, I say, reasoned in this way: Wealth is the fruit which comes from the land for the use of men; the labour of man alone possesses the capacity to increase wealth. Thus the more men there are, the more labour will there be; the more labour there is, the more wealth there will be. The way to achieve prosperity is therefore: (1) to increase men; (2) through these men, to increase productive labour; (3) through this labour, to increase wealth. In this position I felt myself invulnerable, and I gaudily decorated my political edifice with marriages, sumptuary laws, and the rest, just as I wanted to. Never did Goliath go into battle with as much confidence as I did when I sought out a man [Quesnay] who, I had been informed, had written on the margin of my book these insolent words: The child has been suckled on bad milk; the force of his temperament often puts him right so far as results are concerned, but he understands nothing as to principles. My critic did not beat about the bush with me, and told me quite plainly that I had put the cart before the horse, and that Cantillon, as a teacher of the public was nothing but a fool.   (Meek 1962: 17)

These words directed by Quesnay at Mirabeau were harsh. The latter, after an evening of deliberation, accepted his new master's criticisms and became his disciple in the promotion of what would become known as the Physiocratic doctrine. The above passage contains a major paradox, for it presents Quesnay's cursory dismissal of Cantillon as 'nothing but a fool'. These were somewhat hollow words since the basis for Quesnay's future formulation of the 'Tableau économique' was Cantillon's verbal description of the circular flow of income in the *Essai*.

The 'Tableau économique'

The 'Tableau économique', the 'Economic Picture', was Quesnay's visual representation of the macroeconomy. The traditional interpretation of the 'Tableau' suggested that Quesnay's inspiration for it came from his medical knowledge on the circulation of blood—he had, after all, written a treatise on bloodletting. While this medical background may have helped, it appears that Quesnay was more directly inspired by mechanical models. Rieter (1990) and Charles (2003) have shown how Quesnay may have been influenced by his recollection of the rolling-ball clocks and hydraulic water machines in the Grollier collection in Lyons that he may have viewed on a visit to the city with his patron the duc de Villeroy in 1735. Alternatively, Quesnay may have been able to inspect the diagrams of these machines by reading Grollier's book on the Lyons collection, which had been assembled by his father, Nicolas Grollier de Servière, in 1719. The key element linking Quesnay to Grollier was his borrowing of the terms 'tableau' and 'zigzag'. These terms, key elements of the 'Tableau', appear, as Charles shows, to have been directly inspired by Grollier's book. Grollier had written as follows:

One sees . . . that the body of the third clock is more or less like the one of a *tableau*. There are several small tracks channelled on its surface and placed diagonally on each other in zigzag: these tracks conduct two balls made of copper that travel into the tracks alternately, one after the other, and descend by the virtue of their natural weight. . . . The movement of this clock is regulated by the movement of the balls according to the principles we have described, and mark the hours on a dial placed below the *tableau*.

(Grollier 1719: 15–16; trans. Charles 2003: 534)

Quesnay, inspired by Grollier's mechanical descriptions and Cantillon's verbal description of the circular flow of income process, was able to link the two to create the 'Tableau économique'. Aside from the small number of privately printed copies mentioned above, Quesnay never issued any specific book for public circulation with the title 'Tableau économique'. The first time that it was actually published arose when Mirabeau incorporated it into the sixth part of *L'Ami des hommes* under the title 'Tableau Oeconomique avec ses explications' (1760). Following on from this, it appears that Mirabeau and Quesnay intended to produce a work with the specific title *Le Grand Tableau économique*. Unfortunately, however, this title was abandoned and was replaced by the far less informative *Philosophie rurale* (1764). Though Mirabeau was credited as the author of this work, it is quite clear now that Quesnay played such a huge role in writing it that he may be regarded as the real author (see the editors' discussion of this issue in Quesnay 2005: ii. 639–42).

The 'Tableau économique' clearly shows a visual circular flow of income, expenditure, and output. It was the first macroeconomic diagram showing the importance of expenditure, the interrelationships between income, expenditure, and output, and the interdependencies between different sectors of the economy. Figure 6.1 outlines what Kuczynski and Meek (1972) have described as the 'third edition' of the 'Tableau économique'. It is reproduced because it is a more user-friendly version of the 'Tableau' than the first or second editions. The first point to note about the diagram is that it is an expenditure-driven diagram. Three sources of expenditure are outlined: (1) 'productive expenditure' relative to agriculture; (2) expenditure by landlords; and (3) 'sterile expenditure', defined as expenditure on manufactured commodities, housing, clothing, interest on money, servants, commercial expenses, foreign produce, etc. From a socio-economic perspective, three classes—farmers, landlords, and the sterile sector, the latter representing a catch-all grouping incorporating all economic activity emanating from outside agriculture, i.e. industry and the service sectors—are presented as the drivers of expenditure.

Economic behaviour is skewed in two ways in the 'Tableau'. First of all, the expenditure impetus so crucial for sparking economic activity is centred on the activities of the landlords' expenditure of the rents that they receive from the agricultural sector. As in Cantillon's approach, the landlords are at the centre of the major expenditure decisions. These decisions are simplified in the 'Tableau'. In what constitutes the first round of expenditure, the landlords are deemed to spend half of their expenditure on products produced by the agricultural sector ('bread, wine, meat, etc.') and the other half on products produced by the sterile sector ('clothing, furnishings, utensils, etc.'). Though the landlords are at the centre of the expenditure pyramid, dictating the amount of expenditure that goes to the two economic sectors, the real productive base of the economy is skewed to the left of the table, where the activities of the farming sector are concentrated. It is the farmers, and only the farmers, who produce net product. The 300 units spent by the landlords on agricultural products constitutes income for the farmers. The national income identity with income creating expenditure was thus activated, with the expenditure of the landlords transformed into income for the farmers.

TABLEAU ŒCONOMIQUE

Provided by agriculture, grasslands, pastures, forests, mines, fishing, wood, livestock, raw materials for manufactured commodites, etc. On corn, drink, meat, etc.

Mutual sales from one expenditure class to the other, which distribute the revenue of 600 livres to both sides, giving 300 livres to each, in addition to the advances which are maintained intact. The proprietor subsists on the 600 livres which he spends. The 300 livres distributed to each expenditure class can support one man in each; thus 600 livres of revenue can enable three heads of families to subsist. On this basis 600 millions of revenue can enable three million families to subsist, estimated at three persons per family. The costs of the productive expenditure class which are also regenerated each year, and about half of which consists of wages for men's labour, add 300 millions, which can enable another one million heads of families to subsist at 300 livres each. Thus these 900 millions which are annually generated from landed property could enable 12 million persons of all ages to subsist, in conformity with this order of circulation and distribution of the annual revenue. By circulation is here meant the purchases paid for by the revenue, and the distribution which shares out the revenue among men by means of the payment for purchases at first hand, abstracting from trade, which increases sales and purchases without increasing things, and which represents nothing but an addition to sterile expenditure.

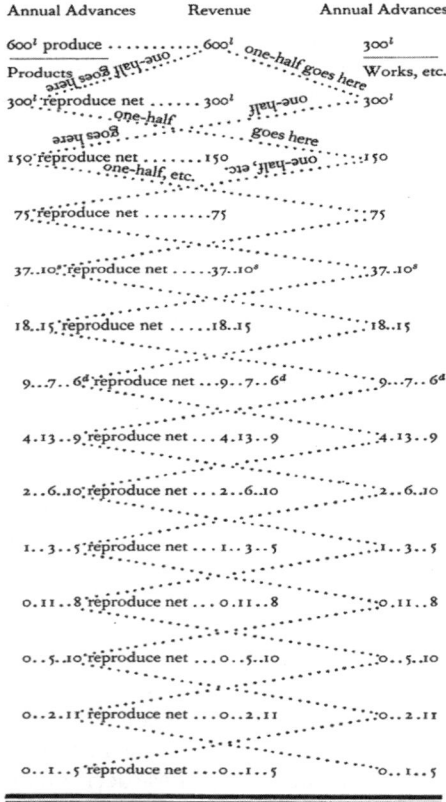

EXPENDITURE OF THE REVENUE
after deduction of taxes, is divided between productive expenditure and sterile expenditure

PRODUCTIVE EXPENDITURE		STERILE EXPENDITURE
Annual Advances	Revenue	Annual Advances

600¹ produce .... 600¹ *one-half goes here* 300¹

Products *goes here, etc.* .... Works, etc.

300¹ reproduce net ..... 300¹ *goes here* 300¹
one-half

150 reproduce net .... 150 *goes here* ...:150
one-half, etc.

75 reproduce net .... 75 .... :75

37..10° reproduce net ..... 37..10° ....:37..10°

18..15 reproduce net .....18..15 ....:18..15

9...7..6ᵈ reproduce net ...9..7..6ᵈ ....9...7..6ᵈ

4.13..9 reproduce net ... 4.13..9 ....4.13..9

2..6..10 reproduce net ... 2..6..10 ....2..6..10

1..3..5 reproduce net ... 1..3..5 ....1..3..5

0.11..8 reproduce net ... 0.11..8 ....0.11..8

0..5..10 reproduce net ... 0..5.10 ....0..5.10

0..2..11 reproduce net ... 0..2.11 ....0..2.11

0..1..5 reproduce net ... 0..1..5 ....0..1..5

Total reproduced .... 600¹ of revenue and the annual costs of agriculture of 600 livres which the land restores. Thus the reproduction is 1200 livres.

On manufactured commodities, house-room, clothing, interest on money, servants, commercial costs, foreign produce, etc.

Mutual purchases by one expenditure class from another distribute the revenue of 600 livres.

The two classes spend in part on their own products and in part mutually on the products of one another.

The process of circulation sends 600 livres to this column, from which 300 livres have to be kept back for the annual advances. 300 livres remain here for wages.

The taxes which ought to be included in this class are taken out of the revenue which is obtained through reproductive expenditure, and get lost in circulation, except for those which come back into circulation, where they are regenerated in the same way as the revenue, and are distributed in the same way to the two classes. But they are always detrimental to the proprietor's revenue, or to the cultivator's advances, or to economy in consumption. In the two latter cases they are destructive, because they reduce reproduction in the same proportion. It is just the same with those which are transferred abroad without any return, and which are held back in the monetary fortunes of the tax-farmers who are responsible for their collection and expenditure; for these parts of the taxes, diverted or stolen from productive expenditure through saving, or taken out of the cultivator's advances, extinguish reproduction, fall back on and cause a double loss to the proprietors, and in the end destroy the mass of revenue which provides the taxes, which ought to fall only on the proprietor, and not on reproductive expenditure, where they ruin the cultivator, the proprietor, and the state.

Figure 6.1 François Quesnay's 'Tableau économique'

Quesnay then postulated that this income produced two consequences. Firstly, it enabled the farmers 'to reproduce' another 300 units—depicted by the horizontal line running from the 300 units on the left. Secondly, it enabled the farmers to spend 150 units, i.e. half of the income that they had received, on the products of the sterile sector. This latter expenditure behaviour is marked by the zigzag line to the sterile sector culminating in the appearance of 150 units of income on the right of the diagram under the sterile sector. Thirdly, the other half of the income of the farmers was destined to pay for the consumption of their own products from the agricultural sector. This activity is not outlined in the 'Tableau'; it takes place off-stage.

Moving back to the top of the expenditure pyramid, the 'Tableau' shows the other half of the landlords' rental income spent on the sterile sector. In this case the sterile sector does not reproduce any further output: there is no horizontal link emanating from this sector. Quesnay, using medical terminology, deemed this sector to be incapable of producing any net output, hence the term 'sterile'. In the second round of expenditure the sterile sector spends half of its income on goods purchased from the agricultural sector and half on its own output; again the latter is not depicted in the 'Tableau'.

After this second round of income and expenditure, third, fourth, etc. rounds are activated, with the farmers spending half of their income on the products of the sterile sector and the sterile sector spending half of its income on the products of the agricultural sector. In each case the agricultural sector is also reproducing whatever comes to it in the form of income, a process marked by the horizontal lines moving from the agricultural sector to the centre of the 'Tableau'. In this format the 'Tableau' presented a static interpretation of the way in which the system could reproduce itself. At the end of the income–expenditure process the agricultural sector has produced 600 units in income and reproduced another 600; the sterile sector, on the other hand, has generated just 600 units of income. The net product of the agricultural sector (600) then constitutes the rent for the landlords to restart the income–expenditure process. At this stage of the analysis the 'Tableau' showed the self-equilibrating nature of the system given the stylistic assumption that half of the income earned by both the productive and the sterile sectors is spent on the products of the other sector.

But that was only the first stage of the analysis, because Quesnay also wanted to show how the economic circle of income, output, and expenditure could be either contracted or expanded further. For him, bad policies such as those of Colbertism and its bias towards encouraging industry (the sterile sector) could contract the economy, whereas good policies, i.e. those recommended by Quesnay to increase the role of agriculture, could increase economic activity. The introduction of these dynamic elements produced a great deal of excitement for its readers because it suggested that it was possible to expand the circle of economic activity through an expansion of the agricultural surplus. This expansion could be achieved through either increased consumption expenditure on agricultural products, a higher price for agricultural products, and/or increased investment expenditure in agriculture. So the very positive element of the 'Tableau' was Quesnay's demonstration that economic activity was not a zero sum game and that economic growth could occur. He was able to demonstrate that, if consumption expenditure on agricultural products increased, it would generate a greater agricultural surplus and hence promote economic growth. Similarly, he showed that, if consumption expenditure on agricultural products fell, then economic activity would be reduced. In a footnote Quesnay suggested to his readers that they work out the consequences of less spending on agricultural products:

> Draw up the *Tableau Economique* on the basis of 400 millions of net product and 400 millions of burdensome assessments, which makes a total of 800 millions, of which 200, constituting one-half of the net product, pass into the hands of the productive expenditure class, and 600 into those of the sterile expenditure class. When the distributions between the two classes are drawn in, the reproduction of the productive expenditure class will amount to only 665 millions instead of 800. (Kuczynski and Meek 1972: 7)

Alternatively, if the price of agricultural products increased, then this would help produce a greater agricultural surplus and more growth. Quesnay always favoured the *bon prix*, the right price, for agricultural products and believed that the market for agricultural goods should be liberalized so as to enable French farmers to export from France and so generate further surpluses.

On an initial analysis of the 'Tableau', it appears to be consumption-driven, but care needs to be exercised here because Quesnay very clearly also wanted to incorporate investment into the analysis. This may be seen from observing the inclusion of 'annual advances' under both productive expenditure and sterile expenditure in Figure 6.1. Annual advances represented investment in seeds, fertilizers, and the subsistence of the labour. As such, this type of investment represented circulating capital. In his earlier work for the *Encyclopédie*, Quesnay had emphasized the huge importance of capital investment for agriculture in his articles on farmers and cereals. Eltis (1975*a*: 1) has shown how Quesnay distinguished between low capital-intensive farming (*la petite culture*), using oxen, and more capital-intensive farming (*la grande culture*), using horses to draw the plough. He produced a variety of statistics to show how the returns from agriculture increased the more intensive the capital investment. His message was clear that the greater the capital intensity of agriculture, the greater the economic surplus that would be generated. He prioritized the size of capital investment (*avances*) when he posed the question, what were the key elements contributing to the prosperity of the nation:

> In what does the prosperity of an agricultural nation consist? *In large advances to perpetuate and increase revenue and taxes; in a free and unobstructed internal and external trade; in the enjoyment of the annual wealth from landed property; and in ample monetary payments of revenue and taxes.* (Kuczynski and Meek 1972: 17)

Quesnay also realized that there was a need for *avances originales*, in the form of animals, ploughs, and farm buildings, and that there was also an even longer type of capital, the *avances foncières*, which involved investments such as draining lands to prepare them for cultivation. It was not a case of just putting workers in the fields to produce agricultural output. Proper agricultural management required capital investment in the form of the three types of *avances*, plus the entrepreneurial flair of the farmer:

Thus it is not to these poor peasants that you should entrust the cultivation of your land. It is animals which should plough and fertilise your fields; it is consumption, sales, and free and unobstructed internal and external trade which ensure the market value which constitutes your revenue. Thus it is wealthy men whom you should put in charge of the enterprises of agriculture and rural trade, in order to enrich yourselves, to enrich the state, and to enable inexhaustible wealth to be generated.   (Kuczynski and Meek 1972: 20)

Earlier, in the *Encyclopédie* article 'Les Grains', Quesnay had stressed the role of entrepreneurship in farming:

We do not see the rich farmer here as a worker who tills the soil himself; he is an entrepreneur who manages his undertaking and makes it prosper through his intelligence and his wealth. Agriculture carried on by rich cultivators is an honest and lucrative profession, reserved for free men who are in a position to advance the considerable sums the cultivation of the land requires, and it employs the peasants and gives them a suitable and assured return for their work.   (trans. Eltis 1975a: 174)

It is quite clear that, although Quesnay stressed the importance of land in unleashing the net product of agriculture, he was more than conscious of the need to add these two further factors of production, capital and enterprise, in order to maximize this net product. From this point, economists could preach a new positive message for what Quesnay referred as 'the science of economic administration', namely, one of economic growth. This excitement had to be tinged, however, by the disappointment of Quesnay's confinement of the process of economic growth to agriculture. For him, agriculture was the only sector capable of producing economic growth. His myopia on this issue, fashioned in large part by his acute distaste of Colbert's policies aimed at encouraging industry, may be gleaned from the following words extolling the importance of agriculture, words that he emphasized in capital letters in the third edition of the 'Tableau économique':

Of all the occupations by which gain is secured, none is better than *Agriculture*, none more profitable, none more delightful, none more becoming to a freeman...for my part, at least, I am inclined to think that no life can be happier than that of the farmer, not merely from the standpoint of the duty performed, which benefits the entire human race, but also because of its charm, and the plenty it gives of everything that tends to the nurture of man and even to the worship of the gods.   (Kuczynski and Meek 1972: 15)

Quesnay had earlier warned of the dangers of spending too much on commodities produced by the sterile sector:

It can be seen from the distribution delineated in the *Tableau* that if the nation's expenditure went more to the sterile expenditure side than to the productive expenditure side, the revenue would fall proportionately, and that this fall would increase in the

129

same progression from year to year successively. It follows that a high level of expenditure on luxury in the way of ornamentation and conspicuous consumption is ruinous. If on the other hand the nation's expenditure goes to the productive expenditure side the revenue will rise, and this rise will in the same way increase successively from year to year. Thus it is not true that the type of expenditure is a matter of indifference.

(Kuczynski and Meek 1972: 12)

The productive versus sterile dichotomy constituted an unhappy differentiation of economic activity for future generations to build on. Even Adam Smith, who was not prepared to accept the singular reproductive powers of agriculture, adopted this terminology, distinguishing between productive and unproductive output, an attitude of mind that lauded tangible output in the form of goods and was highly critical of intangibles in the form of services.

Quesnay's unidimensional bias towards the reproductive potential of agriculture enabled him to produce a simple policy message. As agriculture was the only sector capable of producing a surplus, income from it should be the subject of a single tax (*l'impôt unique*), a proposal which must have had Petty, a strong opponent of excessive taxation of the agricultural sector, turning in his grave. His dismissal of the contributions of the industrial and services sectors made little sense and, ultimately, greatly reduced the appeal of the dynamic income-generating possibilities of the 'Tableau'.

Lionel Robbins (1998: 101), in his lectures, maintained that, though you have to tackle the 'Tableau économique' at some stage or another, 'you need a towel round your head to read Quesnay'. This is all too true, but Quesnay did leave a strong legacy. He influenced Adam Smith to the extent that Smith would have dedicated the *Wealth of Nations* to him if Quesnay had lived until 1776; he was a source of inspiration for Leontief's input–output table of the United States economy in 1941 (Leontief 1941: 9); he left macroeconomists with their first diagrammatic representation of the economy; and he eliminated the zero sum game mercantilistic mentality that economic growth was not feasible. These, and his many other contributions, should encourage readers to take out their towels and read him.

References

Boisguilbert, Pierre de (1705), *Factum de la France*.
Butler, Rohan (1980), *Choiseul, i: Father and Son 1719–54* (Oxford).
Charles, Loïc (2003), 'The Visual History of the "Tableau Économique"', *European Journal of the History of Economic Thought*, 10/4.
Eltis, Walter (1975a), 'François Quesnay: A Reinterpretation. 1: The *Tableau Économique*', *Oxford Economic Papers*, 27 (July).
—— (1975b), 'François Quesnay: A Reinterpretation. 2: The Theory of Economic Growth', *Oxford Economic Papers*, 27 (Nov.).

Faccarello, Gilbert (1999), *The Foundations of Laissez-Faire: The Economics of Pierre de Boisguilbert* (London).

Grollier, Gaspard (1719), *Recueil d'ouvrages curieux de mathématiques et de mécanique; ou, Description du cabinet de monsieur de Grollier de Servière avec des figures en taille-douce* (Lyons).

Kuczynski, Marguerite, and Ronald L. Meek (1972), *Quesnay's Tableau Économique* (London).

Leontief, Wassily W. (1941), *The Structure of the American Economy 1919–39* (New York).

Meek, Ronald (ed.) (1962), *The Economics of Physiocracy: Essays and Translations* (London).

Mirabeau, Victor Riquetti (1756–60), *L'Ami des hommes.*

Quesnay, François (2005), *Œuvres économiques complètes et autres textes*, ed. Christine Théré, Loic Charles, and Jean-Claude Perrot, 2 vols (Paris).

Rieter, Hans (1990), 'Quesnay's *Tableau Économique* als Uhren-Analogie', *Studien zur Entwicklung der okonmischen theorie IX* (Berlin).

Robbins, Lionel (1998), *A History of Economic Thought* (Princeton).

Smith, Adam (1976), *An Inquiry into the Nature and Causes of the Wealth of Nation* (1776), ed. R. H. Campbell, A. S. Skinner, and W. B. Todd (Oxford).

Anne Robert Jacques Turgot

7

Anne Robert Jacques Turgot: The Importance of Capital

Let us imagine that we are in the impoverished French district of the Limousin in 1769. We are sitting besides the 42-year-old administrator for the area, a man deeply moved by the plight of the poor in his district, some of whom have had to eat acorns to stay alive during the periodic famines that have hit this region. This administrator firmly believes that the science of economics has to be used to address the problems of unemployment and economic stagnation not only in his administrative area, but, across France. He is a voracious reader of and commentator on economics works. He has been reading his friend Du Pont de Nemours's *Du commerce et de la Compagnie des Indes. Seconde édition revue, corrigée et augmentée de l'histoire du système de Law* (1769). The mention of John Law evokes for our writer disturbing links with his childhood.

We are in the presence of no less a figure than that of Anne Robert Jacques Turgot (1727–81), baron de l'Aulne, one of the great Enlightenment writers, who six years later will, like Law, become Contrôleur Général des Finances, a position equivalent to that of prime minister. As he reads Du Pont's account of Law's System, he can remember his father, the *prévôt des marchands* (the equivalent of the mayor) of Paris at the time, railing against the way in which Law had destroyed his plans to rebuild Paris. The collapse of Law's System meant that there was no money to finance his father's pre-Haussmannian plans—Turgot *père* had already been responsible for mapping the city of Paris through his Plan de Turgot (commonly known as Le Plan de Paris, 1734–9). His father's vision of a newly rebuilt Paris was destroyed by Law's vision for a new financial system, and Turgot can recollect his father attacking the notion that metallic money could be replaced by paper money and bank credit. Law, who had left the nation bankrupt and without funds for any rebuilding operation, was a detested word in the family home.

Now, as he reads Du Pont's assessment of Law, Turgot's anger rises. Taking up his quill, he writes, 'I found your development of Law's System very good and written to please the public, whom, as you explain so well, had no idea of this magician's spell' (Turgot 1913–23: iii. 375). The specific words he uses with reference to Law's System are *ce grimoire*. *Le Grand Vocabulaire françois*, published in 1770, defines a *grimoire* as a 'Livre dont on dit que les Magiciens se servent pour évoquer les demons, les ames des morts, etc.'. Translated into English, this means that a *grimoire* was 'a magician's book used to call up demons, the souls of the dead etc.'. The dictionary goes on to explain that it is believed by the public that only ecclesiastical people can read such a book and converse with the demons without causing harm to themselves; if a layperson is imprudent enough to open and read the *grimoire*, they will be dragged down to hell by devils. This is heavy stuff indeed. The nearest English equivalent might be to describe Law's work as a book of spells. *Grimoire* is therefore a very pejorative term, associating the work with the dangerous scribblings of magicians and witches. This link between Law and a veritable Tolkienesque underworld of magic, spells, sleight of hand, illusion, etc. is deliberate, for it shows not just Turgot's disagreement with the Scotsman's work, but also an intense animosity, bordering on a pathological hatred.

At one level it could be contended that Turgot was just following a tradition that had started when contemporary pamphleteers likened Law to the devil incarnate (Beelzebub), when Montesquieu in the *Lettres persanes* (1721) compared him to Aeolus, the god of wind, and the Dutch engravers in *Arlequyn Actionist* (1720) caricatured Law as defecating paper money and shares to an excited and ignorant audience wishing to make its fortune from the Mississippi System (Murphy 1997). At a deeper level it will be contended that this word *grimoire* personified a mental block in Turgot's system of thought that prevented him from considering the possible ways in which banks and financial innovation could help the process of capital formation. This created the paradox that Turgot, the creator of the term 'capital' and the champion of capital formation, could envisage only one of three possible methods of financing capital formation, namely, that produced through savings. The other two methods, financing from the banking system and the capital market, he did not consider, wishing to avoid Law's illusory banking world of financial innovation and to concentrate on what he perceived as the real world, one represented by real savings and investment. It is more than striking to note that in the *Réflexions sur la formation et la distribution des richesses* (Reflections on the Production and Distribution of Wealth, 1769–70) Turgot never once mentioned the words 'bank' or 'credit', significant lacunae given the book's emphasis on the importance of savings and capital formation.

So we start the analysis of Turgot with a flaw. Some commentators might feel that this is unfair to him. Surely he should be better treated, given that the *Réflexions* has been recognized as a great work of economic analysis that greatly assisted economists' understanding of the importance of capital formation in generating economic growth? The greatness of the *Réflexions* is not questioned, but it could also be contended that the book could have been an absolutely outstanding work of genius if Turgot had not suffered from this family hang-up about the evil nature of John Law's System.

The enormous merit of Turgot's *Réflexions* (for a modern English translation, see Turgot 1977) lies in the central role that he gave to capital in the process of stimulating economic growth. Quesnay had been the first to recognize the critical importance of a type of capital (*les avances*) in the development of agriculture. However, the term 'capital', defined as representing replacement of depreciated capital plus new investment, made its first appearance in economic discourse in Turgot's work. Furthermore, unlike Quesnay's conception of capital, it was not solely confined to the agricultural sphere. Henceforth capital would be seen as a key factor of production, and Adam Smith would highlight it in the *Wealth of Nations* (1776).

Turgot's analysis of the role of capital formation and his attendant discussions on savings and the rate of interest will be highlighted. Paralleling these developments, his reluctance to accept the new world of money and banking will also be outlined. The origin of his deep antipathy towards money in the form of paper banknotes, credit, and financial innovation will be traced back to his first work on economics, written in 1749, the 'Dissertation sur le papier-monnaie', which he addressed as a second letter to the elder abbé de Cicé and dated Paris, 7 April 1749. His continuing antipathy towards paper credit may be traced through his subsequent works up to and after the *Réflexions*. Two reasons for Turgot's strong opposition to banks and their credit expansion potential will be suggested. The first has already been indicated. The second, interlinked with the first, was that the failure of Law's System had halted the progression of the standard banking model based on credit expansion in France. Unlike in Great Britain, where the fall of the South Sea Company had not brought down the Bank of England, the collapse of the Mississippi Company resulted in the liquidation of the Royal Bank, a development that deepened and entrenched French hostility to financial innovation. Rather than the banks developing in eighteenth-century France, the financial system went backwards, with the French notaries (*les notaires*) providing a type of surrogate banking system. In such an institutional environment it was very hard for Turgot to envisage the new banking developments that were emerging in Great Britain, and in particular in Scotland.

Turgot's Background and Career

Anne Robert Jacques Turgot was born in Paris on 10 May 1727 into a family of Norman aristocracy. The Vikings, the ancestors of the Normans, had been responsible for the name, a combination of two words: Thor-Got, the god of Thor. Thor was the Viking god of thunder and lightning. Turgot's father, Michel-Étienne (1690–1751), was a highly influential figure in Paris, serving in the role of *prévôt des marchands de Paris* (1729–40), a post that made him responsible for policing and directing the navigation, trade, and provisioning of Paris by the waterways. In 1718 Michel-Étienne married Françoise-Madeleine Martineau de Brétignoles, who bore him four children, the youngest of whom was Anne Robert Jacques.

As the youngest in his family, Turgot was pointed towards an ecclesiastical career. At the age of 16, showing all the signs of a precocious talent, he started his theological studies. By the age of 19 he was ready to present for his degree in theology, but, as he had not reached the minimum age of 20, he had to spend the year waiting in the seminary at Saint-Sulpice. There he studied the works of Descartes, Spinoza, Maupertuis, Buffon, and Locke (Poirier 1999: 31). From Saint-Sulpice, Turgot moved across the Latin Quarter to the Sorbonne, where the seminarians represented a significant part of the French intellectual elite and Turgot was able to spend his time reading in the university's well-stocked library. He also engaged in discussion and debate with fellow seminarians such as Loménie de Brienne, who would later become not only a cardinal but also the Contrôleur Général des Finances; the Cicé brothers, the elder of whom would become bishop of Auxerre and the younger the bishop of Rodez; and André Morellet, who would become a leading economic writer and close friend of Turgot. Outside the Sorbonne there was an even more exciting world awaiting Turgot. Under the direction of Diderot and d'Alembert a large group of intellectuals had started to write the *Encyclopédie*, the book of books of what came to be known as the French Enlightenment.

Although he had earlier been created a prior at the Sorbonne, Turgot decided that he wished to abandon his ecclesiastical career, and shortly after his father's death in 1751, he left the Sorbonne and directed his activities towards the law. He was fortunate to be able to obtain a significant position in the legal hierarchy owing to a dispute between Louis XV and the Parlement de Paris. The latter judicial body, using its right of remonstrance, which it had exacted from Philippe, duc d'Orléans, in return for supporting the decision to appoint him Regent during the minority of Louis XV, refused to accept the king's ruling relating to the Jansenists. As a result, many of the *parlementaires* were exiled and a new layer of magistrates had to be created to fill the void. One of these was Turgot, who was able to buy his office (*charge*) for 100,000 *livres*.

While in Paris during the early 1750s, Turgot came into contact with Jacques-Claude-Marie Vincent de Gournay, who would have a very formative influence on him. Gournay had been a merchant in Cadiz and had had the good fortune to inherit his friend Jametz de Villebarre's estate when the latter died childless in 1746. He was then able to add the name Gournay, after the lands in the estate that he had inherited, to his family surname of Vincent. So he became known as Vincent de Gournay. As Vincent de Gournay he married the widow of his deceased friend. Gournay bought one of the offices of councillor of commerce in 1749 and was then appointed an *intendant* of commerce.

Gournay, a man with a magnetic personality, was not typical of the normal run of *intendants* for he had an intense belief in the desirability of freeing trade from all the shackles that had been imposed on it. He promoted and popularized the doctrine of *laissez-faire, laissez-passer* (freedom to manufacture, freedom to trade) in the 1750s. He motivated writers such as Bûtel-Dumont, Dangeul, Forbonnais, Morellet, and Turgot to write, translate, and edit books on economic issues, including Cantillon's *Essai sur la nature du commerce en général* (1755). It was this group that became collectively known as the *économistes*, the first time the term was used to describe a group of writers on economic issues. These economists were strongly opposed to the Colbertist approach of heavy intervention and regulation of the French economy. They wished to introduce a more competitive structure and, like Boisguilbert, strongly favoured a system of *laissez-faire, laissez-passer*. Unlike the Physiocrats, they had no hang-ups about the so-called exclusive productivity of the soil. However, Gournay's early death at the age of 47 in 1759, along with Quesnay's formulation of the 'Tableau économique', gave the initiative to the group of writers and administrators in Quesnay's circle. This was unfortunate, because Gournay's group appears to have been less doctrinaire than the Physiocrats and certainly did not subscribe to the view that only agriculture was capable of producing a net product. If Gournay had lived longer, he might have been able to keep the development of economic theory at a more balanced level, one which viewed all sectors of the economy as capable of producing a net product.

Turgot would turn out to be Gournay's prize pupil, following in his footsteps to become an *intendant du commerce*. Turgot's debt to Gournay is evident from the 'Éloge de Vincent de Gournay', which he wrote for the *Mercure* in August 1759, shortly after Gournay's death. This death left the other inspiring writer on economics at that moment, François Quesnay, as the new rallying centre for the *économistes*, many of whom became followers of Quesnay and his doctrine, which would be termed Physiocracy (*la physiocratie*) by Du Pont de Nemours in 1766. Turgot never became a fully fledged member of the Physiocrats, for he had too powerful a mind to be subject to some of the constraining elements of this doctrine.

In his tribute to Gournay, Turgot summed up the new approach of Gournay, which was based on the promotion of individual's self-interest and the principle of *laissez-faire*:

All of [Gournay's] so called system was based on this maxim: a man knows better his own interest than any other man who is entirely indifferent to it.

From this M. de Gournay concluded that where the individual interest coincides with the general interest the best thing to do is to leave each individual to do that which he wishes. (Turgot 1913–23: i. 602)

Later in the 'Éloge' Turgot added:

M. de Gournay concluded that the only object of the administration should be (1) to give to all branches of commerce that precious liberty...which they have lost; (2) to favour industry...by promoting the greatest possible competition...resulting in the greatest perfection in production and the cheapest price for the buyer; (3) to give at the same time to the latter the greatest possible number of competitors, by opening to the seller all the markets for his produce. (Turgot 1913–23: i. 606–7)

Turgot had quickly learnt about Gournay's approach to economic policy, for he had been invited to accompany him to the districts in France where he was supervising trade from 1753 to 1756. These visits provided him with considerable hands-on experience to policy-making which he was able to use when, in 1761, he was appointed *intendant de justice, police, et finances* for the district of Limoges. He held this position until 1774. Turgot had attempted to become *intendant* in richer areas and was disappointed when he was sent to the Limousin, a district in the central western area of France comprising the modern departments of Haute-Vienne and Corrèze, along with parts of Creuse and most of Charente. Necker estimated its population at 646,500. Far from Paris, an unhappy Turgot wrote to Voltaire, 'There has been a change in my situation and I have had the misfortune to become an *intendant*. I call it misfortune because in this age of quarrels, the only good fortune is to live philosophically between study and one's friends.' Voltaire wrote back to him, 'One day you will be Contrôleur Général, but then I will be dead.' This prescience was limited to Turgot's future appointment, for Voltaire lived to see his friend become Contrôleur Général.

Initially, as this quotation shows, Turgot hated the idea of leaving Paris and its intellectual life, and his mother, working as mothers do on their sons' behalf, persuaded the authorities to give him a better *intendance* in a richer region. Turgot, however, turned the offer down. The plight of the people of the Limousin must have affected him greatly and he had decided to assist them as much as he could. This was a formidable task as the Limoges district was one of France's poorest regions and its agriculture was in a very backward state. He fought hard to reduce progressively the taxes that the region had to pay to the government and was successful in reducing the tax burden. He also recognized that there was a highly onerous tax in kind that labourers had to pay. This was the *corvée*—the word is still used in French meaning an undesirable job or task—which obliged labourers to work a certain number of days a year repairing and building roads. It was the equivalent of working in a chain gang and they could be asked to do such work in the most inclement conditions. The poor hated the *corvée*. Turgot saw this and was successful in having it abolished in the Limoges district. Later, when he became Contrôleur Général des Finances, he was successful in ensuring its abolition for all of France.

Turgot was born with a sense of mission, remarking, 'I really believe that I was born to regenerate France' (Ségur n.d.: 142). Overshadowing this ambition to transform the French economy was his sense of urgency that he needed to accomplish his objectives quickly, for he believed that he was destined for an early grave owing to his family's hereditary gout problems. His father and one of his brothers had both died at the age of 49. Turgot's fears turned out to be justified, for he died on 20 March 1781, at the age of 54.

This is not the place for a biography of Turgot's life, and in particular his courageous efforts, inspired by his economic principles, to liberalize the grain trade during his all too brief period as Contrôleur Général. There have been many biographies and studies on Turgot and his policies that provide detailed insights into this great Enlightenment figure, though a definitive biography will necessitate reopening his archives, which are presently under seal in the Château de Lantheuil. Here the main intention is to show Turgot's sizeable contributions to the development of macroeconomics. In order to do this, it is necessary to start with the letter to his friend the abbé de Cicé that marked the start of his lifelong interest in economics.

Letter to the Abbé de Cicé

Turgot's letter to the abbé de Cicé was written on 7 April 1749, when he was only 22 years old. This was the year when he was elected prior of the Sorbonne. It is a short work and incomplete. Turgot wrote to his friend, 'I read the three letters that the Abbé Terrasson published in favour of Law's System some days before the famous order of 21 May 1720, which as you may well know, poured ridicule upon him.' From a bibliographical viewpoint Turgot's analysis was imprecise, as the letters were published separately in the *Mercure de France* during the months of February and May at key points in the evolution of the history of the System. The first three were then published as a collection shortly before the May 21 *arrêt*, ratified by the Council on 22 May.

The letters have been attributed to the abbé Jean Terrasson, but who was he? Born in Lyons in 1670, Jean Terrasson was elected a member of the Académie des Sciences in 1707. He was appointed professor of philosophy at the Collège de France in 1721, and was elected to the Académie Française in 1732. According to the *Biographie universelle*, Terrasson made a fortune out of the Mississippi System but he kept his new-found wealth in shares and paper money and lost all when the System collapsed at the end of 1720. Given the enthusiasm for shares at the time, it is not surprising to find a man of letters plunging into the stock market with zeal. In England the poet John Gay and the scientist Isaac Newton were prominent investors in the South Sea Company, with the latter losing a considerable fortune in the 1720 speculation.

Given the fortune that Terrasson was making in the Mississippi Company, was it not natural to find him defending its operations in the pamphlets that he wrote? Piossens (1749: v. 233) suggested that the rumours indicated that the letters were written by Terrasson. Furthermore, given Terrasson and Turgot's clerical connections—they were both *abbés* at this time and Terrasson was still alive in 1749—it is interesting to note that Turgot was in no doubt about attributing them to Terrasson. Paul Harsin did not accept this and published all the letters in his three-volume edition of Law's *Œuvres* (1934). Harsin was emphatic on this score: 'There is no doubt in our mind with respect to Law's paternity of [the letters]' (Law 1934, vol. i, p. lxiii).The abbé Terrasson has also been credited with being the author of a later pamphlet, *Mémoire pour servir à justifier la Compagnie des Indes contre la censure des casuistes qui la condamnent* (1720), which is also about Law's System.

I agree with Harsin that Law either wrote or directed the writing of the letters. We may surmise that, in that grand tradition of French political figures who use ghostwriters (*les nègres*), he may have used Terrasson as an intermediary for pushing his own ideas into the public arena.

Although Turgot had attributed the letters to Terrasson, he knew that he was, in reality, attacking John Law:

I believe that the principles that he presents are the same as those of Law since, undoubtedly, he wrote in concert with him; and arising from this I cannot stop thinking that Law never had sufficiently sure and developed ideas for the enterprise that he undertook.   (Turgot 1913–23: i. 144)

Thus, with all the brashness of a 22-year-old, Turgot attempted to belittle and deride Law's ideas. To do this satisfactorily he should have read *Money and Trade* (1705), which had been translated and published in French as *Considérations sur le commerce et sur l'argent* (1720). This might have prevented him from criticizing Law for not recognizing that gold depreciated when its supply increased and for not reading Locke on this issue. In *Money and Trade* Law specifically recognized that increases in silver and gold from the Spanish Americas had caused a fall in the value of these precious metals over a 200-year period. Furthermore, he was quite specific in his attack on Locke for his inability to distinguish between 'demand' and 'vent'. Turgot contented himself with reading the letters, although he was also critical of Du Tot, who, in the *Réflexions politiques sur les finances et le commerce* (1738), had shown that he was a strong apologist of Law.

The core of Turgot's attack was directed against the view that it was possible to replace metallic money with paper credit. He did not believe that Law had discovered the Philosopher's Stone. He believed that money had to be a commodity possessing intrinsic value in order for it to be used as a medium of exchange. He opposed the view that the Crown should issue paper money as a substitute for metallic money: 'First of all I consider that it is absolutely impossible that the King substitutes paper in place of gold and silver' (Turgot 1913–23: i. 147). He contended that both theory and experience indicated that the public would never accept paper in place of metallic money.

In Turgot's letter to the abbé de Cicé he produced a crude metallist argument in favour of gold and silver and showed little refinement in his dismissal of paper money. Du Pont de Nemours, in the *Mémoires sur la vie et les ouvrages de M. Turgot* (1782), said of the 'Dissertation sur le papier-monnaie' that from reading it one could easily recognize 'the man destined to become a great Minister of State' (Du Pont 1782: 19). However, the strong metallist stance in it meant that Turgot lacked a true understanding of the monetary economy and the scope for monetary policy. Indeed, Turgot appears to have recognized this limitation and intimated that he intended to write a great deal more on banks and Law: Schelle noted that in 1769 Turgot had plans to write a 'Traité de la circulation', which was to include sections dealing with banks, Law's System, credit, foreign exchange trade, and luxury (Turgot 1913–23: i. 29). (The work is listed in his 'Ouvrages à faire'.) Though he never wrote this work, he continued through his life to show a deep antipathy towards Law and his System. Turgot's further dismissal of Law will be shown in our discussion of the *Réflexions*, but, prior to discussing this work, it is important to show the type of financial architecture that was in place in France when Turgot was writing. This financial architecture made it difficult for writers to glimpse any potential for an alternative banking and credit system, for in it the dominant players were not bankers but notaries.

France Chez les Notaires

The hostility towards money and the rate of interest, allied with the failure of Law's Royal Bank, created an environment in which the standard evolution of banking from goldsmiths to credit-creating deposit banks did not take place in France in the eighteenth century. Between 1720 and the revolution, aside from bankers who discounted bills of exchange—an important medium of exchange for merchants—and one or two scattered sightings of banks such as the Caisse d'Escompte, eighteenth-century France existed without a formalized banking structure. While the Geneva-based Protestant bankers became major lenders to the government and big merchant companies, the question arises as to how the more mundane business of banking was carried out in the absence of clearly constituted banks in France during this century. In the tumult resulting from the overall collapse of Law's System the financiers, the Paris brothers, had dismantled the System and made a retrograde move to the old financial system of the *ancien régime*. This meant that once again the financiers played a predominant role in managing the tax system through the privatized tax farms, as well as lending money to the Crown to finance

141

budgetary deficits. The legacy of Law's System was that no one wished to talk of banks, paper money, credit, and financial innovation.

An alternative quasi-banking system was provided by France's notaries. Because of the usury laws, the lending of money at interest had to be concealed through a variety of legal stratagems that separated apparent interest payments from money lent. Chief among these were annuity payments (*les rentes*), which provided an income stream for savers with surplus funds. The notaries were central to the establishment and processing of annuities and each *constitution de rente* had to be duly authorized in the presence of the notary. The usury laws meant that a lender of funds could not simultaneously stipulate both the rate of return and the duration of the financial contract. Turgot—in a passage which was later excised from the *Réflexions* when published in the *Éphémérides* (1769–70), but was included in the 1788 edition and the English translation of 1793, showed his familiarity with this type of monetary transaction:

You have indeed one method to make the receipt of interest lawful, it is to lend your capital for an indefinite term, and to give up all right to be repaid it, which is to be optional to your debtor, when he pleases, or when he can. If you find any inconvenience on the score of security, or if you foresee you shall want your money in a certain number of years, you have no other course to take but not to lend: It is better for you to deprive this merchant of this most fortunate opportunity, than to commit a sin by assisting him.

(Turgot 1793, sect. 75)

If a rate of return was covertly packaged in the form of an annuity, it could not, to satisfy the usury laws, specify a redemption date. This meant that the loan had been converted into an annuity redeemable whenever, if ever, the borrower, or his heirs, so deemed. Alternatively, the jurisprudence concealed the rate of return by stipulating specific amounts to be repaid at given dates, suggesting in some way that the lender was not charging a rate of interest but participating in a share of the profits of the borrower. As a result, financial instruments were created in the form of different types of annuity to manoeuvre around the usury laws. These financial instruments had to be notarized in the presence of the notary.

Because he was central to the channelling of surplus funds from lenders to borrowers, the notary assembled a strong information base on the assets and creditworthiness of potential borrowers. Hoffman et al. (2001) maintained that this notarial lending system produced an alternative banking system that worked well. This assessment needs to be qualified for, notwithstanding the pervasiveness of their intermediating activities, the notaries were for the most part only demi-bankers acting as a conduit for savers with surplus funds to borrowers, most notably the state. They were usually not principals in these transactions, nor did they did act as bankers in the sense of lending credit to some multiple of the funds deposited with them. Furthermore, most of the lending activity that they arranged was of a long-term nature. Their banking role was narrowed down further in that most of the lending that they intermediated was to the government on a long-term basis through the acquisition of annuities or loans for the purchase of lands or property. Above all, it must be pointed out that the notarial system was not a banking system in the sense of providing a flexible structure for the expansion of credit. All the notaries did was to increase the velocity of circulation of money by making it easier for some borrowers to access savers. However, they were not principals in the financial transactions and were in no way capable of lending money against reserves deposited with them.

The financial architecture that Turgot faced in France in the 1760s reflected the strong pessimism that had become ingrained in French society resulting from the failure of Law's Royal Bank and the Mississippi Company. No banks had been created since the closure of the Royal Bank, equity financing through the stock market had largely disappeared, and financial innovation was avoided. This was the primitive institutional financial setting in France when Turgot came to write the *Réflexions* in 1766.

Reflections on the Production and Distribution of Wealth

In fairness to Turgot, it could be contended that it is unjust to judge him by his letter to the abbé Cicé because it is the work of a very young man that was not intended for publication. The *Réflexions sur la formation et la distribution des richesses* is a work of far greater maturity, showing the mind of a confident economist at work. Turgot wrote it, in 1766, to help out two young Chinese students, Ko and Yang, who had been brought over to France by the Jesuits and were returning to Canton. He wrote to his friend Du Pont about this work on 9 December 1766:

I have been spoiling a lot of paper since I last saw you. Independently of an explanation of large-scale and small-scale cultivation that I made for a memoir on taxes in the Limousin...I drew up questions for these two Chinese that I mentioned to you, and to make sense of them, I preceded them with a type of sketch analysing society's work and the distribution of wealth. There is no algebra and there is no *Tableau économique* except for the metaphysical part; again I have left aside many questions that could be discussed to make this work more complete, but I developed in depth all that concerns the formation and function of capitals, the interest on money, etc.; it is a sketch...

(Turgot 1913–23: ii. 26)

It is interesting to note that Turgot had envisaged the possibility of using algebra to explain economic problems at the time but then felt it was better to provide an easy-to-understand account of the issues that he wished to discuss. Among these issues he was emphasizing the role of capital and the rate of interest. Unlike Adam Smith, who was busy researching and reading in the tranquil setting of his mother's house in Scotland, Turgot had little time to concentrate on writing books given his administrative responsibilities as the *intendant* for the Limousin. As Turgot wrote, he considered it just a sketch rather than a deeply researched book. Some people have argued that the *Réflexions* was privately published in 1766, but most professional antiquarian book dealers do not accept this view and contend that it was initially published in the *Éphémérides*, in three issues, volumes 11 and 12 of 1769 and volume 1 of 1770.

The style is spartan and the book, when published in English in 1793, amounted to fewer than 23,000 words. The use of the term 'reflections' in the title indicated that Turgot did not intend it to be a treatise. His ideas are presented in paragraph format, rather similar to the laying down of aphorisms relating to economic theory. His friend Du Pont, much to the annoyance of Turgot, included a number of editorial footnotes in an attempt to ensure that Turgot's ideas did not move out of line with the Physiocratic doctrine.

It is an exciting book, for in it we find the utilization of terms such as 'capital', 'utility', and 'equilibrium' in their appropriate economic contexts. Notwithstanding its sparse literary style, the *Réflexions* produced a major analytical impetus for the eighteenth-century economic debate in France.

One senses in the *Réflexions* the tension between Turgot the follower of Gournay, and Turgot the reader of Quesnay. There are strong threads of Physiocracy running through the work, though some of the reasoning, such as his views on the primacy of the land in the creation of output, may be seen also to emanate from Cantillon's *Essai*, which starts: 'Land is the source or matter from whence all wealth is produced' (Cantillon 1931: 3). Nonetheless, though pushing for Physiocratic reforms during his administrative career, Turgot remained an outlier to the Physiocratic debate.

Turgot's great debt to Quesnay arose out of the latter's formulation of the role of advances (*les avances*) in the productive process. Quesnay, in his article on farmers for the *Encyclopédie*—a work that Turgot mentioned specifically in his 'Éloge de Vincent de Gournay'—emphasized the role of capital intensity in promoting the growth of output. As farming moved from the small-scale production of oxen-drawn ploughs (*la petite culture*) to the large-scale cultivation of horse-drawn ploughs (*la grande culture*), the corresponding benefits in terms of increased agricultural production were plain to see. Turgot, in an article written for the *Éphémérides* (5 (1767)), about the same time as he was writing the *Réflexions*, showed that he had grasped the essential elements of Quesnay's distinction but contended that the real factor distinguishing *la petite culture* from *la grande culture* was the role of entrepreneurship. The former system was operated by sharecropper tenant farmers, whereas the latter was organized by entrepreneurial farmers; 'these farmers are the veritable entrepreneurs of cultivation' (*Éphémérides*, 5 (1767), 79–80). The entrepreneur farmers had sizeable quantities of capital to invest in *la grande culture*, but it is important to note the emphasis Turgot placed not only on capital but on entrepreneurship in the production process.

In the 'Tableau économique' Quesnay had positioned annual advances in a prime position to show the importance of this type of investment in the generation of the net product. Thus, Quesnay was one of the first to highlight the prime role of capital in generating economic growth. Turgot went much further than Quesnay. He was responsible for the introduction of the terms *capital* and *capitaux* into economic discussion. It is interesting to note that at one point in section 58 he referred to savings as 'capital', whereas the heading for the next section is 'Another employment for money in advances for enterprises of manufacture or industry'. Capital and money in 'advances' appear to have been synonyms for him.

Turgot on Capital Formation

Turgot's introduction of capital was not a mere semantic addition to the economists' lexicon. He was able to describe in detail the link between savings and capital formation. Crucial to this process was the role of the rate of interest. He was not prepared to accept that the rate of interest was determined by the supply and demand for money. Instead he saw it as determined by the supply of and demand for loanable funds. This savings–capital formation analysis would prove to be one of his outstanding contributions. It would provide the basis for the classical theory of savings and investment for most of the nineteenth century.

Turgot was quite aware that he had to integrate his theory of money with his theory of capital. He recognized that, without the use of gold and silver as mediums of exchange, capital formation would be very weak.

It is almost unnecessary to remark that undertakings of all kinds, but especially those of manufacturers, and above all those of commerce, must unavoidably be very confined before the introduction of gold and silver in trade, since it was almost impossible to accumulate considerable capitals, and yet more difficult to multiply and divide payments as much as is necessary to facilitate and increase the exchanges to that extent, which a spirited commerce and circulation require.   (Turgot 1793: 69)

Economic society had effectively stagnated prior to the arrival of metallic money as a medium of exchange because of the difficulty of accumulating and transforming surplus product into future capital. In a monetary economy the use of money facilitated the flow of surplus product into investment channels. Money was the means to facilitate the flow of real savings into real investment. The process of saving and investment starts when income is greater than consumption, enabling saving to take place. Turgot initially posited this as occurring in a moneyless economy:

> Let us now go back to the time after the introduction of money. The facility of accumulating it has soon rendered it the most desirable part of personal property, and has afforded the means of augmenting, by economy, the quantity of it without limits. Whoever, either by the revenue of his land, or by the salary of his labour or industry, receives every year a higher income than he needs to spend, may lay up the residue and accumulate it: these accumulated values are what we name a capital.   (1793: 58)

Turgot then contended that it was a matter of indifference whether this sum of value or capital 'consists in a mass of metal or any other matter, since money represents all kinds of value, as well as all kinds of value represent money' (1793: 36). So, for Turgot, the surplus accumulated through saving could be held in commodities or money. It was a commodity theory of money because money, in the form of gold and silver, was itself an intrinsically valuable commodity. Turgot wanted to demonstrate the way in which savings could be translated into 'capital'. He schematized five methods by which this transformation could take place, as in Figure 7.1.

This classification for the transformation of savings into investment (leaving aside method 1, the purchase of land, which, as he admitted later in the analysis, did not create capital but only facilitated the transfer of existing capital) may be condensed into two models of investment behaviour:

the self-financing investment model,
the loan investment model.

The self-financing investment model embraced methods 2, 3, and 4. Each of these involved direct investment in agriculture, industry, and trade, and in each case the entrepreneurs reinvested their profits in their enterprises. From a corporate finance perspective this involved self-financing. Unlike the landlords, entrepreneurs, using methods 2, 3, and 4, through their frugality were able to retain profits and use them for self-financing of further investment. Indeed, in the last paragraph of the *Réflexions*, Turgot suggested that entrepreneurs channelled their savings immediately (*sur-le-champ*) into investment. Each of these methods implied that entrepreneurs did not need to access any type of money market to obtain funds. They generated the funds internally through their own savings. Their automatic investment of the funds provided a hermetically sealed model where savings could not leak out of

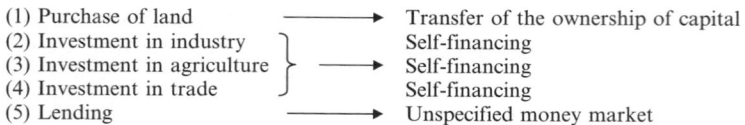

```
(1) Purchase of land              ──────────▶   Transfer of the ownership of capital
(2) Investment in industry    ⎫                 Self-financing
(3) Investment in agriculture ⎬   ──────────▶   Self-financing
(4) Investment in trade       ⎭                 Self-financing
(5) Lending                       ──────────▶   Unspecified money market
```

Figure 7.1 Categorization for the transformation of savings into capital investment

the expenditure stream. The automatic reinjection of savings into investment expenditure led to future generations of economists assuming that there could be no demand-side failures using such a model. Given Turgot's highly stylized assumption of these types of saving automatically finding their way into investment, this inference was correct.

However, besides this automatic self-financing savings–investment model there is a second model, the loan investment model in Turgot's analysis. Method 5 did not involve direct investment because it meant lending savings through unspecified intermediaries to borrowers, who could use them either for consumption or for investment purposes. To understand the loan invest-ment model it is necessary to move back to an earlier part of the *Réflexions* where Turgot outlined his theory of the rate of interest. The initial part of his analysis of the rate of interest involved his attack on the usury laws. In order to show the inappropriateness of these usury laws, Turgot needed to show the determinants of the rate of interest. He was highly critical of the usury laws fixing the rate of interest, believing that the rate of interest on money, like the price of commodities, was determined by supply and demand factors. He was therefore of the view that it could not be arbitrarily fixed through the imposition of usury laws.

Turgot's theory was based on a loanable funds approach where the rate of interest was determined by the supply and demand for loans:

> the price of money borrowed is regulated like the price of all other merchandize, by the balance of the money at market with the demand for it: thus, where there are many borrowers who are in want of money, the interest of money rises; when there are many possessors who are ready to lend, it falls. It is therefore an error to believe that the interest of money in trade ought to be fixed by the laws of princes. It has a current price fixed like that of all other merchandize. The price varies a little, according to the greater or less security which the lender has; but on equal security, he ought to raise and fall his price in proportion to the abundance of the demand, and the law no more ought to fix the interest of money than it ought to regulate the price of all other merchandize which have a currency in trade. (1793: 51)

In this passage he implicitly attacked Hume's profits determination theory of the rate of interest by showing that it was necessary to look not just at the factors influencing demand, but also at those determining the supply of loanable funds for the market. For example, he raised the possibility of a consumption-expenditure-dominated economy where little or no saving would take place. In this low-savings environment, because of this supply-side constraint with respect to loanable funds, the interest rate would be high and prevent profitable investment opportunities from taking place.

On the supply side Turgot maintained that it was not the money supply (i.e. the quantity of silver), but savings generated from income and profits, that constituted the source of loanable funds:

147

It is not therefore the quantity of silver existing as merchandize which causes the rate of interest to rise or fall, or which brings more money in the market to be lent; it is only the capitals existing in commerce, that is to say, the actual value of personal property of every kind accumulated, successively saved on the revenues and profits, to be employed by the possessor to procure him new revenues and new profits. It is these accumulated savings which are offered to the borrowers, and the more there are of them, the lower the interest of money will be, at least if the number of borrowers is not augmented in proportion. (1793: 80)

Turgot stressed this point that loanable funds were produced through savings, which were in turn a function of the 'spirit of oeconomy'. In other words, if people 'economized' and put money aside the supply of savings increased, whereas if they engaged in luxury expenditure the possibility of savings was negated and therefore reduced the potential supply of capital. He concluded from this that 'the lowering of interest proves that in Europe oeconomy has in general prevailed over luxury' (1793: 82). The benefit of increased savings was that, assuming there was no increase in the demand for loanable funds, they lowered the interest rate. A lower interest rate would in turn increase economic activity. To exemplify this, Turgot presented the marvellous metaphor of a country covered by a certain level of water. He then posited that a reduction in the interest rate was the equivalent to lowering the water level in the country, thereby releasing new areas of land for development:

The price of interest may be looked upon as a kind of level, under which all labour, culture, industry, or commerce acts. It is like a sea expanded over a vast country, the tops of the mountains rise above the surface of the water, and form fertile and cultivated islands. If this sea happens to give way, in proportion as it descends, sloping ground, then plains and valleys appear, which cover themselves with productions of every kind. It wants no more than a foot elevation, or falling, to inundate or to restore culture to unmeasurable tracts of land. It is the abundance of capitals that animates enterprise; and a low interest of money is at the same time the effect and a proof of the abundance of capitals. (1793: 60)

So there is clearly no ambiguity in this section dealing with lending. A low interest rate drives the economy to higher rates of economic growth. The low interest rate in turn is a function of high rates of saving. These savings find their way into the market and lower the rate of interest. But, if this is the case, then it suggests that there is a considerable amount of borrowing and lending taking place in an unspecified money market. Hence the paradox. At one point, in the final section, Turgot was highly critical of borrowing as a method of financing investment: 'Those that make their enterprises on borrowed funds, are greatly in danger of failing' (1793: 68). This would seem to indicate that he did not favour borrowing as a method of financing investment. Yet, at an earlier stage, he had unveiled the powerful and colourful vistas of the transformation of the economy through reductions in the rate of interest. Did he actually favour the lending of money or not? At this earlier stage he appeared to favour it, but then, in the latter part of the *Réflexions*, he condemned it. Furthermore, there was no discussion of the specific institutional setting that would facilitate the flow of savings from savers to borrowers.

Did banks have any role to play in this transfer of loanable funds from savers to investors? Banks were conspicuously absent from the *Réflexions*. This lacuna may be more easily understood because France had no formal institutional setting for banks or a money market; it relied, as has been shown, on the informal loan structure created by the notaries.

If we are to judge the *Réflexions* by the final section, then the savings–investment mechanism that Turgot predominantly favoured was a self-financing one. Turgot's ideal *economic transactors* were '[those] absorbed as they generally are, only in their enterprises, and anxious to increase their fortune; restrained by their labour from amusements and expensive passions; they save their whole superfluity, to re-convert it in other enterprises, and augment it' (1793: 67). This was a vision of hard-working, profit-motivated entrepreneurs, frugal in their consumption spending and anxious to expand their businesses by a policy of continuous self-financing investment.

However, the very fact that Turgot was prepared to have an implicit supply of and demand for loanable funds model to determine the interest rate, and that he was also able to contemplate the changed economic habitat that a reduction in the interest rate could produce, suggests that he was not fully happy with specific reliance on self-financing model.

The great merit of Turgot's work was that he opened up macroeconomic theory to the analysis of channels of savings and investment and showed the merit of a policy of capital accumulation. His approach to economic growth was one contingent on the growth of savings which automatically produce investment and hence economic growth. This process would be repeated as economic growth would produce more savings, more investment, and more economic growth. He stated this quite explicitly when he argued that there was just one way to become rich, i.e. to grow the economy through the transformation of savings into capital:

Now, in the present state of things, as all the land is occupied, there is but one way to become rich, it is either to possess, or to procure what is absolutely necessary for subsistence, and to lay up every year in reserve to form a capital, by means of which they may obtain an increase of revenue or annual profit, which will again produce another saving, and become capital. (1793: 56)

Savings were absolutely vital to the process of growth, and the greater the amount of savings, the lower the rate of interest: 'the proprietor who lends money ought to be considered as a dealer in a commodity absolutely necessary for the production of riches, and which cannot be at too low a price' (1793: 65).

Turgot also recognized that there were different rates of return derived from the range of assets that the saver could invest in, but that, despite this, there was an equilibrium relationship between them:

The different uses of the capitals produce very unequal profits; but this inequality does not prevent them from having a reciprocal influence on each other, nor from establishing a species of equilibrium among themselves, like that between two liquors of unequal gravity, and which communicate with each other by means of a reversed siphon, the two branches of which they fill; there can be no height to which the one can rise or fall, but the liquor in the other branch will be affected in the same manner. (1793: 58)

Turgot showed that the rates of return varied according to the risk associated with the investments. For example, the purchase of land was a less risky type of acquisition than investment in industry or trade. According as these rates of return varied, investors would reallocate their resources:

Generally, money converted into property in land, does not bring in so much as money on interest; and money on interest brings less than money used in laborious enterprises: but the product of money laid out in any way whatever, cannot augment or decrease without implying a proportionate augmentation in other employments of money.

(1793: 59)

This meant that, if the interest rate was reduced through savings, it opened up further possibilities for investments in capital projects offering higher rates of return. The rate of interest was therefore a key element in Turgot's analysis. However, the link between money and capital, along with the capital accumulation process, was not fully worked out in the *Réflexions*. This was because of Turgot's difficulty identifying the role of money. He certainly recognized the importance of money. In the final lines of the *Réflexions* he noted that, even though money was a very small part of the total stock of capital, it played a huge role in the formation of capital: 'We have seen what an inconsiderable part money forms in the total sum of existing capitals, but it makes a very large one in the formation of them. In fact, almost all savings are only in money' (1793: 68). Money, therefore, provided the medium for the transformation of savings into investment. Through his attacks on the usury laws and the analysis of the determinants of the rate of interest, it could be argued that he had integrated the rate of interest into his theory of capital, savings, and investment.

However, something is missing in Turgot's analysis, which is frozen in the time warp of eighteenth-century France. The missing ingredient is the role of the banking system. Moneylenders acting in unspecified savings institutions in Turgot's model only exist to transfer money from savers to investors. They are passive intermediaries in the process. They do nothing to increase the potential amount of funds available; all they do is transfer existing funds. So banks were kept out of his model and there was no role for credit creation.

Schumpeter was critical of this, commenting that Turgot's analysis was written as if John Law had not existed: 'Turgot's theory proved almost unbelievably hardy... the theory was not only swallowed by the large majority of economists: it was swallowed hook, line, and sinker. As if Law—and others—had never existed, one economist after another kept on repeating that only (voluntary) saving was capital creating' (1954: 325). It would have been more accurate for Schumpeter to write that Turgot's analysis had this particular bias against credit-creating banks precisely because of the past history of Law and his System. Turgot's earlier views, as expressed in the letter to the abbé de Cicé, had, if anything, hardened. In the *Réflexions*, he formulated a model—just as Cantillon had done before him—in which there was no role for the magicians and their *grimoires*, i.e. for financial innovation on the lines suggested by John Law and his followers such as Melon (1734) and Du Tot (1738). Savings, for Turgot, constituted a real phenomenon. He produced a savings-led model of investment expenditure. Monetary creation, on the other hand, was anathema to him. It produced something from nothing, it was the magician's sleight of hand, it was artificial and inflation-inducing. It produced a money that was not intrinsically valuable. For Turgot, money was the value for which goods were exchanged; he did not accept Law's position that money was the value by which goods were exchanged. The young monetary conservative who had been known as the abbé Brucourt when a seminarian at the Sorbonne was now the staunch monetary conservative *intendant* of the Limousin. Fixated by the collapse of Law's System, a collapse that may, according to Schelle, have prevented his father, Michel-Étienne Turgot, from implementing his plans to improve Paris, and unable to see the potential for a banking system given that France had a surrogate banking structure controlled by the notaries, Turgot was unable to grasp the potential for the banks and the capital market to provide credit in the form of bank loans, equity, and corporate bond issues.

This monetary blockage prevented Turgot, in my opinion, from producing a work of genius. His book is a very great one, but it was frozen in the institutional setting of eighteenth-century France where an intrinsically valuable metallic money was the medium of exchange and no modern-style banking system existed. Turgot did not want to envisage the possibilities of a paper money system and he was hostile to banks and their credit-creating potential. Ironically, when Turgot was Contrôleur Général des Finances between 24 August 1774 and 10 August 1776, he was obliged to abandon some of his hostility towards banks. In 1776 he assented to the creation of the Caisse d'Escompte, an approval probably forced on him by the needs of the French Treasury. It may be noted that two-thirds of the Caisse's proposed capital was to be invested in government paper as security against the Caisse encountering financial difficulties.

References

Cantillon, Richard (1931), *Essai sur la nature du commerce en général*, ed. Henry Higgs (London).

Du Pont de Nemours, Pierre-Samuel (1769), *Du Commerce et de la Compagnie des Indes. Seconde édition revue, corrigée et augmentée de l'histoire du système de Law* (Amsterdam).

—— (1782), *Mémoires sur la vie et les ouvrages de M. Turgot* (Philadelphia).

Du Tot, Nicolas (1738), *Réflexions politiques sur les finances et le commerce* (The Hague).

Hoffman, Philip T., Gilles Postel-Vinay, and Jean-Laurent and Rosenthal (2001), *Des marchés sans prix* (Paris).

Law, John (1934), *Œuvres complètes de John Law*, ed. Paul Harsin (Paris).

Melon, Jean-François (1734), *Essai politique sur le commerce*.

Murphy, Antoin E. (1997), *John Law: Economic Theorist and Policy-Maker* (Oxford).

Piossens, chevalier de (1749), *Mémoires de la Régence*, 2nd edn, 5 vols (Amsterdam).

Poirier, Jean-Pierre (1999), *Turgot* (Paris).

Schumpeter, Joseph (1954), *History of Economic Analysis* (Oxford).

Ségur, marquis de (n.d.), *Au couchant de la monarchie: Louis XVI et Turgot 1774–1776* (Paris).

Turgot, Anne Robert Jacques (1793), *Reflections on the Formation and Distribution of Wealth* (London).

—— (1913–23), *Œuvres de Turgot*, ed. Gustav Schelle, 5 vols (Paris).

—— (1977), *The Economics of A. R. J. Turgot*, ed. and trans. Peter D. Groenewegen (The Hague).

Adam Smith

8

Adam Smith: Land, Labour, Capital, and Social Cement

Let us imagine that we are in a horse-drawn coach on a dusty road near Toulouse in the south-west of France. The date is 5 July 1764 and there are two people accompanying us on this trip. One is a young 18-year-old yawning at the beauty of the surrounding countryside and trying to clear his head of the hangover of the previous evening. The other is a more serious gentleman in his forties. He is also bored, not by the passing vineyards, but by the companionship of his young tutee. The more serious traveller has left behind Scottish academia to be royally paid to accompany this young man on his European tour. They have been based in Toulouse and the weather is extremely warm.

There is also an intellectual warmth in the air, for France is experiencing the great transformation of the eighteenth century, the Enlightenment. The serious gentleman has been reading some of the vast outpouring of books, pamphlets, and journals that mark this intellectual revolution. His stimulation has come not solely from the *philosophes*. He has also been reading the writings of a group of young *économistes* noted for their championing of *laissez-faire, laissez passer*. Their leader is a certain Dr Quesnay, physician to no less a figure than the king's mistress, Madame de Pompadour, who has become the main exponent of what his followers call 'the new science of political economy'. Quesnay, in his sixties, has had the vision to see the importance of promoting this new science. Our voyager has been thinking on similar lines, and has already presented some lectures on these issues in Glasgow University. His head jolts up. He smiles and remarks, 'I know what to do now.' That night he writes to his great friend David Hume, 'I have begun to write a book in order to pass away the time. You may believe I have very little to do' (Smith 1977: 102). Twelve years later this book, *An Inquiry into the Nature and Causes of the Wealth of Nations* (1776), was published. Our passenger is Adam Smith (1723–90), the famous Scottish philosopher, with time on his hands and the intellectual ideas of the French *économistes* resonating in his mind, ready to synthesize their concepts and those of many other authors into a work that many regard as the bible of economics.

Smith's tutee and fellow passenger was Henry Scott (1746–1812), third duke of Buccleuch, stepson of the statesman Charles Townshend. Buccleuch would continue to exercise an enormous influence on Smith, for in many respects Smith became a well-paid retainer and adviser to Buccleuch for the rest of his life. He had given up his professorship in Scotland for the far more lucrative position of tutor to the duke, for which he was paid £500 a year. When no longer needed in his role as tutor, he was paid a pension for life of £300, which freed him from the need to lecture and thereby enabled him to devote himself full-time to writing the *Wealth of Nations*. It was the equivalent of giving a modern academic a research grant for life.

Buccleuch had a high opinion of Smith. He would later write of him that he received 'every advantage that could be expected from the society of such a man . . . a friend whom I loved and respected, not only for his great talents, but for every private virtue' (Douglas 1813: i. 258). At a later stage in Smith's career, in 1773, Buccleuch was instrumental in dissuading him from travelling abroad again, this time as the proposed tutor to the duke of Hamilton. Still later, he was responsible for finding another well-paid position for Smith, that of Commissioner of Customs in Scotland with a salary of £600 per year (see Smith 1977: 252). Now with an annual income of £900, Smith would later write:

Upon my appointment I proposed to surrender the annuity which had been settled upon me by the Tutors of the Duke of Buccleugh, before I went abroad with him, and which had been renewed by his Grace after he became of age, as a thing for which I had no farther occasion. But his Grace sent me word by his Cashier, to whom I had offered to deliver up his bond, that though I had considered what was fit for my own honour, I had not consider'd what was fit for his; and that he never would suffer it to be suspected that he had procured an office for his friend, in order to relieve himself from the burden of such an annuity. My present situation is therefore as affluent as I could wish it to be. (Smith 1977: 252–3)

In the interim Buccleuch would be involved in the collapse of the Ayr Bank, one that generated financial distress, not only in Scotland, but also in the rest of Great Britain. It will be conjectured below that Buccleuch's involvement in this banking collapse and the heavy losses that he suffered as a partner in it were key factors in transforming Smith from a liberal to a conservative in monetary theory and policy and also in promoting his very hostile attitude to the East India Company.

The *Wealth of Nations* is a work of great scholarship and erudition. However, it is not a book brimming over with new ideas. Its greatness lies as a work of synthesis, for few writers have put together the exciting ideas of others in such a coherent fashion. The literature on Adam Smith is vast (for a detailed book on Smith's economics, see Hollander 1973). It is not intended in this chapter to attempt any summary or assessment of this. Instead primary attention will be devoted to Smith the macroeconomist, with emphasis on his ideas on economic growth and monetary theory.

Smith's Background and Career

Adam Smith was born in the small fishing port of Kirkcaldy, Fifeshire, on the Firth of Forth, in the early summer of 1723. He was baptized on 5 June, though his most recent biographer, Ian Simpson Ross (1995), has been unable to determine whether this was the date of his birth or not. His father, also named Adam Smith (1679–1723), had died five months before Smith was born, leaving the economist along with his half-brother, Hugh (1709–50), to be brought up by his mother, Margaret Douglas (1694–1784), who would live to see the publication of her son's great work. Smith would later write of the intensity of the mutual love between himself and his mother. He wrote to his publisher, Strahan, shortly after her death on 23 May 1784, that she was a person 'who certainly loved me more than any other person ever did or ever will love me; and whom I certainly loved and respected more than I ever shall either love or respect any other person' (Smith 1977: 275). Thus, like his great friend David Hume, whose father died when he was 2, Smith would be reared by a dedicated and selfless mother. This mutually strong matriarchal devotion and filial affection may explain in part why neither man married.

Smith was a sickly child and needed a great deal of care to overcome the various illnesses that afflicted him when he was young. Throughout his life he suffered from 'a shaking of the head' a condition which he relieved, when residing in Kirkcaldy, by swimming in the Firth of Forth throughout the year— an impressive performance given the coldness of the sea in that area. Michael Barfoot (1991) has diagnosed Smith's medical state as hypochondriasis, a psychosomatic disorder involving the 'vapours', or 'low spirits', which could at times produce hysterical states. Smith was also the archetypal absent-minded professor, apparently sleepwalking around Glasgow and putting his toast in the teapot and complaining about the taste of the tea. His encounter with a tannery pit will be recalled later.

Smith had an early education in the Classics at the small, two-room school that he attended. At the age of 14 he moved to Glasgow University, where he studied Greek, Latin, mathematics, logic, moral philosophy, and natural philosophy. Here he was a student of the 'never to be forgotten' Irish philosopher Francis Hutcheson, the professor of moral philosophy, who would have a profound influence on Smith's way of thinking. Hutcheson, who coined the expression 'the greatest happiness of the greatest number', had a more modern approach than his contemporaries, a modernism that he showed by lecturing in English rather than Latin as had been the custom. At the age of 17 Smith was awarded a Snell exhibition to Balliol College, Oxford. The purpose of this scholarship was to assist students destined to be ordained in the Episcopalian Church of Scotland, a path that Smith clearly moved away from quickly. He was distinctly unimpressed by the standards of tutoring and lecturing in Oxford, where the staff appeared to compete with the students in heavy drinking. In a letter written in his first year, in 1740, Smith cynically commented on the standards required by the Oxford academics: 'it will be his own fault if anyone should endanger his health at Oxford by excessive study' (Smith 1976a: ii. 761). It was rumoured that he was caught by his academic superiors reading David Hume's *Treatise of Human Nature* in his rooms; the book was confiscated and Smith was severely reprimanded. So much for scholarship. By the time he came to writing the *Wealth of Nations*, he was still distinctly unimpressed by his old alma mater: 'In the university of Oxford, the greater part of the publick professors have for these many years given up altogether even the pretence of teaching' (Smith 1976a: ii. 761).

Smith returned to Scotland in 1746 and within two years was asked by Henry Home, Lord Kames, to present a series of lectures relating to rhetoric and belles-lettres at Edinburgh. There, over the next five years, he made friendships with a number of the leading Scottish thinkers and writers, most notably David Hume. He also met Hume's friend the astute James Oswald, whose father had been one of Smith's guardians.

The *Lectures on Jurisprudence*

In 1751, with the support of Lord Kames, Smith was elected to the chair of logic in Glasgow University. A year later he was elected to the chair of moral philosophy. His first full course of lectures in moral philosophy was presented in the 1752–3 session, and he continued to give them until he left Glasgow about the middle of 1764. According to John Millar, one of Smith's students in his logic class at Glasgow University, Smith divided his lectures on moral philosophy into four parts (see the introduction to Smith 1978). The first three parts were (1) natural theology; (2) ethics—lectures which would form the basis of his *Theory of Moral Sentiments* (1759); and (3) justice—lectures inspired by Montesquieu tracing the evolution of public and private jurisprudence. The fourth part is the most interesting from our viewpoint. Millar described them as follows:

In the last part of his lectures, he examined those political regulations which are founded, not upon the principle of justice, but that of expediency and which are calculated to increase the riches, the power, and the prosperity of a State. Under this view he considered the political institutions relating to commerce, to finances, to ecclesiastical and military establishments. What he delivered on these subjects contained the substance of the work he afterwards published under the title of An Inquiry into the Nature and Causes of the Wealth of Nations. (Smith 1978: 3)

Millar thus raised the fascinating possibility that Smith had delivered the basics of what appeared later in the *Wealth of Nations* in the fourth part of his lectures on Moral Philosophy to students at Glasgow University. Thanks to two sets of lecture notes taken by his students, it is possible to see the material that Smith lectured on in the third and fourth parts of the moral philosophy course. The first set of notes to Smith's lectures, delivered in 1763–4, was edited by Cannan and published in 1896. The second set, to lectures delivered in the 1762–3 session, was edited and published in 1978 by Meek, Raphael, and Stein, along with the first set, under the title *Lectures on Jurisprudence.*

The painting of a great work of art takes time; frequently many canvases are necessary before the artist is satisfied with the ultimate painting that he wishes to create. Analysis of the work of great artists such as Michelangelo show the way that the artist agonized over earlier sketches and painted over work that did not satisfy him. In economics, when dealing with the seventeenth- and eighteenth-century writers, we are rarely presented with the economist's equivalent of work in progress. Books were published and earlier manuscripts that formed the basis for such books were binned and destroyed by their authors. In Smith's case, although he insisted that all his unpublished papers and notes be destroyed by his executors, we do have the equivalent of work in progress because of the two sets of lecture notes taken by his students. They indicate the way in which Smith's ideas had evolved and were developing thirteen to fourteen years before the publication of the *Wealth of Nations*. Through them we can see the way in which Smith's mind had started to work on economic issues. The exciting aspect of the *Lectures on Jurisprudence* is that they contain a significant part of Smith's analysis of the importance of the division and specialization of labour. They demonstrate that, by the early 1760s, he had read and reflected on economic issues and had identified this key element in economic growth. However, Millar was only partially correct in asserting that the lectures contained the 'substance' of the *Wealth of Nations*. It appears to me that the book was conceptualized in two parts over two periods. The first part, Book I, dealing with the role of labour, had clearly been crystallizing in his mind during the Glasgow lectures. The second part, Book II, showing the key role that capital played in the process of economic growth, had to await Smith's visit to France and his meetings with Quesnay and Turgot, along with his reading of their works. The *Lectures on Jurisprudence* show that he had already read economics authors such as Cantillon, Du Tot, Gee, Hutcheson, Law, Locke, Hume, Magens, Mandeville, Montesquieu, Mun, and Paris-Duverney. However, he still had a great deal more to study and learn in order to show that there were elements other than the division and specialization of labour that were necessary to produce economic growth.

In the *Lectures*, Smith defined jurisprudence as 'that science which inquires into the general principles which ought to be the foundation of the laws of all nations' (Smith 1978: 397). He divided the subject into two parts: (1) justice and (2) police. It is the second part that is of interest to us, for it is this section that contains his economic analysis. Police, according to Smith, used to signify the policy of civil government, 'but now it only means the regulation of the inferior parts of government, viz. cleanliness, security and cheapness or plenty' (1978: 486). He very quickly moved away from cleanliness, 'the proper method of carrying dirt from the streets', and security, 'regulations for preventing crimes or the method of keeping a city guard', to the issue of 'cheapness or plenty' (1978: 487). Here, he informed his students, was an issue well worth consideration because investigation of cheapness or plenty led to the analysis of 'the most proper way of procuring wealth and abundance'. Smith was concerned with wealth, the wealth of the nation—though frequently the term he used in the lectures was not 'wealth' but its synonym 'opulence'. 'Cheapness', he wrote, 'is in fact the same thing with plenty.'

Smith's central theme in this part of his lectures was that it was the division of labour which increased 'the opulence of a country'. He produced the example of a pin factory to show how output could be increased through the division and specialization of labour. He argued, as he would later do so in the *Wealth of Nations*, that the division of labour increased output through (1) improved workers' dexterity, (2) the savings in time gained from specializing in one aspect of production, and (3) the invention of machinery. The introduction of machinery into the analysis showed that Smith had an implicit understanding that capital was also vital in order to generate economic growth. Echoing what Quesnay had been writing in France in the *Encyclopédie*, he noted:

The quantity of work is greatly increased by the invention of machines. Two men and three horses will do more in a day with the plow than 20 men without it. The miller and his servant will do more with the water miln than a dozen with the hand miln, tho' it too be a machine. The division of labour no doubt first gave occasion to the invention of machines.   (1978: 491–2)

He would later argue in the *Lectures* that the growth of the wealth of the nation was very much dependent on the accumulation of stock, i.e. the increase in capital. Furthermore, he contended that there was a strong interrelationship between the division of labour and the growth of stock (capital):

This is one great cause of the slow progress of opulence in every country; till some stock be produced there can be no division of labour, and before a division of labour take place there can be very little accumulation of stock.   (1978: 522)

↳ Bernard Mandeville (Dutch Economist)
Fable of the Bees

Earlier in the *Lectures* Smith had criticized what he believed to be Mandeville's unidimensional emphasis on consumption expenditure:

It is commonly imagined that whatever people spend in their own country cannot diminish public opulence, if you take care of exports and imports. This is the foundation of Dr. Mandevilles system that private vices are public benefits. But it is evident that when any man tears and wears and spends his stock, without employing himself in any species of industry, the nation is at the end of the year so much the poorer by it. If he spend only the interest of the money he does no harm, as the capital still remains and is employed in promoting industry but if he spend the capital the whole is gone.
(1978: 513)

In this passage Smith was equating stock with what we call 'capital' and asserting, as Turgot would in the *Réflexions*, that if people used up the capital stock in consumption expenditure the nation would end up losing out in the process. The following sentence in the above quotation shows the introduction of capital into the analysis, but this is financial capital rather than capital as defined in the economic sense of the term. It is clear from this section of the *Lectures* that Smith recognized the importance of capital, but his knowledge on the subject was still at a very elementary stage. It would require a great deal more reading, and discussion with the French economic writers, to develop his knowledge on the subject to the level that it attains in Book II of the *Wealth of Nations*.

Smith had, however, by this stage, linked the division of labour to 'a direct propensity in human nature to barter with another', maintaining that this propensity arose from self-love:

Man continually standing in need of the assistance of others, must fall upon some means to procure their help. This he does not merely by coaxing and courting; he does not expect it unless he can turn it to your advantage or make it appear to be so. Mere love is not sufficient for it, till he applies in some way to your self love. A bargain does this in the easiest manner. When you apply to a brewer or butcher for beer or for beef you do not explain to him how much you stand in need of these, but how much it would be your interest to allow you to have them for a certain price. You do not address his humanity, but his self-love. (1978: 347–8)

From this point Smith's *Lectures* moved into an analysis of the distinction between natural price and market price. This analysis suggests that he had read Cantillon's *Essai*—he had a copy of this book in his library (Bonar 1932: 40–1)—for he appeared to be just transforming Cantillon's distinction between intrinsic value and market price to one of natural price versus market price. Like Cantillon, Smith then demonstrated how differences between these two prices would produce a reallocation of resources:

These two different prices, which appear at first sight to be no way connected nor to have the least dependence on each other, are very intimately related, tho the circumstances which regulate them appear also independent. For if the market price be so high as to be more than sufficient to make up the natural price, and answers all those things for which every tradesman has a demand . . . this will appear to be a vastly profitable trade and all will crowd into it with expectations of making a fortune. As the number of hands increases so will the quantity of work done, and consequently it will become the purchase of a lower rank of men and fall down to its natural price.   (1978: 359–60)

This approach was powerfully developed in chapter vii of Book I of the *Wealth of Nations*. Smith had already adopted a strong *laissez-faire* (a term he never used in the *Wealth of Nations*) approach reminiscent of the earlier Petty: 'the best police would be to leave every thing to its natural course, without any bounty or any discouragement' (1978: 366).

The *Theory of Moral Sentiments*

In 1759 the *Theory of Moral Sentiments* was published. It must be remembered that, according to John Millar, this book constituted the second part of Smith's lectures on moral philosophy. It was a book dealing with ethics. The dominating motive for human action presented in this book was not that of self-love or self-interest—the catalyst for action in the *Lectures on Jurisprudence* and the *Wealth of Nations*—but sympathy. This apparent duality of contradictory motives, sympathy in the *Theory of Moral Sentiments,* and self-interest in the *Wealth of Nations*, has been presented by German scholars as the 'Adam Smith problem'. How can man motivated by an apparently philanthropic motive, namely sympathy, the desire to be well regarded by showing empathy to his fellow man, be transformed into the apparent polar opposite: economic man catalysed by a greed motive, that of self-interest? The reconciliation may be found by regarding the *Theory of Moral Sentiments* as providing the type of social cement for economic society that would emerge out of the *Wealth of Nations*. The moral virtues of Smith's construct of the 'impartial spectator' in the *Theory of Moral Sentiments* correspond to those that are assumed to be at the heart of his legal counterpart 'the reasonable man'. There have to be rules of behaviour for society to function. Man has innate moral sentiments. The inner man's voice of conscience imposes a template for social behaviour, as may be seen from the opening lines of the *Theory of Moral Sentiments*: 'How selfish so ever man be supposed, there are evidently some principles in his nature, which interest him in the fortunes of others, and render their happiness necessary to him, though he derives nothing from it except the pleasure of seeing it' (Smith 1976*b*: 9).

The desire to be well regarded by showing sympathy with one's fellow man has its reciprocal in the hope that one's neighbour will also act in this way. Do unto others as you would expect them to do unto you. If individuals do not act reasonably, with 'reasonableness' defined as the normal behaviour that one would expect from the man in the street, then social anarchy will prevent the economic development of society. The institutionalization of reasonable behaviour in social customs, mores, and laws ensures that human action, be it in the form of economic or leisure activity, can take place in the context of a well-defined set of rules. Moral sentiments take the cudgel away from the individual and only legitimize it as the baton of the policeman. It is reasonable to be able to expect to walk safely down the street. It is reasonable to be able to save money and to buy and sell property with such savings. The apparent anarchy of market forces is bounded by the social and legal structures that have evolved from the development of the concepts of sympathy and reasonable behaviour. It was Smith's great strength as a moral philosopher to be able to show the importance of this concept of 'sympathy' and how it was a prerequisite for the development of the economic society that he would later outline in the *Wealth of Nations*.

There are glimpses of Smith the future economist in the *Theory of Moral Sentiments*, most notably when he discussed how the selfishness of rich landlords unintentionally promote the interests of society:

They [the rich] consume little more than the poor, and in spite of their natural selfishness and rapacity, though they mean only their own conveniency, though the sole end which they propose from the labours of all the thousands whom they employ, be the gratification of their own vain and insatiable desires, they divide with the poor the produce of all their improvements. They are led by an invisible hand to make nearly the same distribution of the necessaries of life, which would have been made, had the earth been divided into equal portions among all its inhabitants, and thus without intending it, without knowing it, advance the interest of the society, and afford means to the multiplication of the species. (1976b: 184–5)

Here it may be seen that Smith, introducing for the first time the 'invisible hand', wanted to show that the pursuit of self-interest by the rich could bring about an overall benefit for society. However, as Raphael and Macfie state, this passage 'refers to the distribution of means to happiness, the *Wealth of Nations* passage to maximization' (Smith 1976b: 184).

Let us recall Millar's description of the taxonomy of Smith's lectures on moral philosophy. The first part dealt with theology. Smith would have been obliged to give such lectures, but the subject had no great intellectual interest for him. He had published the second part of the course, that dealing with ethics, through the *Theory of Moral Sentiments*. The third and fourth parts, dealing with justice and economics, were gestating in his head. There is some evidence that he may have attempted shortly before April 1763 to translate the 'economic' material of his lectures on jurisprudence into book form, though, fortunately for posterity, he did not persist at this stage with this endeavour. There was to be an interlude in his publishing career. He was destined to go to France and there he would see and benefit from the intellectual revolution of the French Enlightenment, particularly that part which was leading to the formal creation of economics as a new science.

It was the *Theory of Moral Sentiments* that would play a key role in a major career move by Smith. Shortly after the publication of this work in 1759, David Hume wrote to him stating that Charles Townshend, a man who would later become the Chancellor of the Exchequer, was so impressed by the book that he wanted to appoint Smith as a tutor to his stepson:

> Charles Townshend, who passes for the cleverest fellow in England is so taken with the performance, that he said to Oswald he would put the Duke of Buccleugh under the author's care, and would endeavour to make it worth his while to accept of that charge. As soon as I heard this, I called on him twice with a view of talking with him about the matter, and of convincing him of the propriety of sending that young nobleman to Glasgow: For I could not hope, that he could offer you any terms, which would tempt you to renounce your Professorship. (Smith 1977: 36)

Townshend went to the trouble of meeting Smith in Glasgow. Here we might imagine Smith's excitement at meeting such a man of quality, but in fact we do not need to do so because the event was later recalled by *The Times* in its obituary of Smith:

> While Mr. Townshend was at Glasgow, the Doctor conducted him to see the different manufactures of the place; and particularly to a very flourishing tan-work. They were standing on a plank which had been laid across the tanning pit, the Doctor, who was talking warmly on his favourite subject, the division of labour, forgetting the precarious ground on which he stood, plunged headlong into the nauseous pool. He was dragged out, stripped, and carried with blankets, and conveyed home on a sedan chair, where, having recovered of the shock of this unexpected cold bath, he complained bitterly that he must leave life with all his affairs in the greatest disorder, which was considered an affectation, as his transactions had been few and his fortune was nothing. (*The Times*, 24 July 1790)

Townshend took Smith's fall in his stride and, notwithstanding it, was determined to hire him. Townshend was extremely solicitous in his duties as stepfather to the young duke, explaining in a letter to Smith that he wanted the young man taken away from London so that 'he should not be long in town, exposed to the habits and companions of London, before his mind has been more formed and better guarded by education and experience' (Smith 1977: 95).

Judging by Hume's letter to Smith, he obviously hoped that Townshend's money would not cause Smith to give up his professorship. This hope was not realized, and four years later, in 1763, Smith resigned from Glasgow University. He would never have to lecture again, and he personally refunded all his students their fees for the year because they had not received a complete course of lectures from him.

The duke of Buccleuch left Eton at Christmas in 1763. In 1764 Smith moved to France on the start of the grand tour with his young tutee. Initially, they stayed for a considerable time in Toulouse. The town and surrounding countryside did not excite him unduly, but towards the end of 1765 Smith was able to travel to Paris with his tutee. There, as the author of the *Theory of Moral Sentiments*, he was invited to all of the great literary salons and he met Diderot and d'Alembert, the editors of the *Encyclopédie*. He became a good friend of François Quesnay, the leader of the young group of *économistes*–Physiocrats who were formally creating the new science of economics. He also met and became friendly with Anne Robert Jacques Turgot, who, in 1766, was writing the *Réflexions sur la formation et la distribution des richesses* (1769–70), a book that would have a profound influence on the *Wealth of Nations*, particularly Book II, dealing with the role of capital.

Smith witnessed at first hand the professional work of Quesnay the physician when he successfully treated the duke of Buccleuch for a fever in Paris. Unfortunately, Quesnay was unable to save the duke's brother Hew Campbell Scott from a similar fever. The young man's death on 19 October 1766 meant that Smith and the duke had to return to England with the body for burial. Smith never revisited France, and spent the next ten years between Kirkcaldy and London preparing the *Wealth of Nations* for publication.

The *Wealth of Nations*

There are a number of dominating elements in the *Wealth of Nations*. These, for the purposes of this book, I have classified under two main groupings, with each group divided into a further two separate areas:

- *The philosophical–economic structure*
  Self-interest as the motivating force to human action
  The role of the price mechanism
- *The road to economic growth*
  The division and specialization of labour
  The importance of capital formation

Although it will be later asserted that the *Wealth of Nations* was primarily a book about economic growth, it is important to recognize that Smith the philosopher also set out to identify the optimal philosophical–economic structure in which economic growth could occur. It is for this reason that initial attention needs to be paid to the philosophical–economic structure of the *Wealth of Nations*.

The Philosophical–Economic Structure

The primary emphasis of Smith's philosophical–economic structure was to analyse transactors' motivations for producing and exchanging commodities. What motivated individuals to trade goods and services with one another? In the *Theory of Moral Sentiments* he had started to analyse this issue when he was still under the influence of Hutcheson's teaching. Words such as 'sympathy' and 'benevolence' were presented as part of the motivations for human action. Having read and reflected a great deal further on the subject, Smith strongly asserted that 'self-interest', or 'self-love', was a greater motivating factor than benevolence when it came to the production and exchange of commodities. Instead of the philosophy of 'do unto others as you would have them do unto you', Smith expressed the basics of the exchange process as 'Give me that which I want, and you shall have this which you want' (1976a: i. 26). Furthermore, the huge benefit of the pursuit of his own self-interest was that *Homo economicus* unconsciously promoted benefits for others across the economy. In one of his most celebrated passages, intimations of which had already appeared in the *Lectures on Jurisprudence*, Smith observed: 'It is not from the benevolence of the butcher, the brewer, or the baker, that we expect our dinner, but from their regard to their own interest. We address ourselves, not to their humanity but to their self-love, and never talk to them of our own necessities but of their advantages' (1976a: i. 27). Smith, as Gray (1931) has noted, transformed the Mandevillean theme that 'private vices are public virtues' into a more specific formula: 'private self-interest is a public virtue'.

At a later stage Smith returned to this theme, stating that, when the individual pursued his own self-interest, he was guided by an 'invisible hand':

> He generally, indeed, neither intends to promote the public interest nor knows how much he is promoting it. By preferring the support of domestic to that of foreign industry, he intends only his own security; and by directing that industry in such manner as its produce may be of the greatest value, he intends only his own gain; and he is in this, as in many other cases, led by an invisible hand to promote an end which was not part of his intention. Nor is it always the worse for the society that it was no part of it. By pursuing his own interest he frequently promotes that of the society more effectually than when he really intends to promote it. I have never known much good done by those who affect to trade for the public good. It is an affectation, indeed, not very common among merchants, and very few words need be employed in dissuading them from it. (1976a: i. 456)

This was Smith's only reference to the 'invisible hand' in the *Wealth of Nations* (on the issue of the invisible hand, see Ahmad 1990; Grampp 2000; Pack 1996; Persky 1989; Rothschild 1994).

One of the many interpretations of the 'invisible hand' is to understand it as a metaphor for the role of the competitive forces in the economy, suggesting that, if individuals are left alone to pursue their own individual self-interest in markets, they will produce solutions that are beneficial for society as a whole. Without knowing it, transactors motivated by their own self-interest produce overall economic harmony for society.

The positive correlation between self-interest and economic harmony induced Smith to propose a strong policy message, that of leaving people alone in the market and not interfering in their economic decisions. The corollary of this viewpoint led to a strong criticism of politicians supposedly acting in the public interest. In the above quotation, following the introduction of the invisible hand, Smith excoriated those people who purport to act for the 'public good', in other words politicians. He warned his readers that, when politicians stand up in front of the electorate and suggest that they want to work on behalf of the public good, they will in fact be pursuing their own self-interest. This pursuit of their own self-interest will not be for the good of society because they will want to interfere in the free workings of the market. Smith urged his readers to keep the politicians out of such activity.

This was a highly cynical approach to politicians, and many well-motivated political practitioners may take deep offence at Smith's cynicism. Is it not possible for a politician to be motivated by the public good without being subjected to the moral censure of Smith and his followers? Is it tolerable that politicians such as Winston Churchill, Mahatma Gandhi, Martin Luther King, and Nelson Mandela should be subjected to such a withering reflection on their political motivations of trading for the 'public good', and all this by a Scotsman who had spent most of his life living as a well-paid retainer of one of Scotland's richest families? Smith, it could be pointed out, rarely had to have recourse to the functioning of the invisible hand because he was supported by the highly visible handouts of the Buccleuch family.

In defence of Smith's cynical tone it may be argued that he was writing at a time when both the political and economic structures were very much open to political interferences which were against the public interest. Free political institutions and free markets were still in their infancy. Politicians bought their way into Parliament through the 'rotten borough' system. Ricardo, later, would be voted into Parliament to represent the constituency of Portarlington in Ireland without ever visiting the place. No doubt a couple of hundred pounds placed in the right hands secured him his seat and released him from the tedium of attempting to convince the electorate of the bona fides of his political objectives. Furthermore, a large part of the economic structure was characterized by the presence of monopolies, such as the East India Company and the Bank of England, well supported by the political establishment in Westminster. In this type of environment a certain degree of cynicism about the behaviour of politicians might be permitted. Would Adam Smith, faced with modern political and economic institutions, be as cynical?

If Smith was prepared to exclude politicians from most economic decision-making, what was the structure of his politician-free economic system? It was one thing to assert that self-interest and the invisible hand sorted out the market problems, but where was the economic structure that underpinned these phenomena? The invisible hand guiding self-interested economic transactors is at the centre of Smith's competitive system. Prices act as signals to market transactors, providing both information and incentives. In chapter vii of Book I, Smith, borrowing very heavily from Richard Cantillon's earlier analysis in the *Essai sur la nature du commerce en général* (1755), distinguished between natural price and market price. The natural price of a commodity was a long-run equilibrium price incorporating the costs of production of a commodity plus a normal profit. The market price was a price determined by the outcome of demand and supply in the market. If the market price moved above the natural price, then this provided extra profit for the producers of the commodity. The extra, or supernormal, profits acted as a signal to producers and consumers. Producers, attracted by the higher profit, would produce more of the commodity, while consumers, put off by the higher price, might be tempted to look for cheaper substitutes. The signals created by such behaviour would lead to more producers moving into producing the commodity, or substitutes for it, until their activity pushed profits back to their normal level. Similarly, resources would move out of the production of commodities where the market price fell below the natural price. The implication of this analysis was very clear. The price mechanism, if left alone, would allocate resources efficiently without the need for any outside intervention. Without using the term *laissez-faire*, Smith provided the basis for the economic philosophy underlying this particular term. In this way, he provided the philosophical–economic structure for his model. However, he wanted to go further than this. He wanted to show how, using this economic structure, it was possible to increase the wealth of nations.

The Road to Economic Growth

Building primarily on the work of Cantillon, Quesnay, and Turgot, Smith's *Wealth of Nations* provided an analysis of how to increase the wealth of the nation, i.e. how to generate economic growth. Both Quesnay and Turgot had shown the possibility for the economic circle to expand. They had given hope by showing that economic activity was not limited to a zero sum game in which the economic circle could not expand. This new hope cleared economics from the pessimistic pall that had hung over it when writers such as Cantillon presented a very existential view of the economy performing around a stationary line with the economic cycle fluctuating above and below this line. For Cantillon, even though he had provided Smith with the basic structure of how markets worked, the line would never move permanently upwards to show the possibility of long-term growth. The new possibilities for economics, presented by Quesnay, Turgot, and Smith, made it an exciting subject, not just for practitioners, but also for the educated public, now that economic writers had started to show the potential for the economy to grow. Smith had the gift to show these possibilities.

There were two key elements in his analysis: (1) the role of labour, and (2) the role of capital. The importance of these elements may be quickly identified by consulting the layout of the *Wealth of Nations*. It consists of five books. The first deals with the role of labour and the second with the role of capital. The other three, dealing with the history of the growth of wealth (Book III), systems of political economy (Book IV), and fiscal issues (Book V), were largely historical and policy-related addenda to the first two books. The analytical core of the *Wealth of Nations* is therefore to be found in Books I and II, demonstrating the importance of labour and capital to the process of economic growth. Smith was the first to provide a clear verbal statement of the production function, which nowadays is represented by:

$$Y = f(L,K)$$

where

Y = Output
L = Labour
K = Capital

If income was to be increased, it would need increases of both labour and capital. Smith started by emphasizing the role of labour in generating income. When first consulting the *Wealth of Nations*, new readers might be excused the reflection that they were reading Karl Marx rather than Adam Smith, for the opening lines are as follows:

The annual labour of every nation is the fund, which originally supplies it with all the necessaries and conveniencies of life which it annually consumes, and which consist always either in the immediate produce of that labour, or in what is purchased with that produce from other nations. (Smith 1976a: i. 10)

This view of the dominating importance of labour appears to be confirmed by the opening lines of chapter v:

The value of any commodity, therefore, to the person who possesses it, and who means not to use or consume it himself, but to exchange it for other commodities is equal to the quantity of labour which it enables him to purchase or command. Labour, therefore, is the real measure of the exchangeable value of all commodities.

(Smith 1976a: i. 47)

Smith wanted to emphasize the primary role of labour because he wanted to show the huge benefits that arose for society through the division and specialization of labour. This he asserted in the very first sentence of Book I chapter i: 'The greatest improvement in the productive powers of labour, and the greater part of the skill, dexterity, and judgment with which it is anywhere directed, or applied, seem to have been the effects of the division of labour' (1976a: i. 13).

It has been shown that the division of labour was a key part of the *Lectures on Jurisprudence*. There was nothing original in this idea, as earlier writers such as Xenophon, Petty, Mandeville, Braddon, Harris, and Massie had already shown the benefits arising from the division of labour. Smith's example of a pin factory to illustrate how many more pins may be manufactured through the division and specialization of labour was not original, as it was to be found in the article 'L'Épingle' in the *Encyclopédie*. However, where Smith differed from earlier writers was that he immediately linked the division and specialization of labour with capital:

> This great increase of the quantity of work, which, in consequence of the division of labour, the same number of people are capable of performing, is owing to three different circumstances; first, to the increase of dexterity in every particular workman; secondly to the saving of the time which is commonly lost in passing from one species of work to another; and lastly, to the invention of a great number of machines which facilitate and abridge labour, and enable one man to do the work of many.   (1976a: i. 19)

Smith deemed capital ('the invention of a great number of machines') to be an essential part of the process for facilitating the division and specialization of labour. He contended that it was the division of labour that produced the need for capital: 'the invention of all those machines by which labour is so much facilitated and abridged, seems to have been originally owing to the division of labour' (1976a: i. 21).

Smith owed a great deal to Quesnay and Turgot for his theory of capital formation. Quesnay had showed in his *Encyclopédie* articles the importance of capital intensity for agriculture. The greater the amount of machinery applied to agricultural production, the greater would be the increase in output. Unfortunately, Quesnay believed that economic growth could only be achieved through the expansion of agriculture. As has been shown, Turgot had coined the term 'capital' as an economic concept and shown how increased capital investment could raise output, not just in agriculture, but across the whole economy. He had also shown the key role of savings in the process of capital formation. Relying primarily on a self-financing model, he believed that savings were produced through an abstention from current consumption. Smith followed Turgot's analysis closely and contended that 'Capitals are increased by parsimony, and diminished by prodigality and misconduct' (1976a: i. 358).

There are two problems with Smith's analysis of this issue. First of all, his growth model is predicated on the growth of capital expenditure. Investment can increase growth, but this process can be interfered with by increased consumption expenditure (prodigality). Not only was he unwilling to accept that increased consumption expenditure could be beneficial to growth, he was prepared to assert that it could be strongly disadvantageous to growth by switching resources away from capital formation to the pursuits of idle consumption behaviour. Here Smith could have found common ground with twentieth-century dictators such as Mao, who believed in forcible reductions of Chinese consumption expenditure to finance heavy capital expenditure. The second problem with Smith's growth model flowed from the first. Because of his belief that investment could only be financed by savings, i.e. abstention from current consumption expenditure, he was not prepared to view the vast and exciting new possibilities that the banking system was creating for the financing of investment expenditure. This brings us to the Achilles heel of Smith's economic analysis, the role of money and banking.

Smith's Views on Money

Smith changed his mind quite dramatically when it came to reassessing the role of money and banks in the *Wealth of Nations*. This change in his approach to money shows the way in which specific financial events arising in the economy may modify a theorist's approach to money. When presenting the *Lectures on Jurisprudence* in Glasgow, Smith produced a relatively liberal stance on the development of banking, paper money, and financial innovation. He extolled, as will be shown, the way in which banks had increased economic activity, not only in Europe, but also in the American colonies. However, by the time he came to putting the finishing touches to the *Wealth of Nations*, he had become a great deal more circumspect about the role of money, banking, and financial innovation. It is suggested that this change in his views on money was caused by a specific financial crisis, that of the financial problems of the Ayr Bank in 1772.

The *Lectures on Jurisprudence* show a confident Smith discussing the benefits of the introduction of paper money and banking, benefits in terms of the release of the 'dead stock' of metallic money for other expenditure purposes when it was replaced by paper money. Here he wanted to show the opportunity cost of using metallic money in terms of a country having less food, clothing, and housing. More use of metallic money meant less expenditure on these items, which contributed to the opulence of the nation:

The more money that is necessary to circulate the goods of any country the more is the quantity of goods diminished. Suppose that the whole stock of Scotland in corn, cattle, money, etc. amounts to 20 millions and if one million in cash is necessary to carry on the circulation, there will be in the country only 19 millions of food, clothes, and lodging, and the people have less by one million than they would have if there be no occasion for this expedient of money. It is therefore evident that the poverty of any country increases as the money increases, money being a dead stock in itself, supplying no convenience of life. (1978: 503)

This passage clearly showed that Smith was of the opinion that the opportunity cost of using metallic money was very high in terms of expenditure opportunities forgone to buy other commodities. The natural implication of this was that paper money was an attractive substitute for money because it freed up the use of metallic money for expenditure purposes. He praised the way paper money had economized on the use of scarce resources:

Money in this respect may be compared to the high roads of a country, which bear neither corn nor grass themselves but circulate all the corn and grass in the country. If we could find any way to save the ground taken up by highways, we would encrease considerably the quantity of commodities and have more to carry to the market. In the same manner as the value of a piece of ground does not lye in the number of highways that run thro' it, so the riches of a country does not consist in the quantity of money employed to circulate commerce, but in the great abundance of the necessaries of life. If we could therefore fall on a method to send the half of our money abroad to be converted into goods, and at the same time supply the channel of circulation at home, we would greatly encrease the wealth of the country. Hence the beneficial effects of the erection of banks and paper credit. It is easy to show that the erection of banks is of advantage to the commerce of a country. (1978: 503)

So at this point in his career Smith was unequivocal in praising the benefits of banks and paper money. Furthermore, he praised the way that banks had 'prodigiously' increased economic activity not just in Europe but also in 'our American colonies' where 'paper circulation' had been a great success:

We find that the commerce of every nation in Europe has been prodigiously encreased by the erection of banks. In this country every body is sensible of their good effects, and our American colonies, where most of the commerce is carried on by paper circulation, are in a most flourishing condition. (1978: 504)

This sentiment was repeated and summarized two pages later: 'From all these considerations it is manifest that banks are beneficial to the commerce of a country and that it is a bad police to restrain them' (1978: 506).

Smith even attacked economic writers who were critical of banks. The note taker of this part of the *Lectures* indicated that Smith had pointed out the absurdity of the views of 'several political writers [who] have published treatises to show the nature of banks and paper money'. These 'absurd' views were ascribed to Sir Thomas Mun and Joshua Gee. There is a problem here in that Mun and Gee never had these views. So, did the student note taker, as is suggested by the editors of the *Lectures* (Smith 1978: 506), report Smith's views incorrectly? Or was it the case that Smith, as he would later do in the *Wealth of Nations*, showed a basic misunderstanding of Mun's views? Irrespective of how one judges Smith in relation to Mun and Gee, it is clear from the *Lectures* that Smith opposed writers who wanted to demonstrate 'the pernicious nature of banks and paper money'. At this stage in the development of his theory of money there was just one caveat, and that related to his fellow countryman John Law. Smith had already formed a negative impression of Law and the Mississippi System: 'This scheme of Mr. Laws was by no means contemptible; he really believed in it and was the dupe of it himself' (1978: 519). Smith devoted a number of pages to explaining Law's System, but these pages are full of errors showing that his knowledge of the System was extremely inadequate and that he was over-reliant on the views of John Law's enemy the financier Joseph Paris-Duverney, who had written the *Examen du livre intitulé 'Réflexions politiques sur les finances et le commerce'* (1740).

The Law caveat apart, it may be contended that the Adam Smith of the *Lectures on Jurisprudence* was ready to welcome the development of paper money and extol the work of banks. This would not be the case of the *Wealth of Nations*, where Smith had become distinctly more circumspect about the benefits of paper money and banks. He still realized the importance of money, but the emphasis had shifted away from paper money and back to metallic money.

Smith realized the importance of money for the division and specialization of labour:

> every prudent man in every period of society, after the first establishment of the division of labour, must naturally have endeavoured to manage his affairs in such a manner, as to have at all times by him, besides the peculiar produce of his own industry, a certain quantity of some one commodity or other, such as he imagined few people would be likely to refuse in exchange for the produce of their industry.   (1976*a*: i. 37–8)

He gave cattle as an example of rudimentary money: 'the armour of Diomede, says Homer, cost only nine oxen; but that of Glaucus cost a hundred oxen'. Salt in Abyssinia, shells in India, dried cod in Newfoundland, tobacco in Virginia, sugar in the West Indies, and hides or dried leather in some other countries were cited as forms of money. Using his local knowledge, he even mentioned a village in Scotland where nails had been used in payment by workmen in the baker's shop and alehouse.

The description of these types of primitive money served as a backdrop to Smith's introduction of metallic money, which, because of its durability and divisibility, had proven to be a far better type of money. The state had become involved in the manufacture of metallic money by providing its stamp to attest to the metallic fineness and weight of the coinage. However, having discussed the historical evolution of the state's involvement in money, Smith castigated it for reducing the value of money:

> For in every country of the world, I believe, the avarice and injustice of princes and sovereign states, abusing the confidence of their subjects, have, by degrees, diminished the real quantity of metal which had been originally contained in their coins...By means of these operations, the princes and sovereign states which performed them were enabled, in appearance, to pay their debts, and to fulfil their engagements, with a smaller quantity of silver than would otherwise have been requisite. It was, indeed in appearance only; for their creditors were really defrauded of a part of what was due to them. All other debtors in the state were allowed the same privilege; and might pay with the same nominal sum of the new and debased coin whatever they had borrowed in the old. Such operations, therefore, have always proved favourable to the debtor and ruinous to the creditor.   (1976a: i. 43–4)

Thus, Smith attacked the state for debasing the coinage, and, through the resulting inflation, reducing its debts. To Smith this was a fraudulent activity by the state.

Book II chapter ii of the *Wealth of Nations* presented Smith's most significant attempt to analyse the role of money in the economy. Using the metaphor of 'the great wheel of circulation', he distinguished between monetary circulation and the revenue of society, i.e. national income:

> Money, therefore, the great wheel of circulation, the great instrument of commerce, like all other instruments of trade, though it makes a part, and a very valuable part of the capital, makes no part of the revenue of the society to which it belongs; and though the metal pieces of which it is composed, in the course of their annual circulation, distribute to every man the revenue which properly belongs to him, they make themselves no part of that revenue.   (1976a: i. 291)

This quotation shows that, even though Smith was not prepared to accept that money was income, he was prepared, nevertheless, to allow that money could be included as part of society's capital. If this is the case, then it is part of capital as a factor of production, but, unlike other forms of capital, Smith was not prepared to allow for money generating an income stream. The paradox of Smith's inclusion of money as capital along with his refusal to allow it to be considered as income-generating may be solved by understanding that, in this instance, he was referring specifically to metallic money. As in the *Lectures*, he realized that there was a very high opportunity cost to using metallic money and that its substitution by paper money would enable the use of this hitherto 'dead' resource. He wanted to demonstrate how financial innovation, involving the substitution of paper money for metallic money, would produce a new and more efficient 'wheel':

> The substitution of paper in the room of gold and silver money, replaces a very expensive instrument of commerce with one much less costly and sometimes equally convenient.

Circulation comes to be carried on by a new wheel, which it costs less both to erect and to maintain than the old one. But in what manner this operation is performed and in what manner it tends to increase either the gross or the neat revenue of the society, is not altogether so obvious, and may therefore require some further explanation.

(1976a: i. 292)

Smith, developing some ideas that he had partially presented in the *Lectures*, set out to give a concrete example of how the substitution of paper money for metallic money could be beneficial to society (on this issue, see Laidler 1981). He hypothesized a specie money supply of 1 million and that this was replaced by paper money of the same amount. The banks were assumed to hold reserves of 200,000 as backing for the paper money that they issued, leaving 800,000 of specie still in circulation. The creation of the paper money meant that there was 1.8 million of money in circulation consisting of:

— Paper money   1.0 million
— Specie in circulation   0.8 million
— Total   1.8 million

Implicitly Smith assumed that the demand for money was 1 million. However, as a result of the creation of paper money, the overall money supply had risen to 1.8 million so that the money supply was greater than the demand for money. This excess, or, to use Smith's language, 'overflow', had to exit monetary circulation. Here one might have expected Smith to use the straightforward Humean self-adjusting specie flow mechanism, for he would later resort to Hume's arguments on this front to dismiss mercantilist arguments. Instead he provided three methods for the money to flow out of the economy:

1. to finance what he referred to as the 'carrying trade', i.e. purchasing goods in one foreign country to sell in another;
2. to purchase goods for domestic consumption—the consumption by 'idle people' of foreign wines, silks, etc.
3. to purchase capital goods—additional stocks of materials, tools, and provisions.

These capital goods could be purchased 'in order to maintain and employ an additional number of industrious people, who reproduce, with a profit, the value of their annual consumption' (1976a: i. 294).

Smith's acceptance of some of the benefits of paper money may be seen as an advance on Hume's theory. However, he was not prepared to go the whole way and to endorse enthusiastically the new financial innovations as he had done in the *Lectures*. In the latter he had been unequivocal in welcoming the use of paper money in that it freed up metallic money to be spent in the purchase of food, clothing, and housing. However, in the *Wealth of Nations* he considerably modified this approach through his distinction between productive and unproductive expenditure. If the freed-up metallic money was used to finance the carrying trade (method 1) or to purchase capital goods such as machinery and tools (method 3), it would be beneficial to the economy. However, if it was spent 'by idle people who produce nothing' on consumer goods such as foreign wines and foreign silks (method 2), then it was not beneficial to the economy. All this expenditure did was to promote 'prodigality, encrease expence and consumption without increasing production' (1976a: i. 294).

This distinction between productive and unproductive expenditure weakened Smith's analysis considerably. It probably arose as a result of his reading of the Physiocrats' distinction between productive (agriculture) and sterile (industry and services) output–expenditure. In fairness to Smith, he was certainly not prepared to accept, like the Physiocrats, that industry was unproductive, but he was a harsh critic of consumerism and, additionally, tended to the view that many parts of the service sector were involved in 'unproductive activity'. Actors and academics came in for much stick from Smith, who was unable to see any potential productive contribution to society from them. Whatever the truth about the productivity of academics, he would undoubtedly be astounded to see how much Hollywood today contributes to the Californian economy. To add to the Smithian confusion, he allowed this 'productive' and 'unproductive' distinction to spill over into his analysis of money through the distinction that he made between 'real' and 'fictitious' bills. In order to understand his need to distinguish between real and fictitious bills, it is necessary to grasp the extent to which his analysis was influenced by the collapse of the Ayr Bank and his patron the duke of Buccleuch's involvement in it.

The Ayr Bank Collapse

Using an electrical analogy, James Boswell, in the *Reflections on the Late Alarming Bankruptcies in Scotland*, described the shock that had hit the Scottish banking system in 1772:

War, famine, and pestilence, used formerly to fill up the number of the general calamities of mankind; but, in the present age, one has been added, viz. bankruptcy. The year 1772 will ever be remembered as a year of confusion, dismay, and distress. All Scotland has been shaken by a kind of commercial earthquake, while, like a company connected by an electrical wire, the people in every corner of the country have almost instantaneously received the same shock. (Boswell 1772: 1)

How had this arisen? On 6 November 1769 the firm of Douglas, Heron, and Company, which became popularly known as the Ayr Bank, opened for business. It had an issued nominal capital of £150,000, of which £96,000 had been subscribed. The Bank was established at a time when credit was tight and there was a feeling that there was a need for a new bank that could unleash some of

the potential of land ownership. The Ayr Bank was to be a bank th
create credit backed by the collateral of the land owned by its partn
from the rich, landowning nobility. With the motto 'Pro bon publicc , -.
its objective 'the support of the trade, manufactures and agriculture of the
County'. A contemporary anonymous pamphlet illustrated the nature and
objectives of the Bank:

In this situation of the country, the Bank of Douglas, Heron and Company opened, with
a very large subscription to its capital, and under very liberal management, and the good
effects of the aid it administered to the improvements in husbandry, and the support of
the manufacturers and traders soon appeared to a degree that gave satisfaction to every
well-wisher to the country.   (Anon. (n.d.): 22)

Checkland has noted the links between the objectives of the Company and
John Law's plan for a land bank: 'In a sense, the Ayr Bank, represented the
dream, held since the time of John Law, of a Scottish land bank, for the acres of
all these noblemen and lairds were backing for the company' (Checkland
1975: 125). In keeping with this aristocratic backing for the Company, two
dukes and two earls were included in the partnership. The first ducal partner
and chairman of the Company was the duke of Queensberry, a rich landowner
who had been the governor of the British Linen Company. The duke of
Buccleuch was the second ducal partner. One of the largest landowners in
Scotland, the duke had been a natural target for the proposers of the bank,
based as it was on the land bank concept in which the credit of the bank was
backed by the collateral of large tracts of land. He became one of the leading
partners in the Company, initially subscribing £1,000 of its capital. Smith's
very keen interest in the history of the Ayr Bank was due not only to its
subsequent collapse and the consequences that it had for the British economy
and banking, but also to Buccleuch's considerable financial involvement in
the Bank as an unlimited partner. Unlike the other major Scottish banks—the
Bank of Scotland, founded in 1695; the Royal Bank, established in 1727; or the
British Linen Company, founded in 1746—the Ayr Bank was not a limited
liability company. It was a partnership, and this made its partners subject to
unlimited liability for its losses.

   The Ayr Bank engaged in an expansive issue of banknotes so that, within a
short time, 'they were said to represent two thirds of the currency of the
country' (Hamilton 1956: 409). By June 1772 the Bank had issued £1.2 million
through advances and bills of exchange. However, in order to lend these sums
of money, the Bank had been obliged to borrow around £600,000 from its
London correspondents. These borrowings were expensive, costing the Bank
on average around 8 per cent, and, as the Bank was lending at 5 per cent, the
long-term position was untenable. On 8 June 1772 the London bankers Neale,
James, Fordyce, and Downe, with whom the Ayr Bank had been closely connected, failed. By 25 June the Ayr Bank was obliged to suspend its payments.

To shore up the bad loan book of the Ayr Bank, its partners had to put up the collateral of their lands, which, in time, would be sold to meet the Bank's losses. Thus, the collapse of the Ayr Bank was not only a tragedy for banking in Scotland but also a personal tragedy for many great Scottish landowning families. In much the same way as the collapse of some of the insurance 'names' partnerships at Lloyds of London in the 1990s led to the sale of many country estates, the collapse of the Ayr Bank forced many of Scotland's richest landowners to dig very deep into their sporrans. As a retainer (remember Smith was on an annual pension of £300 from the duke) and adviser to Buccleuch, who was only 26 years old in 1772, Adam Smith would have heard a great deal about the Ayr Bank.

The difficulties which the Ayr Bank found itself in in June 1772 necessitated the issue of annuities to finance the liquidity needs of the bank:

the copartners in the said company, in order to raise money to satisfy the demands made upon them, and thereby prevent the bankruptcy of many, which their stopping payment would necessarily have occasioned, did raise, on granting annuities for one and two lives, the sum of 450,000 l. and upwards. (*Scots Magazine* (1774), 197)

The situation further deteriorated so that, by 23 July 1772, the *Glasgow Journal* was noting 'The Bank of England's proceedings against the Dukes of Buccleuch, Queensberry and Dumfries for £300,000 sterling'. This was a sizeable sum of money, even for the rich dukes who were the defendants in the action. The duke of Buccleuch was obviously a central figure in the efforts to settle the affairs of the Ayr Bank. On 12 August 1773, when a meeting was held to discontinue the banking business of the Company and to wind up the affairs of the partnership, the duke was the first named of the twelve partners appointed by the general meeting to oversee these winding-up proceedings. The *Scots Magazine* reported a general meeting of the bank of Douglas, Heron, and Company in Edinburgh on 17 December 1773, noting that 'the proprietors present subscribed 200,000 1. for the relief of the company; whereof 20,000l. by the Duke of Buccleugh. A committee was appointed for managing their affairs, viz. the Dukes of Buccleugh and Queensberry' (*Scots Magazine* (1773), 668–9).

On 9 February 1774 the partners of Douglas, Heron, and Company agreed to the proposal to raise a sum not exceeding £500,000 through a bond issue bearing a rate of interest of 5 per cent. The objective of this bond issue was to use the proceeds to purchase the more costly annuities for lives that had to be issued to repay the Company's debts. The principal on these bonds was to be repaid in four equal instalments in midsummer 1778, 1779, 1780, and 1782. Lands yielding a rental of £32,000 per annum were to be subject to a mortgage, and the proceeds of these land sales would be used to repay the bonds issued. Adam Smith's direct interest in this meeting is testified to by the fact that he had in his library Richard Glover's 'speech introductory to the proposals laid before the annuitants of Messrs Douglas, Heron and Company... on the ninth of February 1774' (see Goldsmith's Library Catalogue, item 11,135).

On 25 February 1774 the dukes of Buccleuch and Queensberry, on behalf of themselves and the other co-partners of Douglas, Heron, presented a petition to the House of Commons 'to issue bonds for a sum not exceeding the sum of 500,000 l. and not under the sum of 50 l. in each bond, for redeeming their [Douglas, Heron's co-partners'] annuities'. The debate on this proposed bond issue heated up when, on 25 March 1774, the East India Company objected to the petition on the grounds that the 5 per cent interest paid on these new bonds would 'most materially affect and prejudice the interest and credit of the petitioners by reducing the value of their bonds which now are issued at an interest of three per cent only' (*Journals of the House of Commons* (1804), 34: 594). This was followed by a petition of certain merchants, bankers, and traders of London 'alledging, that if the bill should pass it would be highly injurious to the trading part of this country, and depretiate the value of the national funds' (*Scots Magazine* (1774), 196). So Buccleuch and his co-partners found that both the East India Company and many merchants and bankers in the City of London were hostile to their petition for facilitating the winding up of the Company. No wonder Adam Smith had a hostile attitude to the East India Company and to the merchant class. Notwithstanding this opposition of the East India Company and the merchants and bankers, the House of Commons passed the bill (Ayes 176, Noes 36) on 28 March. It went through the Lords without amendment, and was passed into law by royal assent on 31 March 1774.

The need to raise such a large sum of money to repay the debts of the Ayr Bank shows the extent to which it had encountered serious financial difficulties. These difficulties had considerable repercussions for the partners of the Bank, and by August 1775 only 112 of the original 226 shareholders remained solvent (see Hamilton 1956: 415). A broadsheet, compiled in Edinburgh on Christmas Day 1780, for the benefit of the partners gave the extent of the losses to that date. This broadsheet, entitled *States of the Affairs of Messrs Douglas, Heron, and Company at August 1773, when they finally gave up Business*, shows that in the course of the previous six years the Ayr Bank has paid off £602,821 of their debts. Additionally, another £146,874 had been put aside to meet further bad debts. Thus, a total of £749,695 had been lost by the Bank. These losses had to be made good by the sale of the lands of the Company's debtor partners, which the managers of the Company stated 'in the present times is attended with considerable difficulty'. Thus, Buccleuch, as a major shareholder of Douglas, Heron, and Company (the Ayr Bank) would have been obliged to sell valuable lands in order to meet his liabilities as a partner of the company.

It is surmised that the financial problems created by the Ayr Bank and the knock-on effects that they had for many Scottish banks were instrumental in causing Smith to rethink his analysis. One can visualize frequent conversations between the young Buccleuch and Smith over the period 1772 to 1780 about the very significant financial implications that the Ayr Bank's collapse was posing for Buccleuch and his family.

These discussions are confirmed by a letter that Smith wrote to his friend William Pulteney on 3 September 1772: 'Tho I have had no concern myself in the public calamities, some of the friends for whom I interest myself the most have been deeply concerned in them; and my attention has been a good deal occupied about the most proper method of extricating them' (Smith 1977: 163). This is an obvious reference to Buccleuch. At the end of the letter Smith explained that these efforts, alongside his own illness, were responsible for delaying the publication of the *Wealth of Nations* 'for a few months longer'. In fact it would be another four years before it was published, so it may be surmised that the Ayr Bank's difficulties presented further obstacles to Smith's finishing the book.

David Hume had been quick to note that the Ayr Bank's collapse might cause Smith to reconsider his monetary views. He had written to Smith earlier that summer, on 27 June 1772, observing the consequences of the collapse, not just in Scotland, but also in London, and in particular for the Bank of England:

We are here in a very melancholy situation: continual bankruptcies, universal loss of credit, and endless suspicions. There are but two standing houses in this place [Edinburgh], Mansfield's and the Couttses... The case is little better in London. It is thought that Sir George Colebroke must soon stop; and even the Bank of England is not entirely free from suspicion. (Hume 1932: ii. 476)

Intriguingly, Hume asked Smith if the financial crisis would cause him to change his thinking on monetary theory: 'Do these events any-wise affect your theory? Or will it occasion the revisal of any chapters?'

Given the huge problems in note-issuing of the Ayr Bank, it is easy to understand how Smith, the relatively liberal monetary theorist of the *Lectures on Jurisprudence*, transformed into a conservative monetary theorist in the *Wealth of Nations*. Praise for paper credit in such circumstances would have appeared as a smack in the face for Smith's patron, Buccleuch, who was so deeply involved in the losses arising from the excessive credit of the Ayr Bank.

It is conjectured that Smith felt obliged to intellectualize the reasons for the failure of the Ayr Bank. This intellectualizing led to his adoption of the contemporary distinction between real and fictitious bills of exchange to explain how bank lending should be predicated on the former rather than the latter. He regarded lending against the latter as undesirable; however, he was prepared to allow that bank lending could be beneficial to the economy when it was in the form of real bills:

When a bank discounts to a merchant a real bill of exchange drawn by a real creditor upon a real debtor, and which, as soon as it becomes due, is really paid by that debtor; it only advances to him a part of the value which he would otherwise be obliged to keep by him unemployed, and in ready money for answering occasional demands. The payment of the bill, when it becomes due, replaces to the bank the value of what it had advanced, together with the interest. The coffers of the bank, so far as its dealings are confined to such customers, resemble a water pond, from which, though a stream is continually running out, yet another is continually running in, fully equal to that which runs out; so that, without any further care or attention, the pond keeps always equally, or very near equally, or very near equally full. Little or no expence can ever be necessary for replenishing the coffers of such a bank.   (1976*a*: i. 304)

Thus, a real bill was a bill drawn by a real creditor upon a real debtor. A fictitious bill was a bill for which 'there was properly no real creditor but the bank which discounted it; nor any real debtor but the projector who made use of the money' (1976*a*: i. 312). His argument appears to be that lending against real bills freed up 'dead stock'. If the merchant had to keep a quantity of cash available to meet payments for goods instead of having the facility of drawing a bill of exchange based on the goods, then this money was inactive:

It is not by augmenting the capital of the country, but by rendering a greater part of that capital active and productive than would otherwise be so, that the most judicious operations of banking can increase the industry of the country. That part of his capital which a dealer is obliged to keep by him unemployed, and in ready money for answering occasional demands, is so much dead stock, which, so long as it remains in this situation, produces nothing either to him or to his country. The judicious operations of banking enable him to convert this dead stock into active and productive stock; into materials to work upon, into tools to work with, and into provisions and subsistence to work for; into stock which produces something both to himself and to his country.   (1976*a*: i. 320)

Smith extended the analogy from the banks to the country in general. All the gold and silver of the country may be regarded as 'dead stock'. It is part of the capital of the country, but 'produces nothing for the country'. However, by substituting paper for gold and silver, a great part of this 'dead stock' can be converted into 'active and productive stock'. His prose flowed at this point:

The judicious operations of banking, by substituting paper in the room of a great part of this gold and silver, enables the country to convert a great part of this dead stock into active and productive stock; into stock which produces something to the country.
(1976*a*: i. 321)

Extending the highway metaphor that he had presented in the *Lectures*, Smith compared the use of money in this way to the creation of an air route that could be used to improve the transportation system. At a time when air travel was unknown, the metaphor was striking:

The gold and silver money which circulates in any country may very properly be compared to a highway, which, while it circulates and carries to market all the grass and corn of the country, produces itself not a single pile of either. The judicious operations of banking, by providing, if I may be allowed so violent a metaphor, a sort of wagon-way through the air; enable the country to convert, as it were, a great part of its highways into good pastures and corn fields, and thereby to increase very considerably the annual produce of its land and labour.   (1976*a*: i. 321)

But, having produced this striking metaphor, Smith qualified the scenario by saying that the commerce of the country was less secure when 'suspended upon the Daedalian wings of paper money' than upon 'the solid ground of gold and silver'. This quotation (and perhaps it should have been the Icarian rather than the Daedalian wings) shows that Smith had moved back to a preference for the solidity of metallic money. Paper money and credit had their uses, but ultimately he had a stronger preference for metallic money. Where was his previous confidence, as expressed in the *Lectures on Jurisprudence*, about paper money and banks? It had disappeared in the air, in this case the Air Bank, as it was contemporaneously spelt by many, including Hume.

Smith attacked the Ayr Bank in the *Wealth of Nations*, condemning it as more 'liberal than any other had ever been' and as seeming 'to have made scarce any distinction between real and circulating bills' (1976*a*: i. 313). He was particularly scathing about the Bank and its customers. Its borrowers were described as 'chimerical projectors' who employed their money in 'extravagant undertakings'. The Bank's activities, including those of lending heavily to investors in the Bank, only succeeded in transferring money from 'prudent and profitable to imprudent and unprofitable undertakings' (1976*a*: i. 316–17).

Like many other developments in the *Wealth of Nations*, the real versus fictitious bills distinction was already well known to bankers. However, Smith attempted to give it intellectual weight and to use it as a rule of thumb for bankers to distinguish between good and bad lending policy. If banks were prudent and lent only on the security of real bills, then there would be no problem. If, on the other hand, banks lent on the basis of fictitious bills, where there were no real goods underpinning the loan transaction, then problems would arise in terms of insolvencies, bankruptcies, and the knock-on effects of such developments.

Smith then progressed from analysing the failures of the Ayr Bank to those of John Law: 'The ideas of the possibility of multiplying paper money to almost any extent, was the real foundation of what is called the Mississippi scheme, the most extravagant project both of banking and stock-jobbing that, perhaps, the world ever saw' (1976*a*: i. 317). He described Law's ideas in *Money and Trade* (1705) as 'splendid but visionary' and blamed them for contributing in part 'to that excess of banking which has of late been complained of both in Scotland and in other places' (1976*a*: i. 317–18). Poor John Law; close to fifty years after his death he was indicted as one of the guilty parties behind the collapse of the Ayr Bank.

Smith was reluctant to allow credit to fall into the hands of the ordinary citizen. He divided circulation into two branches: (1) the circulation of the dealers with one another, and (2) the circulation between the dealers and consumers. The first type of circulation he accepted, but he warned against the latter. Furthermore, he was against banks issuing small-denomination notes:

> Where the issuing of bank notes for very small sums is allowed and commonly practised, many mean people are both enabled and encouraged to become bankers ... the frequent bankruptcies to which such beggarly bankers must be liable, may occasion a very considerable inconveniency, and sometimes even a very great calamity to many poor people who had received their notes in payment.   (1976a: i. 323)

Despite Smith's reservations about banknotes, it is interesting to observe that there is a Scottish £50 banknote with Smith's portrait and recently, in 2006, the Bank of England replaced a £20 banknote depicting the composer Edward Elgar with one bearing Smith's portrait against a background combining machines and labour with the following words: 'the division of labour in pin manufacturing: (and the great increase in the quantity of work that results)'. Doubtlessly, the Bank of England would contend that at least it did not issue a small-denomination note bearing Smith's likeness.

Notwithstanding Smith's reservations about banknotes, he advocated free competition in banking because such competition, he felt, would reduce the moral hazard problem. With many banks competing for business, it behoved banks to be more careful in their practices so as to guard themselves against malicious runs:

> The late multiplication of banking companies in both parts of the united kingdom, an event by which many people have been much alarmed, instead of diminishing, increases the security of the publick. It obliges all of them to be more circumspect in their conduct, and, by not extending their currency beyond its due proportion to their cash, to guard themselves against those malicious runs, which the rivalship of so many competitors is always ready to bring upon them.   (1976a: i. 329)

That said, Smith earlier suggested that there would be a need to regulate banks even though such regulation might be construed as an interference with natural liberty:

> But those exertions of the natural liberty of a few individuals, which might endanger the security of the whole society, are, and ought to be, restrained by the laws of all governments; of the most free, as well as of the most despotical. The obligation of building party walls, in order to prevent the communication of fire, is a violation of natural liberty, exactly of the same kind with the regulations of the banking trade which are here proposed.   (1976a: i. 324)

Smith went a great deal further than his advocacy in favour of the regulation of the banking sector. He also expressed a strong preference for the imposition of maximum interest rates. This was a strange stance, as Bentham, in his *Defence of Usury... To Which is Added A Letter to Adam Smith, Esq.; LL.D.* (1787), would later point out, for such a partisan of free competition.

Smith's distinction between real and fictitious bills, allied to his preference for metallic money rather than paper money, exposed his monetary theory to a full-frontal intellectual assault by Henry Thornton sixteen years later in the *Paper Credit of Great Britain* (1802), the subject matter of the next chapter.

It has been shown above that the East India Company had attempted to block the bond issue of the Ayr Bank in the House of Commons in 1774. Given Smith's closeness to Buccleuch, it is not surprising to find him take a distinctly hostile line to the East India Company. A further factor that may have stoked up Smith's hostility to the Company could have been his disappointment at not being appointed a member of a commission to study the affairs of the Company in 1772. In a letter to William Pulteney on 3 September 1772 he had written that he was 'very much honoured and obliged to [Pulteney] for having mentioned me to the east India Directors as a person who could be of any use to them' (1977: 164).

Smith's attack on the East India Company appeared late in the *Wealth of Nations* when he expressed considerable reservations about joint stock companies. He was only prepared to accept that joint stock companies could be beneficial in four instances: (1) banking, (2) insurance, (3) canals, and (4) urban water suppliers. In all other cases he felt it was unreasonable to allow for the establishment of joint stock companies. Smith's conclusion on publicly quoted companies came in Book V of the *Wealth of Nations*: 'The joint stock companies, which are established for the publick spirited purpose of promoting some particular manufacture, over and above managing their own affairs ill, to the diminution of the general stock of the society, can in other respects scarce ever fail to do more harm than good' (1976a: ii. 758) This conclusion was mild in comparison with the criticism that he directed at the East India Company, which he accused of being 'the plunderers of India':

No other sovereigns ever were, or, from the nature of things, ever could be, so perfectly indifferent about the happiness or misery of their subjects, the improvement or waste of their dominions, the glory or disgrace of their administrations; as, from irresistible moral causes, the greater part of the proprietors of such a mercantile company are, and necessarily must be. (1976a: ii. 752)

He went on to add a tirade about how the company had abused its exclusive position in India:

With the right of possessing forts and garrisons, in distant and barbarous countries, is necessarily connected the right of making peace and war in those countries. The joint stock companies which had the one right have constantly exercised the other, and have frequently had it expressly conferred upon them. How unjustly, how capriciously, how cruelly they have commonly exercised it, is too well known from recent experience.

(1976a: ii. 754)

Smith's analysis of joint stock companies was distinctly unimpressive. It has been shown that his friend David Hume regarded the stock market as an utterly redundant organization. Smith did not go so far, but his reluctance to allow for joint stock companies outside the four areas of banking, insurance, canals, and water supply displayed a very narrow understanding of the benefits of joint stock companies on his part.

The collapse of the South Sea Bubble had been responsible for the introduction of the Bubble Acts, which confined the establishment of joint stock companies after 1720 to those that could secure a costly royal charter. Smith linked monopoly privileges with the establishment of joint stock companies by charter. This had been true of the big chartered companies such as the East India Company and the Bank of England. However, Smith had difficulty recognizing that joint stock companies did not need such privileges, a development that would take place over fifty years later when the Bubble Acts were repealed. Once again, Scotland's major Enlightenment figures Hume and Smith failed to recognize the huge potential of corporate finance. Banks and paper money had been largely rejected by Hume, and given at most a lukewarm reception by Smith. The stock exchange had been rejected completely by Hume, while Smith believed that there were only four areas in which joint stock companies could be tolerated.

Imagine how limited the London, New York, and other stock exchanges would be if the strictures with respect to PLCs of the so-called founder of modern capitalism had been followed. Modern capitalism could not have developed in such a limited environment. Can we really say that such views formed part of the Scottish Enlightenment? Presumably the Enlightenment involved taking forward-looking positions with respect to the future of money, banking, and finance. Yet, in all these three areas, Hume most definitely, and Smith to a lesser degree, failed to grasp the extent to which there was an underlying financial revolution taking place in Great Britain, one that would be the basis for the growth and future prosperity of the British economy.

References

Ahmad, Syed (1990), 'Adam Smith's Four Invisible Hands', *History of Political Economy*, 22/1 (Spring).
Anon. (n.d.), *An Inquiry into the Late Mercantile Distresses in Scotland and England* (London).
Barfoot, Michael (1991), 'Dr. William Cullen and Mr Adam Smith: A Case of Hypochondriasis?', *Proceedings of the Royal College of Physicians of Edinburgh*, 21.

Bonar, James (1932), *A Catalogue of the Library of Adam Smith* (1894; repr. New York, 1966).

Boswell, James (1772), *Reflections on the Late Alarming Bankruptcies in Scotland* (Edinburgh).

Checkland, S. G. (1975), *Scottish Banking: A History*, 1695–1973 (Glasgow).

Douglas, Sir Robert (1813), *The Peerage of Scotland*, rev. J. P. Wood, 2nd edn, 2 vols (Edinburgh).

Grampp, William D. (2000), 'What Did Smith Mean by the Invisible Hand', *Journal of Political Economy*, 108/3 (June).

Gray, Alexander (1931), *The Development of Economic Doctrine: An Introductory Survey* (London).

Hamilton, Henry (1956), 'The Failure of the Ayr Bank, 1772', *Economic History Review*, new ser., 8/3.

Hollander, Samuel (1973), *The Economics of Adam Smith* (Toronto).

Hume, David (1932), *Letters of David Hume*, ed. J. Y. T. Greig, 2 vols (Oxford).

Laidler, David (1981), 'Adam Smith as a Monetary Economist', *Canadian Journal of Economics*, 14 (May).

Pack, Spencer J. (1996), 'Adam Smith's Economic Vision and the Invisible Hand', *History of Economic Ideas*, 4/1–2.

Persky, Joseph (1989), 'Retrospectives: Adam Smith's Invisible Hand', *Journal of Economic Perspectives*, 3/4 (Autumn).

Ross, Ian Simpson (1995), *The Life of Adam Smith* (Oxford).

Rothschild, Emma (1994), 'Adam Smith's Invisible Hand', *American Economic Review*, 84/2, Paper and Proceedings (May).

Smith, Adam (1896), *Lectures on Justice, Police, Revenue and Arms delivered in the University of Glasgow by Adam Smith*, ed. E. Cannan (Oxford).

—— (1976a), *An Inquiry into the Nature and Causes of the Wealth of Nations* (1776), ed. R. H. Campbell, A. S. Skinner, and W. B. Todd., 2 vols (Oxford).

—— (1976b), *The Theory of Moral Sentiments* (1759), ed. D. D. Raphael and A. L. Macfie (Oxford).

—— (1977), *The Correspondence of Adam Smith*, ed. E. C. Mossner and I. S. Ross (Oxford).

—— (1978), *Lectures on Jurisprudence*, ed. R. L. Meek, D. D. Raphael, and P. G. Stein (Oxford).

LONDON. Published by James Asperne. Nº 32. Cornhill 1.ª March 1813.

Henry Thornton Esq.ʳ

Late one of the Representatives for the

BOROUGH OF SOUTHWARK . —

Engraved by T. Blood for the European Magazine, from the original Picture
By Jnº Hoppner, R.A. — in the possession of Mʳˢ Thornton.

Henry Thornton

9

Henry Thornton: The Lender
of Last Resort

Let us imagine that we are in the leafy London suburb of Clapham with a splendid view of Battersea Rise—it is, after all, the start of the nineteenth century—in the presence of a well-known banker and Member of Parliament. He is agonizing over a draft of a future book on paper credit. Here we have a banker writing on paper credit nearly a hundred years after John Law investigated this type of subject. Inspiration comes slowly to him; in his own words, he is having 'a hard fag' of it. His problem is a guilt complex induced by his belief that he is not praying enough. As his personal diaries show, his war against sin is tormenting him, a torment that will last all his life. Maybe he has the bars of a song he sings with his co-religionists on Sundays ringing in his ears:

> Satan, who now tries to please you,
> Lest you timely warning take,
> When that word is past, will seize you,
> Plunge you in the burning lake:
> Think, poor sinner, Thy eternal all's at stake.
>
> (Meacham 1964: 22)

Our writer's concern with the dark Satanic forces that could foil his chance for everlasting salvation is interfering with his dispassionate analysis of the British banking system that he knows so well. We are now in the study of Henry Thornton (1760–1815), evangelical and economist, a man who firmly believes in the priority of evangelicalism over economics. What does it benefit a man if he gains the whole world but loses his soul?

Henry Thornton had a remarkable career.[1] Philanthropist, Member of Parliament, successful anti-slavery abolitionist, creator of that quintessentially British institution the Sunday School, founder of the Clapham Sect, treasurer

---

[1] A significant amount of this chapter is based on Murphy (2003).

of the Bible Society, the Church Missionary Society, the Religious Tract Society, founding chairman of the Sierra Leone Company, banker, and economist. Meacham (1964) wrote a biography on him with particular emphasis on his evangelicalism and his political career. In this chapter an attempt is made to analyse Thornton's macroeconomic contributions as presented in *An Enquiry into the Nature and Effects of the Paper Credit of Great Britain* (1802). These were immense, serving, *inter alia*, to show the need for a central bank to intervene in financial markets and act as a lender of last resort. For many, his measured analysis laid out the parameters within which a prudent central bank should act in formulating an appropriate monetary policy for the macroeconomy. But just as Thornton had continuous religious turmoil in his mind, so also his economics was subject to an intense mental dialectical process, which has led to difficulties in the classification of Thornton's exact stance.

When it comes to the categorization and classification of economists, historians of economic thought are like wine connoisseurs attempting to find a little bit of this, a concentration of that, a *soupçon* of the other. The emphasis in many writings is on the association of a writer with a particular strain or tradition. When it comes to classifying the 'vintage' to which Henry Thornton belongs, immediate difficulties arise. Some writers, such as Hayek (1939) and Rist (1938), have identified him closely with the classical vintage. Others, such as Hicks (1967) and Beaugrand (1981), feel that there is definite evidence of the roots that would later prosper in the Keynesian vineyard. Reisman (1971: 70) found that, against a background of monetary orthodoxy, Thornton was 'strikingly unorthodox', while Laidler (1987: 634) suggested that Thornton has claims to be regarded as 'the most important contributor to monetary economics between David Hume (1752) and Knut Wicksell (1898)'. The reason for this wide range of opinions on Henry Thornton is that *Paper Credit* may be subjected to a number of different interpretations. This chapter suggests that it is possible to identify three Mr Thorntons appearing in various parts of this fascinating book.

Initially when reading *Paper Credit* I believed that there were two Henry Thorntons to be found. The first is the concerned anti-deflationist, showing many pre-Keynesian insights and unwilling to accept the current dogma of his time regarding the need to reduce the Bank of England's note issue whenever the price level increased, as indicated by a rise in the market price of bullion relative to the mint price. The second, whom even Sir John Hicks would call 'the hard currency man', emerges in the latter part of *Paper Credit*, when he adopted the role of the worried anti-inflationist warning against the over-issue of Bank of England banknotes. The identification of these two Mr Thorntons, alluded to by Thornton himself in the preface, and later highlighted by Hicks (1967), is easy enough to detect. However, lurking in the shadows of the book I believe there may be a third Mr Thornton. This is

Henry Thornton the paper credit emancipator and financial innovator struggling to push monetary economics away from the accepted orthodoxy of the gold standard system. The title of *Paper Credit* reveals this third Mr Thornton, a writer who wished to inquire into 'the nature and effects of the paper credit of Great Britain'. Here was a banker writing on the metamorphosis of the monetary economy from a gold-based system to one driven by paper credit in which gold played an increasingly diminishing role. This was not the work of a metallist; rather it was the work of a writer who realized that paper credit had taken over from metallic money in constituting the main part of the monetary system. This third Mr Thornton is at his best when systematically deconstructing and exposing as fallacious many of the major tenets of monetary economics advanced by Adam Smith. Thornton the banker was suggesting to his readers that Adam Smith, along with some of the other leading commentators on money, Locke, Montesquieu, and Hume, had misinterpreted monetary developments and did not understand the extent of the paper credit revolution that was taking place under their eyes. The converse of these attacks was the view that it was paper credit rather than metallic money that drove the system.

Ultimately, none of the Mr Thorntons dominate the book, and a more reasoned interpretation might be to insist that there is an overall synthesis in Thornton's work that makes it the most remarkable work on monetary economics of the nineteenth century, an assessment all the more remarkable when it is realized that it was written in the second year of the new century. One would not necessarily disagree with the view of the book's greatness, but, as was the case with Turgot, there is a thin dividing line between greatness and genius. Thornton was very close to the latter. His greatness was to show the danger of deflationary monetary policies based on an inappropriate understanding of the causes of a rising price level. Consistently with this, he recommended intervention by the Bank of England, a prototype for the modern central bank, to provide liquidity to financial markets in its role as a lender of last resort. His genius might have been to develop his analysis of monetary theory and policy in the context of a full paper credit economy.

Thornton wrote at a time when convertibility had been suspended, and so he had a unique opportunity to show the extent to which the banking system and the different forms of paper credit had progressed in taking over from metallic money. He did so in a remarkable fashion and gave some indications of the future course of monetary developments. However, he did not progress the analysis to the point of suggesting that the new paper credit system could completely replace gold and silver. Some conjectures are made in the latter part of this chapter as to why Thornton did not make the complete progression to a specie-less economy.

Thornton's Background and Career

Henry Thornton was born into a 'City' family. He would later remark, 'We are all City people and connected with merchants, and nothing but merchants on every side'; one of Henry's grandfathers, along with his brother, was a director of the Bank of England.

John Thornton, father of Henry, was a very prominent City merchant specializing in trade with Russia. He was described in the *Gentleman's Magazine* on his death as 'the greatest merchant in Europe, except Mr. Hope of Amsterdam' (Meacham 1964: 2). He was a noted benefactor of the poor and is reputed to have given a sum estimated between £100,000 to £150,000 to charity. This was consistent with his evangelicalism. John Thornton had three sons. Samuel (1754–1839) was, like his father, a 'Russian' merchant and Member of Parliament for Hull; he was also a director and later a Governor of the Bank of England. Significantly his governorship was from 1799 to 1801, the period when Henry was writing *Paper Credit*. Hayek (1939) pointed out that many economics writers, starting with McCulloch, confused Samuel with Henry, to the point of maintaining incorrectly that the latter was a director and Governor of the Bank of England. Despite the fact that the Bank of England was a joint stock bank with shareholders, Thornton would maintain that the directors of the Bank of England were first and foremost motivated by *pro bono* considerations of stabilizing the monetary environment rather than the mere pursuit of profit-maximizing objectives:

They are men, therefore, who feel themselves to be most deeply interested not merely in the increase of the dividends or in the maintenance of the credit of the Bank of England, but in the support of commercial as well as of public credit in general. There is, indeed, both among them and among the whole commercial world, who make so large a portion of this country, a remarkable determination to sustain credit, and especially the credit of the bank; and this general agreement to support the bank is one of the pillars of its strength, and one pledge of its safety. The proprietors of it themselves are not likely to approve of any dangerous extension even of their own paper; both they and the directors know the importance of confining the bank paper, generally speaking, within its accustomed limits, and must necessarily be supposed to prefer its credit, and the paper credit of the nation to the comparatively trifling considerations of a small increase in their own dividends; an increase which would prove delusory, if it should arise from that extravagant issue of bank notes which would have the effect of depreciating all the circulating medium of the country, since it would thus raise upon the proprietors of bank stock, as well as on others, the price of all the articles of life. (Thornton 1939: 110)

Keynes, over a hundred years later, professed a similar view when he wrote in *The End of Laissez-Faire*:

It is almost true to say that there is no class of persons in the Kingdom of whom the Governor of the Bank of England thinks less when he decides on his policy than of his shareholders. Their rights, in excess of their conventional dividend, have already sunk to the neighbourhood of zero.   (Keynes 1926: 44)

The second brother, Robert, was a Member of Parliament for Colchester and at one stage a governor of the East India Company. Despite his prominence in the City, he later lost his fortune, speculated heavily, and emigrated to America, where he died.

Henry was born on 10 March 1760. He did not go to university and his experience of the university of life started with his cousin's 'counting-house'. Thornton was greatly perturbed by his father's 'Jack of all trades' approach, along with his speculative ventures in commodities such as tobacco and wheat—enterprises in which the father lost substantial sums of money. He decided to move away from the career of merchant to that of banker, a career move that was against his parents' wishes, who felt that banking was a station in life below that of the merchant. At the age of 22, following his brothers' examples, he became a member of the House of Commons, representing Southwark. The first vote he cast in the House of Commons was 'in favour of the treaty of peace with America'. Two years later, at the age of 24, he joined the bank of Down and Free, which soon became Down, Thornton, and Free. Thornton started in banking, according to Clapham (1944: i. 165), with 'only the very moderate sum of £6,000'. This was a large sum of money for the man in the street of the time, and Thornton was further enriched when he inherited around £40,000 on his father's death. With that type of capital base, he had the money to develop his bank, Down, Thornton, and Free, to become an established financial institution in the City of London. Thornton created a network of agents to develop his business across Great Britain. He would later write: 'We owed much to the kindness of our friends . . . and much also to the circumstance of many country banks rising up at that time, with which we were wise enough to become connected' (Clapham 1944: i. 165). He appeared to have it all, an apparently brilliant banker, as well as a very active parliamentarian ever concerned with the plight of those less fortunate than he or his family. Thornton, like his father, was a noted philanthropist. Up to the age of 42 he is reputed to have given away six-sevenths of his income to charity. This amount was reduced when he married, but he continued to put aside considerable sums for charity.

In 1791 Thornton, then aged 31, was appointed the chairman of the newly established Sierra Leone Company, with William Wilberforce and the prominent emancipationist Thomas Clarkson also serving on the board. The objective of this company was to provide African Americans who had fought on the British side during the War of Independence, in return for obtaining their freedom from slavery, with the possibility of moving from Nova Scotia to establish a new life in the colony of Sierra Leone. For a recent discussion of this project, see Schama (2005). Thornton, who temporarily retired from banking, was obviously a highly effective chairman because the company initially raised a capital of £42,000 from its Quaker and evangelical supporters. This sum was then increased to £235,000. These funds enabled a fleet of ships, commanded by John Clarkson, a brother of Thomas Clarkson, to set sail from Nova Scotia in 1791 for Sierra Leone. Despite very adverse conditions, John Clarkson succeeded in establishing a community of 'free black British African-Americans' in the new environment of Freetown, Sierra Leone (Schama 2005: 406).

When John Clarkson left the colony, in late December 1792, to return to London to report to the company, the whole colony of Freetown came together to wish him a safe voyage and a quick return. It appears that almost to a man the new colonists wished for John Clarkson's return as the governor, and their leaders wrote to Henry Thornton to that effect. Despite initially receiving John Clarkson with considerable civility and promising that he would be returned to the colony as the governor, Henry Thornton and William Wilberforce changed their minds and refused to allow Clarkson to return. What happened to change their minds? After all, they had sent the very young Clarkson to organize the former North American slaves in Nova Scotia to travel to Freetown. He had done this with the utmost professionalism, and had shown himself to be a very humane and sympathetic representative of the company in organizing the colony in Freetown. Apparently, Thornton was turned against Clarkson by correspondence from Freetown by his fellow Clapham 'Saint' Zachary Macaulay, the father of Thomas Babington Macaulay. Zachary Macaulay accused Clarkson of promising the former slaves too much. Thornton, in opting to favour Macaulay's criticisms of Clarkson, showed a deep personal flaw on this issue. Clarkson had almost lost his life in the transportation of the colonists to Freetown, he had shown considerable skill in meeting the massive logistical problems that the new colonists faced, and he was extremely popular with them. Despite this, Thornton's judgement was swung by his friendship with Macaulay. Clarkson was never allowed set foot in Sierra Leone again.

Schama is highly critical of Macaulay and Thornton, maintaining that, while they wanted to abolish the slave trade, they were not prepared to push this to its logical development, namely the full freedom of the black people:

Although, as Evangelicals, they were committed to the abolition of the slave trade, neither Zachary Macaulay nor Henry Thornton was much interested in freedom. Looking askance at the monsters brought forth in revolutionary France by the abuse of liberty, their tepid enthusiasm became icy hostility. What stirred the Clapham Saints was commerce and Christianity, sustained in mutual nourishment, until they had converted the pagan continent into godly civility and prosperity. (Schama 2005: 422)

Certainly Thornton's behaviour towards Clarkson was inexcusable. It shows a hesitancy on Thornton's part indicating that, while he favoured freedom for slaves, he was not prepared to push this to the point that the freed slaves of Sierra Leone had a full constitutional democracy. Was Thornton's hesitancy on this issue an intimation of some of the hesitancy that he later showed in *Paper Credit* when presenting both a strong anti-deflationist and a strong anti-inflationist line of reasoning?

Thornton was a firm ally of Wilberforce in Parliament in his opposition to slavery (for the latest biography on Wilberforce, see Hague 2007). In 1792 Thornton purchased a small estate called Battersea Rise in the London borough of Clapham. William Wilberforce shared his residence with him there for five years, and a variety of other friends lived in houses on the estate. This grouping of evangelicals became known as the Clapham Sect, and was to the fore in leading the anti-slavery agitators in Parliament. Ultimately they succeeded in ensuring the passing of the Slave Trade Bill in 1807. Thornton also favoured popular education and was responsible for the foundation of the Sunday School Society (of which he was the first president). Consistently with these good works, Thornton has been presented as the economist–banker par excellence, someone to look up to and include among the greats worthy of a posthumous Nobel Prize in Economics. Here it is necessary to pause for thought. Was Thornton a great banker? Appearances can be deceptive, for, while emphasis has been attached to his charitable work and the sums he gave to the poor, indicators of the profit he made as a banker, the reality is that Thornton died leaving his bank essentially bankrupt. This was not owing to any corrupt behaviour on his part, and most of the blame may be attributed to his managing partner Peter Free, who over-lent to Everth and Company. The loss on the Everth and Company account ultimately proved to be £72,000, far greater than Thornton's 1815 estimate of £50,000, and ultimately helped to precipitate the crash of Pole, Thornton, and Company in the crisis of 1825. However, as the senior partner, Thornton should have exercised far stricter control over the bank's activities so that the account with Everth and Company did not assume crisis proportions.

Shortly before his death, in 1815, Thornton wrote a letter to Peter Free in which he expressed considerable concern for the extent to which Free had over-lent to the company of Everth and Hilton. It is quite clear that, by this stage, Thornton realized that there was insufficient collateral to back up these loans, and that he partly blamed himself for this state of affairs: 'I have been led perhaps by occupations in other quarters, & especially by committee business at former times in the house of commons, to take too superficial view of some of our affairs, but I cannot now with my eyes open, see this matter even run on, much less grow still more heavy' (Acaster 1975, pt 3, 60). This letter was written in June 1814. By 24 October, Thornton estimated that the loss through Everth and Hilton amounted to £50,000. On 16 January 1815 Thornton died in Wilberforce's house. His bank's loss on the Everth and Hilton account actually amounted to £70,000. Further bad debts, including one of

£6,865 contracted by his brother Robert, meant that the capital base of Down, Thornton, and Free of £72,000 was completely lost.

Acaster, who has examined the issue of Thornton's banking activities, recognized that Thornton attempted at one stage to arrest the problem but that, ultimately, he was insufficiently decisive in solving the problem: 'True it was entirely due to him that any real curb was placed upon the swelling debt, but recognition appears to have come late, the treatment urged to have been ineffective or ignored, and the overseeing of the situation lax' (Acaster 1974, pt 2, 50)

The Writing of *Paper Credit*

An Enquiry into the Nature and Effects of the Paper Credit of Great Britain was published in 1802, just twenty-five years after the publication of the *Wealth of Nations*. Hayek (1939), relying on a quotation in J. C. Colquhoun's *Wilberforce and his Friends* (1866), suggested that *Paper Credit* may have been started as early as 1796. However, examination of Thornton's manuscripts in Cambridge University Library does not provide any evidence of this; indeed, the Thornton manuscripts provide evidence that he wrote at least most of the book in 1801. His wife, Marianne, notified the Thorntons' great friend the writer Mrs Hannah More, on 5 March of what appears to be the year 1801, that 'Mr. Thornton had a bad night or a moderate one as it happens but is working hard on paper credit' (Cambridge University Library, Thornton MSS, Add. MS 7674/ I/L3, vol. 2, fo. 135). In a letter, on 30 March 1801, Thornton himself wrote to Hannah More, 'I am also going on with paper credit' (ibid., vol. 2, fo. 141). In a further letter to Mrs More, on 1 September, he wrote, 'poor paper credit gets on but slowly' (ibid., vol. 2, fo. 150). In an undated letter to his wife, Marianne, apparently written in early 1801, he wrote, 'After my letter to you yesterday I had a hard fag at Paper Credit' (ibid., vol. 3, fo. 10). Again, on 21 August 1801, he detailed to his wife the amount of work that he was putting into *Paper Credit*: 'At night I worked at some remnants of paper credit papers which I have here . . . Thank God I slept better and rose soon after 7. I wrote a little on Paper Credit before breakfast' (ibid., vol. 3, fos 11–12). As all the diary entries appear to refer to a period from March to September 1801, and as there are no earlier mentions of the work antecedent to this date, it is highly probable that Thornton wrote all, or at least the bulk, of the work in 1801. Textual confirmation for this may be adduced from his reference to the problems of the 'spring of 1801' (Thornton 1939: 227), when there was the possibility of a repeat of the difficulties that the British economy experienced in 1793. The importance of situating the writing of *Paper Credit* around this period is that Thornton's brother Samuel was Governor of the Bank of England during the period 1799–1801.

Thornton's Criticisms of Adam Smith's Monetary Economics

To understand Thornton it is necessary to grasp the extent to which he believed that Adam Smith was incorrect in his interpretation of monetary economics. Although Smith's *Inquiry into the Nature and Causes of the Wealth of Nations* (1776) had already been established as a classic, this did not prevent Thornton from engaging in a strong critique of the dead Scotsman's monetary ideas. Even the title of his book *An Enquiry into the Nature and Effects of the Paper Credit of Great Britain* has some parallels with Smith's title, though Thornton was focusing attention on a narrower topic, the nature and effects of paper credit. This critique highlighted Henry Thornton the experienced banker taking issue with Adam Smith the academic theorist. Thornton primed his readers for his attack on Smith from the very start of the book. In the preface he commented that he had referred to several passages of Smith in the book—a gross understatement—and also made some observations on Hume's writings on money and the balance of trade, Sir James Steuart's *An Inquiry into the Principles of Political Oeconomy*, and the writings of Locke and Montesquieu. Writing about these works, he observed that 'we ought not to be surprised, if, in treatises necessarily in some degree theoretical, or written for the purpose of establishing a particular truth, certain incidental observations should not be just, nor even if some main principles should have been laid down in terms not sufficiently guarded' (Thornton 1939: 69).

Note the way Thornton was prepared to attack not just 'certain incidental observations' but more importantly 'main principles' that were insufficiently guarded. It needs to be understood that he was not just some practitioner–banker critical of theorists' understanding of certain aspects of the monetary economy, but that he was prepared to take them on with respect to 'principles' and their understanding of these. For a man imbued with principles, his attack on previous economic writers for their misunderstanding of principles shows the extent of his disagreement with earlier authors. He added, in the preface, that someone who differs from such 'authorities' and who intends 'to correct the public opinion on the important subject of paper credit' needs to be careful that he does not propagate new errors when trying to remove old ones, expressing the hope that *Paper Credit*'s 'leading doctrines' are just. Thornton's use of terms such as 'main principles' and 'leading doctrines' implies that he intended *Paper Credit* to present a major reassessment of monetary theory and policy. While prepared to acknowledge the contributions of Smith, Hume, Steuart, Locke, and Montesquieu, he felt that they had an insufficient understanding of the actual mechanisms of the monetary economy to present a proper account of it. This is confirmed by the final sentence of the preface: 'It may not be irrelevant or improper to observe, that the present work has been written by a person whose situation in life has supplied information on several of the topics under discussion, and that much use has been made of those means of correcting the errors of former writers which recent events have afforded' (Thornton 1939: 69). In other words, Thornton felt it was appropriate for someone with the practical experience of banking that he possessed to take issue with those writers who had written on monetary economics solely from an academic rather than a practitioner's viewpoint.

It will be shown later how Thornton was at his imperious best when criticizing three fundamental parts of Smith's monetary economics; namely, (1) the limited conceptualization of the definition of the money supply, (2) the real bills of exchange doctrine, and (3) the neglect of the role of the velocity of circulation. Here was someone drawn from the real world of banking more than capable of castigating Smith's understanding of money and banking. Here was someone who was able to see the complexities of defining money and the multiple uses of bills of exchange from the standpoint of the banking habitat in which he worked. Here was someone quite prepared to propose a break with previous monetary theories. Thus, it would be wrong to place Thornton in the filiation of classical economists from Hume to Smith. He represented a break, one that could perhaps have become an even more radical fissure if he had decided to progress further his theory away from a structure in which metallic money had a role.

Eighteenth-century Britain, and in particular Scotland, had been a land of great financial innovation where bankers, without the aid or direction of economists, had been developing new approaches to the business of lending and creating money. This was a changing monetary environment that the more academic theorists such as David Hume and Adam Smith worried about, one where paper credit was supplanting gold as the medium of exchange. Both Hume and Smith had reluctantly acknowledged the benefits of paper money, but, and this needs to be stressed, both equivocated when it came to theorizing about whether it could replace gold. Both were metallists at heart, fearing the damage to the economy emanating from excessive issues of paper credit.

This tension between the use of gold and paper credit had been brought to the fore not only by the Ayr Bank failure in June 1772, but, more notably, by the French revolutionaries' excessive issues of paper money, the *assignats*. The hyperinflation generated by the *assignats*, which had been initially successful in financing the French Revolution between 1790 and 1793, must have convinced many of the dangers of paper money. John Law's earlier experiment to leave France specie-less in 1719–20 presented the sceptics with further evidence of the dangers of paper money. More recently the tension between gold and paper credit had been reinforced by the war-induced suspension of convertibility in 1797, a suspension that would last until 1821. It was, in other words, a time of profound change, forcing people to ask questions about the nature of money and the degree to which the monetary system could and should be based on gold. Thornton the banker had the confidence to understand developments on the ground and then to ~~encapsulate~~ *expressed* them in his theory of money and banking.

Theory develops as a result of challenges to accepted theory. Just as Adam Smith hoped to develop his approach to a free market system by challenging the theories of the retrospectively named mercantilists, and in particular Sir Thomas Mun, so also Thornton developed his views by challenging the existing orthodoxy on money as encapsulated in Smith's *Wealth of Nations*, and further down the line by Hume in the *Political Discourses* (1752). This led him to question systematically some of the main Smithian tenets relating to money. Unlike Smith, Thornton did not accept that real bills could be distinguished from fictitious bills, or that there was a unique quantity of money needed in the economy, or that this quantity of money should be determined in some mechanical way by reference to the stock of gold. Furthermore, he did not believe that there should be an automatic rule for the Bank of England to reduce its note issue when prices rose, as indicated by an increase in the market price of gold above the mint price.

Thornton the professional banker was obviously bemused by the academic Smith's division of bills of exchange into real bills—bills drawn in consequence of a real sale of goods—and fictitious bills—bills drawn for the same purpose as the real bill, i.e. their potential discountability, but which had not been 'drawn up in consequence of an actual sale of goods' (Thornton 1939: 85). Although the theorist in Smith may have wanted to show that there were some bills based on real transactions and others that were not, the banker in Thornton dismissed this distinction. He did not accept the view that real bills were drawn up on the collateral of a specific bundle of goods. The reality of the bill of exchange market was that the same bundle of goods could be used for the issuance of a multiplicity of bills of exchange:

Suppose that A sells one hundred pounds worth of goods to B at six months credit, and takes a bill at six months for it; and that B, within a month after, sells the same goods, at a like credit to C, taking a like bill; and again, that C, after another month, sells them to D, taking a like bill, and so on. There may then, at the end of six months, be six bills of £100 each existing at the same time; and every one of these may possibly have been discounted. Of all these bills, then, one only represents any actual property.   (1939: 86)

Furthermore, Thornton argued that the number of these bills could be increased through the extension of the duration of credit given on the sale of goods. Supposing, he argued, the period of credit was a year rather than six months, this would be the equivalent of doubling the amount of credit given relative to the first period.

This opening skirmish, while dismissing the Smithian distinction between real and fictitious bills, gives intimations of Thornton's attack on Smith for not understanding the wide range of financial instruments that could be used as money along with their different velocities of circulation. Acknowledging that

Smith had discussed the substitution of paper banknotes for gold, Thornton criticized him for limiting the choice to one between banknotes and gold. Smith had omitted to consider the substitutability of bills of exchange for gold:

Dr. Smith, although he discusses at some length the subject of paper circulation, does not at all advert to the tendency of bills of exchange to spare the use of bank paper, or to their faculty of supplying its place in many cases. (Thornton 1939: 91)

Thornton the banker then showed the way in which the bill of exchange could be used as money as it circulated from the grocer to the corn factor, to the sugar baker, to the merchant, to the country banker:

Let us imagine a farmer in the country to discharge a debt of £10 to his neighbouring grocer, by giving to him a bill for that sum, drawn on his cornfactor in London for grain sold in the metropolis; and the grocer to transmit the bill, he having previously indorsed it, to a neighbouring sugar-baker, in discharge of a like debt; and the sugar-baker to send it, when again indorsed, to a West India merchant in an outport, and the West India merchant to deliver it to his country banker, who also indorses it, and sends it into further circulation. The bill in this case will have effected five payments exactly as it were a £10 note payable to bearer on demand. (1939: 92)

Having shown the parallels between bills of exchange and paper banknotes in their use as mediums of exchange, Thornton then introduced the velocity of circulation into the discussion. He contended that there was not only a wide range of potential money substitutes to gold, but that each of these had varying degrees of rapidity of payment, i.e. differing velocities of circulation. The bill of exchange bore a rate of interest that the banknote did not. This meant that the velocity of circulation of a bill of exchange, particularly those drawn for large amounts, could be slower than that of the banknote. Furthermore, as the bill of exchange moved towards its maturity date, there was an increasing incentive for transactors to hold it so as to benefit from the interest paid on it rather than to use it as a medium of exchange.

By showing the multiplicity of alternative mediums of exchange to gold along with their varying velocities, Thornton was then able was to question Smith's proportionality argument that there was some 'regular proportion' between the circulating medium of a country and its quantity of trade and payments. Thornton attacked Smith for his view that: 'The *whole* paper money of *every kind* which can *easily* circulate in any country, never can exceed the value of the gold and silver of which it supplies the place, or which ('the commerce being supposed the same') would circulate there, if "there was no paper money"' (Thornton 1939: 95; emphasis added by Thornton). Thornton asked what Smith intended to include in the 'whole paper money'. Was it to include bills of exchange? In a sentence showing many affinities with John Law's definition of the broad money supply, Thornton questioned whether it should also include interest notes, exchequer bills, India bonds, and other mediums which resembled bills of exchange.

Thornton contended that it was not possible to quantify some fixed sum of 'the whole paper money' because of (*a*) the wide variety of different paper mediums of exchange, and (*b*) the differing velocities of circulation of these mediums of exchange: 'the same note may either effect ten payments in one day, or one payment in ten days; and one note, therefore, will effect the same payments in the one case, which it would require a hundred notes to effect in the other' (1939: 96). The state of confidence in the economy had a considerable influence on velocity. In times of crisis the public hoarded not only gold and silver but also Bank of England notes, as had been the case during the banking crisis of 1793. These hoarding propensities would reduce the velocity of circulation of both coins and banknotes. He would later criticize Montesquieu for not realizing the importance of velocity in the determination of the overall value of money in an economy: 'It is on the degree of the rapidity of the circulation of each [different type of money], combined with the consideration of quantity, and not on the quantity alone, that the value of the circulating medium of any country depends' (1939: 267).

Thornton was trenchant in criticizing the view that there was some rigid rule regulating the amount of gold required in the economy and that 'the appearance of gold is the only test of wealth' (1939: 110). He wrote of this:

> It is perfectly well understood among all commercial men, that gold coin is not an article in which all payments (though it is so promised) are at any time intended really to be made; that no fund ever was or can be provided by the bank which shall be sufficient for such a purpose; and that gold coin is to be viewed chiefly as a standard by which all bills and paper money should have their value regulated as exactly as possible; and that the main, and indeed, the only, point is to take all reasonable care that money shall in fact serve as that standard.   (1939: 111)

So to Thornton there was 'no fund' which could be provided by the Bank to ensure that all payments were made in gold coin. At most, gold was 'a standard' by which other media of exchange could be valued rather than the main medium of exchange. Gold constituted just a small part of the overall money supply.

The need for the CB to act as LOLR.

The First Mr Thornton: The Concerned Anti-Deflationist

From this foundation, incorporating a wide definition of the money supply, Thornton criticized Adam Smith's plan to have a stipulated money supply heavily reliant on the gold stock of the country. This plan necessitated cutting back on the excess banknotes issue of the Bank of England when it was perceived that gold was moving out of the British economy. This policy, he believed, could have highly deflationary effects and generate undesirable contagion fears in the banking environment. He believed that the Bank of England's policy to reduce the banknote issue in 1793 was due to Smith's influence:

> The bank, on this occasion, pursued, though only in a small degree, the path which a reader of Dr. Smith would consider him to prescribe, as in all cases the proper and effectual means of detaining or bringing back guineas. They lessened the number of their notes. (1939: 113)

This, he believed, was an undesirable policy in the circumstances of the time because there was a direct relationship between the Bank of England's bank-notes and the pyramid of paper credit that emanated from it to the London banks and on to the country banks. These banknotes issued by the Bank of England were analogous to high-powered money which, when reduced, endangered the London banks' activities, even leading to insolvency:

> A reduction of them which may seem moderate to men who have not reflected on this subject—a diminution, for instance, of one third or two-fifths, might, perhaps, be sufficient to produce a very general insolvency in London, of which the effect would be the suspension of confidence, the derangement of commerce, and the stagnation of manufactures throughout the country. (1939: 114)

Because of the possible deflationary and contagion effects induced by a sudden decrease in the Bank of England note issue, Thornton rejected the view that it was necessary to have some automatic relationship between gold and the Bank of England's note issue:

> The idea which some persons have entertained of its being at all times a paramount duty of the Bank of England to diminish its notes, in some sort of regular proportion to that diminution which it experiences in its gold, is, then, an idea which is merely theoretic. (1939: 116)

Note Thornton's dismissal of 'men who have not reflected on this subject' in the earlier quotation and 'some persons' in the latter extract. These are refer-ences to Adam Smith, the main proponent of this approach.

Thornton's rejection of Smith's gold–banknotes relationship did not imply a failure to understand the classical arguments in favour of deflation. He under-stood this approach very well, but he was not prepared to accept it:

> That a certain degree of pressure will urge the British merchants in general who buy of the manufacturers, as well as the manufacturers themselves, to sell their goods in order to raise money; that it will thus have some influence in lowering prices at home; and that the low prices at home may tempt merchants to export their articles in the hope of a better price abroad, is by no means an unreasonable supposition. (1939: 118)

However, Thornton, at least in this first part of *Paper Credit*, argued against deflationary policies for the following three reasons. The first reason related to the way in which deflation could adversely affect the overall state of demand when an eagerness to sell was matched by a reluctance to buy in the economy. This had knock-on effects, in that merchants would delay their orders from manufacturers and/or require them to give extended credit. In Keynesian terms, there was an increase in liquidity preference, and because of the tightened credit conditions the manufacturer, facing cash flow problems, might be unable to give such extended credit, causing his sales to fall:

But, then, it is to be observed . . . first that this more than ordinary eagerness of all our traders to sell, which seems so desirable, is necessarily coupled with a general reluctance to buy, which is exactly proportionate to it: it must be obvious, that, when the general body of merchants, being urged by the pecuniary difficulties of the time are selling their goods in order to raise money, they will naturally also delay making the accustomed purchases of the manufacturer. They require of him, at least, that he shall give them a more than usually extended credit; but the manufacturer, experiencing the same difficulty with the merchants, is quite unable to give this credit. The sales of the manufacturer are, therefore, suspended; but though these are stopped, his daily and weekly payments continue, provided his manufacture proceeds. In other words, his money is going out while no money is coming in; and this happens at an aera when the general state of credit is such, that he is not only able to borrow, in order to supply his extraordinary need, but when he is also pressed for a prompter payment than before of all the raw materials of his manufacture. Thus the manufacturer, on account of the unusual scarcity of money, may even, though the selling price of his article should be profitable, be absolutely compelled by necessity to slacken, if not suspend, his operations. To inflict such a pressure on the mercantile world as necessarily causes an intermission of manufacturing labour, is obviously not the way to increase that exportable produce, by the excess of which, above the imported articles, gold is to be brought into the country. (Thornton 1939: 118)

The second reason advanced against deflationary policies related to wage stickiness, a reason providing considerable resonance for modern Keynesians:

The tendency, however, of a very great and sudden reduction of the accustomed number of bank notes, is to create an unusual and temporary distress, and a fall of price arising from that distress. But a fall arising from temporary distress, will be attended probably with no correspondent fall in the rate of wages; for the fall of price, and the distress, will be understood to be temporary, and the rate of wages, we know, is not so variable as the price of goods.   (1939: 119)

Hicks (1967) argued that Thornton had advanced two Keynesian arguments, liquidity preference and wage stickiness, to counter the doctrine that deflationary policies would work. Thornton invoked a further Keynesian argument suggesting that a general deflation would reduce the marginal efficiency of capital. This would happen when uncertainty and business pessimism lowered the prospective returns on capital. This in turn would cause investment decisions to be changed or suspended:

When a time either of multiplied failures, or even of much disappointment in the expected means of effecting payments arises, plans of commerce and manufacture, as well as general improvement of every kind, which had been entered upon, are changed or suspended, and part of the labour which had been bestowed proves, therefore, to have been thrown away. (1939: 120)

[handwritten: ~ Believed in necessary as 1 Ms in genics.]

[Thornton criticized the Bank of England for following in 1793 'what seems likely to have been the advice of Dr A. Smith' by emphasizing 'too much restricting its notes in the late seasons of alarm, than on that of too much enlarging them'] (1939: 127). This is a theme which he reiterated five pages later: 'the bank, at the time of the failure of its cash payments, had lent too little rather than too much' (1939: 132).

The importance that Thornton gave to his dismissal of Smith on this issue is further borne out, in chapter v, in his discussion of the balance of trade. There Thornton returned to his criticism of Smith's recommendation to reduce the banknote issue when the market price of gold was above the mint price: 'Dr. Smith, as was remarked in the beginning of the former chapter, in some degree leads his reader to assume the Bank of England to be in fault (that is, to have issued too many notes) whenever an excess of the market price above the mint price of gold takes place' (1939: 148). Thornton questioned whether it was desirable to reduce the banknote issue in such circumstances. The balance of trade deficit could have been caused by overseas remittances to finance the war effort and/or an adverse harvest. In such circumstances deflating the economy by reducing the banknote issue rather than rectifying the situation would only cause a further deterioration. Thornton's explanation went as follows:

> In order, then, to induce the country having the favourable balance to take all its payment in goods, and no part of it in gold, it would be requisite not only to prevent goods from being very dear, but even to render them excessively cheap. It would be necessary, therefore, that the bank should not only not encrease its paper, but that it should, perhaps, very greatly diminish it, if it would endeavour to prevent gold from going out in part of payment of the unfavourable balance. And if the bank do this, then there will arise other questions, which Dr. Smith leaves totally out of his consideration; namely, whether the bank, in the attempt to produce this very low price, may not, in a country circumstanced as Great Britain is, so exceedingly distress trade and discourage manufactures as to impair, in the manner already specified, those sources of our return-ing wealth to which we must chiefly trust for the restoration of our balance of trade, and for bringing back the tide of gold into Great Britain. (1939: 151–2)

Thornton's argument appears to be that the crisis of 1797 was one provoked by the war, which necessitated monetary remittances overseas to finance the war and which caused interferences in foreign trade, thereby exacerbating the balance of payments problem. Add to these problems the harvest failures of 1799 and 1800 to come up with a set of exogenous circumstances producing a balance of payments that in Thornton's view had nothing to do with the Bank of England's banknote issue. This balance of payments deficit, caused by the overseas war payments and the import of corn to make up the deficiency caused by the bad harvests, put pressure on the exchange rate. The market price of gold went above the mint price of gold, and gold bullion was exported from Great Britain. Smith held that, if the market price of gold was above the mint price, then this was evidence of an excessive quantity of paper issued by the Bank of England. His solution was for the Bank of England to reduce the quantity of its banknotes in circulation. Thornton inveighed against this approach, remarking that there was 'much of inaccuracy and error in the doctrine of Dr. Smith on this subject' (1939: 150). Smith, he felt, was unable to make the distinction between a high market price of gold caused by (1) an excess quantity of banknotes in circulation, or (2) a balance of payments deficit caused by external factors such as an act of nature that produced a bad harvest. In not looking at the causes behind the high price of gold, Thornton believed that Smith's remedy, namely, the reduction of the bank-note issue, would create an excessive deflation, which would 'so exceedingly distress trade and manufactures as to impair, in the manner already specified, those sources of our returning wealth to which we must chiefly trust for the restoration of our balance of trade, and for bringing back the tide of gold into Great Britain' (1939: 152).

Monetary Policy

Thornton went on to add that, even if the Bank greatly restricted the note issue, there could be a considerable lag before the full effects of the restriction were felt. By this time the situation may have righted itself and the deflationary

Time lag.

effects produced by the note reduction would not be necessary. Thornton believed that it was very desirable that the Bank of England should avoid excessive contractions of the note issue, also noting that the Bank of England's banknotes acted as a type of high-powered money for the country banks which, if reduced, 'may possibly annihilate, before it is aware, a part or even almost the whole of the circulating country bank notes' (1939: 152). Even when the exchange was against Britain, the right policy may have been to expand credit rather than restrict it. In such circumstances the right approach of the Bank was to compensate for the loss of gold through an expansion of credit, in other words to act as a lender of last resort so as to maintain the stability of the banking system. Even if the gold reserve was exhausted, the policy should not be stopped. Instead, suspension of convertibility could be introduced.

In the headings of chapter viii Thornton continued to highlight the 'errors of Dr. A Smith on the subject of excessive paper'. By page 200 he was attacking Smith's discussion of the tendency of an excessive paper circulation to send gold out of the country as being 'particularly defective and unsatisfactory'. There were two kinds of error relating to the Bank of England, and in attacking them one sees Thornton directing his attention again to Adam Smith:

Two kinds of error on the subject of the affairs of the Bank of England have been prevalent. Some political persons have assumed it to be a principle, that in proportion as the gold of the bank lessens, its paper, or, as is sometimes said, its loans ... ought to be reduced ... A maxim of this sort would lead to universal failure. A sentiment has prevailed among other persons, which has bordered on a very different extreme. They have complained of nothing, except the too scanty liberality of the bank, and have seen no danger in almost any extension of its discounts, or profusion in the issue of its paper, provided only the bills discounted ... were real bills, and were those also of sufficiently safe and responsible houses.   (1939: 227)

Later Thornton observed:

Dr. A. Smith ... has asserted the necessity of a limitation of paper ... but he has done this in terms which are inaccurate, and he has given an erroneous and inadequate idea of the evil which may result from a very extended emission.   (1939: 245)

Thornton's low esteem for Smith as a monetary economist was one that would have been further reinforced by Smith's support for the usury laws, which Thornton condemned later in the book.

The Second Mr Thornton: The Concerned Anti-Inflationist

So far the discussion has highlighted the first Mr Thornton, the concerned anti-deflationist, critical of Adam Smith's recommendations and critical of the Bank of England in 1793 for following Smith's implied recommendation of reducing the money supply by cutting back at the Bank of England's note issue.

Before discussing the second Mr Thornton it is apt to remind readers that the first Mr Thornton had effectively deconstructed the quantity theory of money:

$$MV = PY$$

He had shown how, on the left-hand side of this equation, it was possible for a wide range of financial instruments to be used as money (M), and therefore questioned the viewpoint that there was one unique quantity of money for the economy. He had also introduced a variable velocity of circulation of money (V), and this alongside an ever-changing money supply rendered the left-hand side of the equation highly unstable. On the right-hand side he had introduced shocks to the system in the form of harvest failures and war that greatly affected both P and Y. Thornton's deconstruction of the quantity theory of money showed the dangers of dogmatic pursuit of a monetary policy that aimed at controlling the money supply. Consistently with this approach, he praised the Bank of England for its policy during 1799 and 1800 in not reducing the banknote issue at a time when the market price of gold had risen out of line with the mint price.

From this point onwards, however, the tone of the book changes. Hicks (1967) surmised that this change in tone, manifest in the second half of the book, was due to the fact that it was written shortly before its publication and by this time the harvest crisis was over and the Peace of Amiens had been signed in March 1802. I do not really accept this viewpoint because examination of the Thornton manuscripts, as shown above, appears to indicate that the book was written in 1801. An alternative, and perhaps more plausible, view may be that Thornton wished to protect his eldest brother Samuel, the Governor of the Bank of England from 1799 to 1801, from criticism of a policy which Thornton believed was very necessary at the time. By the end of 1801 Samuel was no longer the Governor, and Thornton could embark on showing the danger of a policy of maintaining inconvertibility. The problem was that inconvertibility created an environment in which over-issue could thrive, thereby generating inflation. There was, therefore, in Thornton's opinion, the need to control the note issue.

Thornton metamorphosed in the second half of the book—until the final chapter—from a gentle anti-deflationist to a more orthodox anti-inflationist preaching against the excessive issue of paper money. Gone was the concern about the impossibility of defining the money supply, the problem of a variable velocity of circulation, and the difficulties created by supply shocks on the right-hand side of the equation of exchange. Instead, Thornton reconstructed the quantity theory, placing great emphasis on the potential of the left-hand side of the equation (M and V) to generate inflation. The second Mr Thornton had started to appear in *Paper Credit*. As noted above, Thornton had recognized, in the preface, that the book incorporated these dual personalities, the anti-deflationist and the anti-inflationist:

The earlier parts of the work having tended to shew the evil of a too great and sudden diminution of our circulating medium, some of the latter chapters are employed in pointing out the consequences of a too great augmentation of it. (1939: 68)

That said, it is difficult to understand the rapidity of Thornton's transformation into an anti-inflationist:

It has thus been admitted that paper possesses the faculty of enlarging the quantity of commodities by giving life to some new industry. It has, however, been affirmed, that the encrease of industry will by no means keep pace with the augmentation of paper. The question now to be considered is, whether, if we suppose thirty five millions of new paper to be suddenly issued, the fresh industry which would, consequently, be excited, would create a quantity of goods, the sale of which would give employment to all the new paper. (1939: 239)

In fact at this point Thornton appears to lose the reasoned logic that characterized so much of the first half of the book. This occurs through his reintroduction of the concept of the velocity of circulation of the new paper money.

As shown, he had been very effective in focusing attention on the velocity of circulation of money in the first half of the book. Taking up a concept that had been first introduced into economic theory by Sir William Petty and John Locke, Thornton had shown that Smith's viewpoint, that there was a unique quantity of money necessary in the economy, was erroneous. The actual quantity of money required was related to its velocity of circulation. A high velocity of circulation could accommodate a low stock of money and vice versa.

But he then assumed that, when there was a new issue of banknotes, it would be accompanied by a very considerable upward hike in the velocity of circulation of money. In his example he suggested that an increase of £35 million of new paper 'will thus effect in a year the sale of goods to the extent of two or three thousand millions' (1939: 240). This meant that the velocity of circulation of the new credit to the increased banknote issue varied between 57 and 85. He arrived at this amount by assuming that the new money generated new expenditure every three days, so that a potential expenditure of billions could be created by the initial injection of paper money into the system.

> In order, therefore, to account for the employment of the thirty-five millions, we must assume, if we allow no rise in prices to take place, such a new quantity of goods to be called into existence by the magic influence of the new paper, as to become a subject for purchases, amounting, in a year, to no less than these two or three thousand millions.
>
> (1939: 240)

While admitting that the case he presented was inaccurate in that he had not taken into consideration 'the numberless sums borrowed and repaid', he then assumed that such transactions bore a 'nearly uniform proportion to those of the other class' and that therefore the general inference that he intended to make was 'just'. Milton Friedman has used the analogy of excess money burning a hole in the pockets of transactors. To push this analogy further, Thornton seemed to be suggesting that the excess money would act as a type of flame-thrower, vastly increasing expenditure in the economy.

In discussions on this issue Professor David Laidler made the point to me that he believed Thornton was adopting a very heavy-handed ironic approach, attempting a *reductio ad absurdum* argument against those who claimed that increases in the Bank of England note issue were never responsible for increases in prices. This is a possible interpretation of this passage, but it may be countered that irony and *reductio ad absurdum* were not part of Thornton's literary toolbox. Thornton was a very serious individual, not, in my opinion, prone to Swiftian irony. There is a difficult choice of interpretation here. If the irony argument is accepted, then the passage can be rationalized as part of Thornton's attack on the inflation-generating potential of an increase in the money supply. If it is not, then it appears that Thornton has abandoned logic on the issue. That is the problem, as I see it, in that Thornton becomes schizophrenic at this point as he moves from the concerned anti-deflationist to the worried anti-inflationist. Skaggs (2005) does not accept this possible schizophrenia on Thornton's part.

Thornton concluded that (1) Bank of England paper is such that 'a superfluous quantity of it never be for a long time retained in any quarter', and (2) 'the vast encrease of it, which, for the sake of more convenient discussion, was assumed to take place, cannot possibly create such a new capital as shall furnish the new paper with employment'. In other words, he assumed that there was a very high velocity of circulation of the new paper money because no one wanted to hold it as paper per se, and, concomitantly, the elasticity of output was low so that the increased supply of money, spurred on by its increasing velocity, would find its way into raising prices rather than producing more goods and services.

Thornton then modified his analysis to take into consideration the open nature of the economy, arguing that the excess money supply would also have an adverse effect on the balance of payments, pushing it into deficit, and cause the exchange rate to fall, i.e. the cost of discounting British bills of exchange on foreign markets would increase. He attacked Locke and other writers for analysing this issue incorrectly and confusing the consequence with the cause. According to Thornton, Locke believed that it was the balance of trade deficit that led to a loss of specie and bullion:

> Mr. Locke, however, is very far from leading his reader to conceive that the balance of trade depends on the quantity of circulating medium issued; for he describes an unfavourable balance as resulting from a 'losing trade,' and from an 'over great consumption of foreign commodities;' terms which seem to imply an unprosperous state of commerce, and a too expensive disposition in the people, and which naturally lead to the conclusion, that the prosperity of the country will effectually secure us against the danger of the exportation of our coin, whatever may be the quantity of our paper. (1939: 248)

In the debate on the Bullion Committee Report, Thornton would once again attack Locke on this issue, producing the striking analogy of a French fisherman smuggling £1,000 of brandy into Britain. According to the Lockean approach, it was the brandy which forced out the gold from Britain, and not the gold which attracted the brandy (see Thornton 1939: 353–4). Thornton argued that Locke was confusing the consequence, namely, the import of brandy, with the cause, the excess supply of money. It was not the balance of payments that was the problem, but the excessive increase in the money supply which was producing the balance of payments deficit.

Thornton's use of an exceptional, indeed outlandish, estimate for velocity enabled him to change from the first Mr Thornton of the strong anti-deflationist views to the second Mr Thornton of the strong anti-inflationist views. In my opinion, it is a serious flaw of Thornton's analysis, a flaw that was instrumental in suppressing the full emergence of the third Mr Thornton.

The Third Mr Thornton

The development of the third Mr Thornton may be gleaned from his description of the different types of media of exchange that could be used as substitutes for metallic money, the differing velocities of these media of exchange, and his criticisms of Montesquieu, Hume, and Smith in the final chapter of *Paper Credit*. As shown above, using this analysis Thornton could contend that there was no unique quantity of money for the economy and that gold only constituted a small part of the overall money supply. This part of the analysis shows that he was concerned with determining the nature of different media of exchange and the way in which paper credit had been substituted for gold as the major media of exchange. Thornton, without blowing this trumpet too loudly, believed that paper money had effectively taken over from gold as the main medium of exchange. This was not a view that was accepted at the time. There was a strong metallist lobby. The importance that Thornton attached to paper credit, and his opposition to these metallists who viewed paper credit as a dangerous monetary development, may be clearly seen in an important footnote in chapter vii:

In some of the democratic pamphlets of the present day, bank notes of every kind are spoken of not merely as liable to be carried to excess, or to be issued by irresponsible persons, or as producing particular evils, but as radically and incurably vicious; they are considered in the light of a complete fraud upon the public, which is practised by the rich, and connived at by the government; and the very issue of them has been stigmatised as equivalent to the crime of forgery. The resemblance of bank notes to other paper, and the resemblance of a promise on paper to any other promise, have been touched upon with a view of exposing the absurdity of those doctrines.   (1939: 171)

This third Mr Thornton was the champion of paper credit. He viewed it as the lifeblood of exchange in the banking milieu in which he worked, and, furthermore, a type of money superior to gold in times of crisis:

In a commercial country, subjected to that moderate degree of occasional alarm and danger which we have experienced, gold is by no means that kind of circulating medium which is the most desirable. It is apt to circulate with very different degrees of rapidity, and also to be suddenly withdrawn, in consequence of its being an article intrinsically valuable, and capable of being easily concealed. If, during the war, it had been our only medium of payment, we might sometimes have been almost totally deprived of the means of carrying on our pecuniary transactions; and much confusion in the affairs of our merchants, great interruption of manufacturing labour, and very serious evils to the state, might have been the consequences.   (1939: 276)

If this is the case, why did this third Mr Thornton not go further and push for the demonetization of gold and silver and their complete substitution by paper credit? After all, he was writing in a period when the convertibility of paper banknotes into gold had been suspended by the Bank of England. If society appeared to be working well without gold, why could it not go further and demonetize its use on a permanent basis? Thornton could have become the great emancipator of paper credit. This was not to happen. In my opinion there were three factors, additional to his earlier exaggeration of the velocity of paper money, that suppressed the emergence of the third Mr Thornton. These were (1) the usury laws, (2) the political instability of the period, and (3) Thornton's own position as a leading London banker. The first of these provides a theoretical reason why Thornton did not push his analysis further. The other two factors, while not theoretically important, were also strong constraints on limiting his analysis.

The first complexity that Thornton faced was the imposition by the usury laws of a ceiling rate of interest of 5 per cent on the Bank of England. The continued maintenance of the usury laws meant that the Bank of England could not use the rate of interest to limit the demand for loans when there was excessive demand, or use the rate of interest to attract gold into London when there was an outflow of gold due to a balance of payments deficit.

In analysing this issue, Thornton first of all investigated why the business community demanded loans. The reason was one of profit. Here he was just reiterating the link between the rate of interest and profits that had been earlier presented by Joseph Massie in *The Natural Rate of Interest* (1750) and later by David Hume in the *Political Discourses* (1752). As long as profit was above the rate of interest, then it was in the interest of business borrowers to demand loans. However, there was a major complication in the process in that the Bank could not use the rate of interest to reduce the demand for loans because the usury laws—first imposed in 1545—prevented the Bank from charging more than a 5 per cent rate of interest. This ban remained in place even in time of war. During war, particularly at the time when there was an increased hope for the termination of hostilities, the possibilities of profit increased for merchants. This meant a rightward shift in the demand curve for credit, but, as the interest rate could not be raised above 5 per cent, there was no way in which the demand for credit could be choked off. The rate of interest was too cheap, and, as long as it was, merchants would continue to borrow at this advantageous rate:

It is, therefore, unreasonable to presume that there will always be a disposition in the borrowers at the bank to prescribe to themselves exactly those bounds which a regard to the safety of the bank would suggest. The interest of the two parties is not the same in this respect. The borrowers, in consequence of that artificial state of things which is produced by the law against usury, obtain their loans too cheap. That which they obtain too cheap they demand in too great quantity. (Thornton 1939: 254–5)

On this issue Hayek (1939: 50) suggested that Thornton was making the distinction that Wicksell (1898) would later develop between the market and the natural rate of interest. As the market rate of interest was below the natural rate of interest, which was determined by profits, there was a sizeable and growing demand for credit, which could not be choked off by increasing the market interest rate. Thornton then asked if the increase in loans would not lead to a lower rate of profit because of the increased amount of capital in use. The answer, he believed, was negative because it was necessary to distinguish between the increase in nominal capital generated by the increased loans and the increase in real capital. For him the 'rate of mercantile profit depends on the quantity of this *bona fide* capital and not on the amount of the nominal value which an encreased emission of paper may give to it' (1939: 255). So, from Thornton's perspective, the usury laws greatly weakened the interest rate weapon for the Bank of England when there was an excessive demand for credit. While other banks successfully circumvented the usury laws, the *de facto* 'national bank' status of the Bank of England prevented it from pushing the rate above the maximum 5 per cent allowed by the usury laws:

> The bank is prohibited, by the state of the law, from demanding, even in time of war, an interest of more than five per cent, which is the same rate at which it discounts in a period of profound peace. It might, undoubtedly, at all seasons, sufficiently limit paper by means of the price at which it lends, if the legislature did not interpose an obstacle to the constant adoption of this principle of restriction. (1939: 254)

Earlier, on 31 March 1797, when Thornton gave evidence to the Committee of Secrecy of the House of Commons investigating the outstanding demands of the Bank of England, he had emphasized the difficulty of the Bank's pursuing monetary policy when the rate of interest was fixed. Thornton had been asked a question on the effects of the Bank of England's reducing its discounts below the demand for them. He started his answer as follows: 'I should think there would be no great difficulty in answering that question, if the unnaturally low interest of money resulting from the Usury Laws which confine the Rate of discounting at the Bank to 5l. per cent did not perplex the question' (1939: 307). Note his emphasis on 'the unnaturally low [rate of] interest'. As the usury laws were not repealed until 1854, the specific British institutional environment prevented the Bank from using the flexible interest rate weapon, one that would have given the Bank of England far greater scope in the management of monetary policy, and also helped to reduce the gold stock in its vaults that it needed to keep for emergencies. He also tried to show how speculative attacks against the currency could increase the demand for loans as during this period the possibilities of profit-making would increase. The way to stop such speculative demand for the currency was to raise the rate of interest, but this was not feasible because of the usury laws.

The second factor that may have prevented the further development of Thornton's analysis was the highly unstable political climate. The 1790s had been a period of continuous political problems. The revolution in France, followed by war with France, created a climate of great political uncertainty.

Continued warfare with France meant that the British economy had to ensure that, according to Thornton, there was a certain 'reservoir of gold' to finance the war. Gold was also needed to pay for supplies of corn in the case of harvest failures, two of which had occurred in recent years.

The usury laws, along with the political instability argument, present two good reasons why Thornton would not have been prepared to champion a paper credit system unshackled by the gold anchor. There was a third factor, namely, Thornton's professional standing in the business world. When writing *Paper Credit* and later acting as a member of the Bullion Committee, Thornton presented the stereotype of a leading banker, prudent in thought and in action. While, from a theoretical viewpoint, Thornton could grasp the declining significance of metallic money, particularly during the inconvertibility period, he would have been unprepared in practice to take this to its logical conclusion, that of a specie-less monetary environment. Such a suggestion would have been too daring and innovative for the times he lived in and would have affected his standing in the banking community. Any suggestion that society could in the long run do without gold and silver would have been considered a dangerous doctrine to preach. Thornton would have acquired the reputation of being an impractical dreamer and a dangerous innovator—not the type of reputation that a banker would wish to acquire. He was just one member of the banking community, albeit a well-established insider given the size of his bank, his family's background, and his brother's position as Governor of the Bank of England. He would have become very much an outsider if he had gone round London advocating the permanent break-up of the gold standard.

It may be argued that this exegetical interpretation of the multi-personae Mr Thornton is excessive, but it is quite clear from chapter ix of *Paper Credit* that he did wish to present at least the first two Mr Thorntons: 'It was the object of several former Chapters to point out the evil of a too contracted issue of paper. The general tendency of the present, as well as the preceding one, has been to shew the danger of a too extended emission' (1939: 227). It could also be argued that the first Mr Thornton became less and less prominent at the expense of the second Mr Thornton, and even more so the third Mr Thornton, when he sat on the Select Committee on the High Price of Gold Bullion. Then, along with Horner and Huskisson, he would argue strongly in favour of the return to convertibility. The conclusion of the committee in 1807 was as follows: 'it is, in either case, most desirable for the public that our circulating medium should again be conformed, as speedily as circumstances will permit, to its real and legal standard, Gold Bullion' (Select Committee on the High Price of Gold Bullion 1807: 7).

Was this a case of Thornton the liberal becoming conservative as he became older? Could it have been that the growing problems with his bank forced him to adopt a more conservative public persona? One can only conjecture, but the greatness of *Paper Credit* is that it does provide a view of the mind of an economist who was unprepared to accept the apparent orthodoxy of David Hume and Adam Smith, who outlined the potential for the Bank of England to act as a lender of last resort, who showed the increasingly powerful role of paper credit in the monetary economy, and who gave strong intimations of the further development of a monetary system that did not need to be based on metallic money. It may be further conjectured that, if the usury laws had been abolished prior to Thornton's writing of the *Paper Credit*, the third Mr Thornton might have appeared to take centre stage.

References

Acaster, E. J. T. (1974–5), 'Henry Thornton—The Banker', *Three Banks Review* (Dec., Mar., June).

Beaugrand, P. (1981), *Henry Thornton: Un précurseur de J. M. Keynes* (Paris).

Clapham, J. (1944), *The Bank of England: A History 1794–1914*, 2 vols (Cambridge).

Hague, William (2007), *William Wilberforce: The Life of the Great Anti-Slave Campaigner* (London).

Hayek, F. A. von (1939), Introduction to Thornton, *An Enquiry into the Nature and Effects of the Paper Credit of Great Britain* (London).

Hicks, J. R. (1967), *Critical Essays in Monetary Theory* (Oxford).

Hume, D. (1752), *Political Discourses* (Edinburgh).

Keynes, John Maynard (1926), *The End of Laissez-Faire* (London).

Laidler, D. (1987), 'Henry Thornton', in J. Eatwell, M. Milgate, and P. Newman (eds), *The New Palgrave: A Dictionary of Economics* (London).

Meacham, S. (1964), *Henry Thornton of Clapham 1760–1815* (Cambridge, Mass.).

Murphy, Antoin E. (2003), 'The Multi-Personae Mr. Henry Thornton', *European Journal of the History of Economic Thought*, 10.

Reisman, D. A. (1971), 'Henry Thornton and Classical Monetary Economics', *Oxford Economic Papers*, new ser., 23/1 (Mar.).

Rist, C. (1938), *Histoire des doctrines relatives au crédit et à la monnaie* (Paris).

Schama, Simon (2005), *Rough Crossings: Britain, the Slaves and the American Revolution* (London).

Select Committee on the High Price of Gold Bullion (1807), *Report* (London).

Skaggs, N. (2005), 'Treating Schizophrenia: A Comment on Antoin Murphy's Diagnosis of Henry Thornton's Theoretical Condition', *European Journal of the History of Economic Thought*, 12.

Smith, A. (1776), *An Inquiry into the Nature and Causes of the Wealth of Nations* (London).

Thornton, H. (1939), *An Enquiry into the Nature and Effects of the Paper Credit of Great Britain* (London, 1802), ed. with introd. F. A. von Hayek (London).

Wicksell, K. (1898), *Interest and Prices*, trans. R. F. Kahn (London, 1936).

10

Conclusion: New Ideas from Fascinating People

This book has attempted to show the very considerable legacy that the selected seventeenth- to early nineteenth-century writers left to macroeconomics. It has tried to demonstrate the filiation of ideas from these fascinating people to the subject that would be retrospectively defined as macroeconomics in the 1930s. Drawing together the ideas of the selected economists, we arrive at a formidable list of contributions that they made in providing a skeletal framework for modern macroeconomics. These contributions, along with their authors, may be listed as follows:

National income accounting	Petty, Cantillon, Quesnay
The distinction between income and wealth	Petty
The income = expenditure identity	Petty
The circular flow of income	Petty, Law, Cantillon, Hume, Quesnay
The multiplier approach	Petty, Quesnay
Economic growth	Hume, Quesnay, Turgot, Smith
The role of labour	Petty, Cantillon, Quesnay, Smith
The role of capital	Quesnay, Turgot, Smith
The nature and definition of money	Law, Cantillon, Hume, Turgot, Smith, Thornton
The demand for money	Law, Cantillon

For some commentators, seduced by the technical wizardry of modern macroeconomics, these contributions may represent just a laundry list of ideas. They will glance at the chapters of this book and exclaim 'So what'. So what indeed! Is it not time to give our subject some further colour? Is there no room for observing and analysing the way ideas were conceptualized and then propagated? Is there no role for intuition any more? Good macroeconomics involves considerable intuition, an intuition that develops from investigating blank or blurred spaces and then linking ideas together to fill them. From this perspective there is a great deal to learn from the early macroeconomists. They faced the great blank spaces of economics and creatively imagined ways of filling some parts of them. They imagined, they intuited, they conceptualized, and they created.

They were pioneers. In a way we can imagine them facing a series of macro-economic mountains and then progressively scaling them, peak after peak. Sir William Petty climbed the first peak. Petty wanted to measure the wealth and income of the nation. There was no central statistics office available to him to produce the statistics he needed, and even if there had been, nobody had conceptualized the macroeconomic aggregates that would be necessary to quantify the wealth and the income of the nation. Petty, in true pioneering mode, overcame many of these difficulties. In a couple of pages in *Verbum Sapienti* he set in place many of the foundation stones of macroeconomics, starting with the national income identity:

$$National\ income = national\ expenditure$$

Petty reasoned that, if it was possible to calculate national expenditure, then it would be possible to measure the main sources of national income. As shown in Chapter 2, he used his friend John Graunt's calculation of the total popu-lation and multiplied it by his own estimate of per capita average expenditure to produce his measurement of national expenditure. Then, by dint of meas-uring the income returns from wealth assets such as lands, housing, cattle, etc., he arrived at an estimate for the income derived from non-human wealth. Subtracting this from his estimate for national expenditure, he arrived at an estimate for the income derived by labour. Then, by capitalizing all the differ-ent income streams, he was able to produce an estimate of the wealth of the nation. All of this was achieved in a couple of pages of text. It was a remarkable tour de force.

Some might say that this was just back-of-the-envelope macroeconomics and that the statistics accompanying it were all wrong. Back-of-the-envelope style macroeconomics has a long lineage that Petty started. It would be fol-lowed by Irving Fisher's equation of exchange, $MV = PT$; later by Keynes's national income identity, $Y = C + I$; and still later by Sir John Hicks's IS/LM—all powerful back-of-the-envelope additions to the toolkits of macroecono-mists. As for the statistics, of course they were shaky estimates, but at least they established a base for further analysis.

John Law produced many important concepts for the development of macroeconomics that have been noted above—concepts such as the demand for money, the implications for inflation when the money supply goes out of line with the demand for money, the law of one price, the circular flow of income, and the money in advance requirement. But, above all, he provided vision. He was able to take an overview of the macroeconomic society that he lived in and question whether its monetary system needed to be based on an intrinsically valuable metallic money. He opposed the view that money was the value for which goods are exchanged and replaced it with one where he defined money as the value by which goods are exchanged. His substitution of the preposition 'for' with the preposition 'by' in his definition of money opened up completely new vistas for monetary economy. Why shackle the monetary system to the unpredictable production of the world's gold and silver mines? Money, fiat money, was a matter of confidence between trans-actors. Why not replace metallic money with paper money and bank credit? Law ambitiously tried to do this. That he failed with his visionary system should not be the reason for condemning him to the economic underworld of the wrong ideas of dead men.

One Lawian externality was the way in which he antagonized Richard Cantillon. Initially friends and joint venturers in the colonization project for French Louisiana, their relations deteriorated when Law threatened Cantillon with incarceration in the Bastille while Law was the effective prime minister of France. The relationship deteriorated further when Cantillon turned down Law's offer to return to France and help him restructure the Mississippi System during the summer of 1720. Ultimately Cantillon ended up a very rich man because of his ability to identify and exploit the weaknesses of Law's System. Cantillon's use of his macroeconomic knowledge should serve as an inspir-ation to young economists who believe that they can use their knowledge to make fortunes out of the twists and turns of global financial markets. The tension between Law and Cantillon went further because it motivated the latter to produce his version of the macroeconomic system in his effort to identify where Law went wrong with the Mississippi System. This led to Cantillon producing his extraordinary model-building approach, which serves as a lesson to all model builders on how to identify the very core of the workings of the macroeconomy. The *Essay on the Nature of Trade in General* represents an apotheosis in macroeconomic theory. How do we model the macroeconomy?

Cantillon did of course start with the 'Let us assume' approach. He assumed a single large landed estate, which acted as the model for a primitive com-mand, barter, and closed economy. But, as shown above, he then transformed the single large landed estate into the complexities of a modern economy. He relaxed progressively the initial assumptions so that the command element transformed into a market structure, the barter element converted into a monetary economy, and the closed economy progressed into an open econ-omy. Furthermore, central to the activation of the new market-based open monetary economy was the entrepreneur, the catalyst for production and exchange. The transaction flows derived through this basic market-driven monetary structure were then aggregated to produce Cantillon's macroeco-nomic architecture in the form of the circular flow of income. Cantillon outlined the ways in which flows of income, output, and expenditure would move through the three socio-economic classes that he created: farmers, landlords, and urban producers. His analysis of the circular flow of income was designed so that he could estimate the amount of money required to finance this circular flow. He wanted to determine the equilibrium quantity of money demanded in the economy. Once this was achieved, he could ask questions concerning what happened when the supply of money went out of line with this equilibrium quantity of money demanded. The answers to these questions produced a striking taxonomy of monetary transmission channels. Mark Blaug (1962) tagged this approach the 'Cantillon effect', one that attempted to analyse how changed money balances circulated through different streams of economic activity to end up influencing output, prices, and the balance of payments. Modern commentators discuss it as the 'black box' of the monetary transmission process.

François Quesnay took Cantillon's circular flow of income analysis to a new level by encapsulating it in a diagrammatic format in the 'Tableau économique'. In a way, Quesnay, through the 'Tableau', did to Cantillon's *Essai* what Hicks later did to Keynes's *General Theory* through IS/LM analysis. It meant, in both cases, that the ideas of Cantillon, and later Keynes, could be diagrammatically represented. For generations of economists nurtured on Hicksian IS/LM analysis, the power of such diagrammatic representations should not be underestimated.

Quesnay, while adapting Cantillon's circular flow of income process to a diagrammatic format, went much further than Cantillon. The latter, perhaps excessively influenced by Vico's cyclical analysis of human history, was unable to grasp the potential for the economy to expand. He still had a mercantilist belief that economic activity was a zero sum game, with one individual gaining at the expense of the other and nations doing likewise. Quesnay, through his analysis of agricultural output, was able to grasp the potential for the agricultural economy to produce surplus product in the form of net product. This meant that the zero sum conception of economic activity could be changed. The economic circle could expand; economic growth was possible. This was one of the major discoveries of the Enlightenment, for it showed that mankind could advance not just through the progress of ideas, but also through the expansion of output. The peak that macroeconomics had achieved through the discovery of the circular flow of income had led to the attainment of a further peak, the realization that economic growth was possible. But once on this peak, economists—by the time of the late 1750s they had started to be called such—realized that there were further macroeconomic mountain ranges to be scaled.

Quesnay had provided some insights into what could be developed in these new ranges with his incorporation of the term 'advances' into his analysis. He realized that growth was not just due to human endeavour in the form of the labour input. Labour, combining with machinery, could greatly increase output. Quesnay added that entrepreneurial talent was also a key to the dynamic mix that would expand output. Unfortunately, he was somewhat blinkered in that he believed that it was only the agricultural sector that was capable of generating economic growth. However, one of his contemporaries, Anne Robert Jacques Turgot, was ready and waiting to push the analysis in a different direction.

Turgot, like Cantillon a man of great conciseness, introduced economists to the term 'capital' in his *Réflexions*. The word 'capital' had already been used in its financial sense, but Turgot showed the importance of capital as an economic concept. He showed that increased capital formation was a way to drive the economic growth of the nation. In order to do this, he linked capital together with the rate of interest. Following this, he produced a loanable funds theory for the determination of the rate of interest. Capital formation, economic growth, the rate of interest, and the loanable funds theory of the rate of interest were all put in place by Turgot as he expertly scaled peak after peak showing how increased savings could lower the rate of interest, which would increase capital formation, which in turn would increase economic growth. The topographical analogies that have been presented here are apposite in the case of Turgot. In order to show the importance of the rate of interest, he asked his readers to consider an area of land covered by water and then the gains in arable land to be made by lowering the water level. This reduction in the water level he compared to the effects of a lowering of the rate of interest in the economy.

Parallel to these developments in France, Scotland was producing its own contributions to the Enlightenment through the work of David Hume and Adam Smith. Hume introduced a wide range of discussions on money, inflation, the balance of payments, the rate of interest, the national debt, etc. Using his philosophical approach, Hume posed a range of questions that forced readers to rethink some of the accepted views of his time. What, for example, would happen if the money supply was dramatically increased or decreased, supposing that the money supply of Great Britain was reduced by four-fifths or increased fivefold? These types of question enabled him to outline his views on the way money could influence prices, output, and the balance of payments both in the short and in the long run and how the economy could return to an equilibrium state. Hume also pushed for the liberalization of international trade. He wanted all the European countries to grow together and not at the expense of one another.

Adam Smith posed the question, what constituted the wealth of the nations, and more importantly set out to show how this wealth could be increased. Initially, in the *Lectures on Jurisprudence*, he showed that labour, through the division and specialization of labour, was a key element in growing the wealth of the nation. Then, benefiting from his French sojourn and his readings of writers such as Quesnay and Turgot, he added in capital as a key factor in the production process in the *Wealth of Nations*. Men and machinery would drive the wealth of the nation. The optimal environment for such growth was one in which competition flourished and the price mechanism invisibly did its allocative work. Underpinning this ring of competition, so necessary in the Smithian vision for progress to occur, there was a second ring that produced the social cement in which economic society could flourish. This was the ring of social behaviour, based on the empathy of the 'impartial spectator' of the *Theory of Moral Sentiments*, a ring that produced appropriate rules of moral behaviour along with institutions embodying such behaviour. The behaviour of Smith's 'impartial spectator' has very strong parallels with that of the 'reasonable man' so central to the formulation of the common law system that underpins legal behavioural relations in the Anglo-American world.

Henry Thornton, our last author, was quick to identify Smith's weaknesses in monetary economics. He attacked his definition of the money supply and criticized his lack of understanding of the velocity of circulation of money. As a practising banker, he showed up the artificiality of Smith's distinction between real and fictitious bills. This enabled him to be highly critical of Smith's followers' advocacy of a strict type of monetary rule involving decreasing the money supply when the gold reserves of the Bank of England fell. In many respects Thornton re-examined the issues that Law had attempted to analyse a century earlier. Law wanted to replace the metallic money system of the period with one based on paper money and bank credit. The Napoleonic wars had forced Britain to abandon gold convertibility, leaving Thornton with the task of literally analysing the paper credit of Great Britain. In this new monetary habitat Thornton forced economists to become two-handed by destructuring what would later become known as the equation of exchange in the form $MV = PY$. Economics writers traditionally had viewed this from the left-hand side, contending that problems arose if there was too much or too little money on the left-hand side. Thornton asked how this equilibrium quantity of money could be identified, given that velocity could be changing. Furthermore, who was to know that it was the left-hand side that was causing the problem? Look at the right-hand side, where exogenous shocks in the form of harvest failures, outbreaks of war, etc. could play havoc with prices and output. The strong implication of Thornton's analysis, at least in the first half of *Paper Credit*, was that it was dangerous to have a monetary rule linking paper credit to some quantity of metallic money so that paper credit varied according as the quantity of metallic money rose or fell. Thornton described how there were different layers of paper credit stretching from the Bank of England to the London banks and then on to the country banks. Interferences in the Bank of England's credit, the base of the paper credit system, could cause widespread banking failures and financial contagion. To counter such a possibility Thornton envisaged the Bank of England, which by this stage had become a quasi central bank, acting as a lender of last resort to the banking system in order to prevent panic and contagion from spreading through the banking system and then spilling over to the real economy. Thornton the professional banker knew from experience that the Bank of England, if committed to some dogmatic rule linking the money supply to metallic monetary reserves, could produce all sorts of damaging consequences both for the financial economy, in the form of bankruptcies and loss of confidence, and for the real economy, in the form of reduced output. He provided the template for the emergence of the central bank as a lender of last resort.

Weaknesses and Wrong Directions

The macroeconomic legacy of the authors outlined in this book is very significant, but, in admiring these discoveries, it would be wrong not to recognize that they were also accompanied by weaknesses and wrong directions. Hindsight is always perfect, and it is unfair to look for too much from writers who, with the exception of Adam Smith, were not academics and had full-time day jobs to occupy their minds. With that caveat, there are still regrets.

Sir William Petty showed his extraordinary ability to provide ways of measuring the national income and analysing the macroeconomy. It has to be regretted that he did not go further and present his ideas to his fellow members of the Royal Society to initiate further research into macroeconomic phenomena. He appears to have been interested in the issues he raised only from his own perspective of a private landowner threatened with the possibility of further heavy taxation. It is no coincidence that his two major works on economics, *A Treatise on Taxes and Contributions* and *Verbum Sapienti*, with its title referring to the need for a more equal distribution of taxes, were specifically geared to producing a strong policy message on taxation.

With respect to John Law, it is to be regretted that, even though he was the first writer to conceptualize the price-driven market system in terms of supply and demand, he abandoned his market principles when the Mississippi System started to encounter financial turbulence. Rather than analysing the primary problems in terms of market behaviour, he forced people to accept the System through a variety of restrictive measures such as the prohibition on holding specie and bullion, forced devaluations of silver and the demonetization of gold, guaranteeing the price of Mississippi stock, and the overuse of the printing presses of the Royal Bank. In 1723 Law was nearly given the opportunity to reshape the French economy a second time when the duc d'Orléans, the Regent of France, decided to invite him to return. Unfortunately, the Regent died before Law could accept this new invitation.

Richard Cantillon, though producing a very powerful analytical work, suffered from a lack of faith in the potential of the economy. As shown, he perceived economic activity in the aggregate as basically a zero sum game.

There were winners and losers. But there were no net long-term winners. Nations could gain at the expense of others, but all this was occurring around a horizontal line.

François Quesnay, developing Cantillon's work on the circular flow of income, presented the possibilities of economic growth occurring through shifts in consumption and investment expenditure. This moved economics out of the zero sum mindset but, unfortunately, owing to his blinkered emphasis on the exclusively productive powers of agriculture as against the so-called sterility of the industrial and services sectors, Quesnay was unable to perceive economic growth as emanating from any sector but agriculture. The use of the term 'sterile' to sum up the economic activities of these sectors was unfortunate in the extreme and meant that, apart from its brief marketing success in the 1760s and early 1770s, his Physiocracy could not attract long-term adherents. Ironically, Quesnay appears to have lost interest in his economic doctrine towards the end of his career, switching to the study of mathematics.

Another author who switched away from economics and, in this case, the move was even quicker, was David Hume. Hume's *Political Discourses* was probably the most successful book that he had published up to that point in his career. Prior to the publication of this book in 1752, though writing works which would be regarded as classics by later generations, Hume had been unable to produce a commercial success that would enable him to live from the income of his writings. The *Political Discourses* solved this problem. It was a book that went into many editions and many translations. After its publication Hume was recognized as an author who could sell books. He was encouraged to write further books through attractive advances from his publishers. Alas, these advances were not for economics works but for a series of books on the history of England. Advances of £400 for the first volume and £700 for the second were sufficient to attract him to writing history for the rest of his life. History's gain was economics' loss, for, aside from an additional chapter, 'Of the Jealousy of Trade', for the second edition of the *Political Discourses*, Hume would not write any more books on economics. However, he did attempt to persuade Smith in his correspondence that the collapse of the Ayr Bank, which had produced a financial crisis not just in Scotland but also in London, might cause Smith to think again on these issues. He wrote:

Do these events any-wise affect your theory? Or will it occasion the revisal of any chapters...On the whole, I believe that the check given to our exorbitant and ill grounded credit will prove of advantage in the long run, as it will reduce people to more solid and less sanguine projects, and at the same time introduce frugality among the merchants and manufacturers: What say you? Here is food for your speculation.

(Hume 1932: ii. 263–4)

One wonders if, in writing further economics books rather than history, Hume would have solved some of the ambiguities that he produced on money and financial innovation. As has been shown, he was a metallist at heart and feared the use of paper money. He was strongly opposed to financial innovation as manifested in capital markets and the products of such markets, namely, shares and bonds. His weaknesses in this area, at least from my own perspective, were part of this great monetary fault running through the works of not only Hume but also his great friend Adam Smith and their French friend Turgot.

Anne Robert Jacques Turgot made the critical breakthrough with his analysis of capital. However, owing to his opposition to paper money and financial innovation, his work was stuck in the time warp of eighteenth-century France, one where notaries acted as proxy banks and where entrepreneurs had not access to the capital market. In such an environment Turgot could only foresee investment financed by savings, which in turn arose through abstention from current consumption. He could not see the potential for the banking system and the capital market to provide alternative channels to finance investment. He was not alone with this fixation on savings constituting the sole channel for the financing of investment. His theory was accepted, as Schumpeter (1954) has remarked, 'hook, line and sinker' by subsequent generations of economists. The division between economics and the corporate financing of investment has had a long and unsatisfactory history. Indeed, it was Schumpeter who attempted to force a reconsideration by the profession on this issue.

The great monetary fault line continued through Adam Smith in the *Wealth of Nations*. There is some evidence from the *Lectures on Jurisprudence* that Smith had a more liberal view on money in the early 1760s than in 1776. It has been surmised that Smith changed his views on money after the collapse of the Ayr Bank in 1772, this collapse showing him the dangers of excessive financial innovation. The financial system, in Icarian style, had flown too close to the sun, supported on the wings of paper credit. The collapse of the Ayr Bank suggested to Smith that it was better to anchor the financial system on the solid ground of metallic money. His distinctions between productive and unproductive expenditure and real bills and fictitious bills brought him into troubled waters.

Henry Thornton advanced a positive role for the Bank of England, quickly emerging as a central bank, to pursue a lender of last resort approach when there were real shocks to the economy. But, having opened up this new vista for a central bank to follow, Thornton, in the latter half of *Paper Credit*, became a great deal more conservative when invoking the spectre of inflation. This conservatism would spill over into his subsequent recommendations on the Bullion Committee, where he would show a strong metallist streak. This was a pity, because he had effectively shown in *Paper Credit* that it was possible for Great Britain to function without metallic money. The suspension of convertibility in 1797 had produced this changed monetary environment. Thornton recognized that the monetary system did not need metallic

223

money. Furthermore, he recognized that, if the usury laws were abolished, the Bank of England would be able to use the interest rate in place of contractions of the money supply so as to achieve external balance. The pieces were in place for a modern monetary system. However, the conservative in Thornton took over, and he reverted to recommending the restoration of convertibility. It would take Great Britain another 130 years to break away from the gold standard.

This book has tried to present elements from the lives and conceptualizations of the first macroeconomists from Petty to Thornton. At the theoretical level these people are worthy of inclusion in the pantheon of the early discoverers of economics. Despite their theoretical brilliance, many of them had serious defects at a personal level. Petty, obsessed by his desire to increase his wealth, had little sympathy for the Irish population with whom he lived for a considerable part of his life. He had been the key administrator in designing and implementing the Down Survey, which facilitated the transplantation of sizeable sections of the Irish from their native lands to the barren wastes of the west of Ireland. Although not all of this plan was implemented, the personal costs of this transplantation did not weigh heavily with Petty. Indeed, later on in his career he devised a further plan, this time to transplant the native Irish across the Irish Sea so that England would have a more compact population capable of competing with the Dutch, and also to end Ireland as a seedbed for revolution against the Crown (see Goodacre 2005).

John Law's killing of his fellow 'beau' Edmund Wilson in the duel on Bloomsbury Heath may have been an eighteenth-century contract killing. Law may have been induced by well-placed politicians to challenge Wilson to a duel to rid a 'noble lord' of an embarrassing lover. When developing the Mississippi System, he did not cover himself in glory by implementing policies that resulted in the enforced transplantation of beggars, prostitutes, drunks, etc. from France to French Louisiana. Some of the companies that he took over, such as the Company of Africa and the Company of Senegal, were primarily slave companies exporting unfortunate Africans in the most horrific conditions to the Americas.

Richard Cantillon started his career by doctoring the account books of James Brydges, the Paymaster-General to the Forces Abroad, so as to mislead parliamentary watchdogs of the time. Brydges, who would later become the duke of Chandos, made so much money out of war profiteering that he became one of the richest men in London—rich enough to employ Handel as his private *kapellmeister*. Cantillon helped him to build up his fortune through his adroit manipulation of monies destined for the troops abroad in the Iberian peninsula during the War of the Spanish Succession. Cantillon's creditors, such as Joseph Gage, Lady Mary Herbert, and the Carol brothers, maintained that he sold their shares at the height of the Mississippi boom and did not credit their accounts with the proceeds. The strange events surrounding his apparent demise in Albemarle Street in London in 1734 raise further questions about this enigmatic Irishman (see Murphy 1986).

In contrast, Quesnay, Hume, Turgot, and Smith presented a more humanistic approach by the standards of their time. Henry Thornton has claims to have been the most humanistic of this group of economic writers. Powered by his deeply felt evangelicalism, he championed, alongside his great friend William Wilberforce, the anti-slavery legislation that ultimately resulted in the banning of the slave trade by the British Parliament in 1807, a development captured on screen in the film *Amazing Grace* (dir. Apted, 2007). Thornton would no doubt have regarded the anti-slavery legislation achievement as ranking far higher than his book *Paper Credit*. However, his reluctance to provide real freedom for the former black slaves transported from Nova Scotia to Sierra Leone shows a certain flaw in his personality. He appeared to take the view that slavery was wrong but that full democratic freedom for the former slaves was inappropriate. He wanted the Sierra Leone company that he chaired to exercise considerable control over the freed people of Freetown. Furthermore, unfortunately for Thornton, his parliamentary activities, along with his fervour in designing ways of propagating his religious views, meant that he took his eye off his banking business, which was in a bankrupt state by the time of his death.

These writers, combining very different backgrounds and motivations, left a rich legacy of economic theory. In this book we have concentrated on their contributions to macroeconomics. It is hoped that this book has shown that macroeconomics was not a twentieth-century invention, and that readers wishing to examine the roots of macroeconomic theory and policy need to move back through time to see the rich tapestry of contributions that were made by Sir William Petty, Richard Cantillon, John Law, David Hume, François Quesnay, Anne Robert Jacques Turgot, Adam Smith, and Henry Thornton. New ideas from fascinating people.

References

Blaug, Mark (1962), *Economic Theory in Retrospect* (Cambridge).

Goodacre, Hugh (2005), 'The Spatial-Economic Logic of William Petty's Final Scheme', Paper presented to the European Society for the History of Economic Thought, Stirling, June.

Hume, David (1932), *The Letters of David Hume*, ed. J. Y. T. Greig (Oxford).

Murphy, Antoin (1986), *Richard Cantillon: Entrepreneur and Economist* (Oxford).

Schumpeter, Joseph (1954), *A History of Economic Analysis* (London).

Index

Index

Cantillon, Richard (*Cont.*)
  Essai 3, 4, 78, 105–6, 123–4, 137, 144, 161, 168
  limitations 221–2, 224–5
  motivation 11
  speculator 2, 50, 73
capital:
  advances 3
  concept of 77
  factor of production 135, 219–20
  formation 145–51, 170–1
  growth 160–1
  inflows 87
  intensity 128, 144
  marginal efficiency of 203
  role of 143, 159, 160, 169, 215
  the term 14, 134, 144, 219
Carol brothers 224
Cary, John 46
cash balance effect 89, 106
cash-in-advance requirement model 53
Castel de Saint-Pierre 114
Cesarano, F. 78, 105
Chalmers, George 31
Chamberlen, Dr Hugh 46
Chandos, Lord 74–5
Charles, L. 124
Charles I 4
cheapness or plenty 160
Checkland, S. G. 177
Child, Sir Joshua 39
Choiseul-Romanet, comtesse de 121
Churchill, Winston 167
Cicé, abbé de 135, 139, 151
Cicero 27, 97
circular flow of income 2, 10–11, 50–3, 125, 215, 216, 218
Clapham, J. 193
Clarkson, Thomas 193–4
Clarkson, John 194
Cochin, Maître 90
Colbert 129
Colquhoun, J. C. 196
Company of the West 63–4, 75
consumption 171
contertibility 16–18, 191, 198, 207, 210

Craigie, Thomas 98
credit:
  creation 46
  versus money 49–50
Cromwell, Oliver 4, 24–5
Crozat, Antoine 62, 63

d'Alembert 4, 13, 122, 136, 165
Dangeul 137
d'Argenson 123
Dauphin, Jeanne-Catherine 120
deflation 201–6
Descartes, René 27, 136
Diderot 4, 13, 122, 136, 165
Donne, John 27
Douglas, Sir Robert 156
Douglas, Hugh 157
Douglas, Margaret 157
Du Pont de Nemours 1314, 119, 133, 137, 140, 143–4
Du Tot, Nicolas 11, 66, 69, 103, 111, 140, 151, 159
Dubois, abbé 69
Dumfries, duke of 178

Eagly, R. V. 50
East India Company 179, 184–5
Eatwell, J. 3
economic growth 127, 215, 218
  and interest rates 148
  and savings 149
  in *Wealth of Nations* 159, 168–71
economic model 78–9
economics, the term 29, 78, 99
economists 137, 155
Edinburgh 45–6, 95, 96
Eltis, W. 128
employment 50–3, 54
Enlightenment 218, 219
  French 3, 121–2, 136, 164
entrepreneurs 2, 80–2, 129, 144–5, 217, 219
equation of exchange 220
equilibrium, the term 144
Estrades, comtesse d' 121
exchange rates 90–1
exchange reciprocity 82

228